新闻学与传播学经典丛书·大师系列

新闻学原理
The Principles of Journalism
中文·英文(双语版)

[美]卡斯珀·约斯特(Casper Yost) 著
王海 译

中国传媒大学出版社
·北京·

总 序

新闻与大众传播事业在现当代与日俱增的影响与地位，呼唤着新闻学与传播学学术研究的相应发展和跟进。而知识的传承，学术的繁荣，思想的进步，首先需要的是丰富的思想材料的积累。

"新闻学与传播学经典译丛·大师系列"的创设，立意在接续前辈学人传译外国新闻学与传播学经典的事业，以一定的规模为我们的学术与思想界以及业界精英人士理解和借鉴新闻学与传播学在西方方兴未艾之际的精华，提供基本的养料，便于站在前人的肩膀上作进一步的探究，以免长期在黑暗中自行低效摸索。

将近十年前，在何道宽教授与我的发起和主持下，在司马兰女士的大力支持下，"新闻与传播学译丛·大师经典系列"开始启动，至今已推出十来种名著的中译本，在学界也较有影响。这首先是何道宽教授的贡献，作为英语科班出身、口译笔译俱佳的高手，依然投身于传播学经典的引进；退休后更是一发不可收，每天清晨起床开始工作，每年推出好几本译著，而且专攻技术学派（何老师称之为"环境学派"），不但包办了哈罗德·伊尼斯、马歇尔·麦克卢汉著作的所有中译本，而且还延伸到保罗·莱文森等当代名家。

记得何老师说过，他热爱传播学学术翻译到了这样的程度："不给我钱（稿费）我也愿意翻译。"我当时就感慨，新闻传播学界要是多有一些像何老师这样外语水平高、热衷翻译的专才就好了。可是在目前的学术考核著作下，译者辛苦和稿费低暂且不提，在多数学校还是不被承认科研工作量的。这就妨碍了许多为教学科研和生活所累的年轻学人接续这一事业，尽管也出现了像刘海龙这样的优秀青年译者。

好在随着新闻传播学的发展，越来越多的学人意识到了我九年多前说的两个80%：新闻学与传播学是舶来品，80%的学术和思想资源不在中国；而日见人多势众的研究队伍将80%以上的精力投放到虽在快速发展，但是仍处在"初级阶段"的国内新闻与大众传播事业的研究上。这两个80%倒置的现实，导致了学术资源配置的严重失衡和学术研究的肤浅化、泡沫化；专业和学术著作的翻译虽然在近几年渐成气候，但是其水准、规模和系统性不足以摆脱"后天失调"的尴尬。

如果说当年启动时，我们深感百余年前梁启超呼吁"国家欲自强，以多译西书为本；学子欲自立，以多读西书为功"对于当代新闻传播学的意义，如果说任公所言西学著述"今之所译，直九牛之一毛耳"的巨大落差，如果说新闻学与传播学相关典籍的译介比其他学科还要滞后许多，以至于我们的学人们对这些经典知之甚少，眼界相当狭窄，那么这种状况已经有所改观。如今的新闻传播学，虽然仍属小学科，但是近十年出版的图书数量猛增，其中译著的大量问世是最为引人瞩目的现象。

　　这些新闻传播学译著可能并非本本经典,事实上也出现了些许重复翻译。一些译本的翻译质量存在问题,译校也比较粗糙。但是总体而言,它们对于学术的推动和学科地位的提升功不可没,尤其是比较媒介理论、传播研究方法类译著,直接烘托了和滋润了年轻学子,令他们的研究水准迅速提升。回想十年前,尽管几乎所有新闻传播专业学生言必称传播学"四大奠基人"或"四大先驱",可是当时他们的传播学译著一本也没有被翻译成中文。

　　本译丛将奉献新闻学与传播学大师的经典之作,如哈罗德·拉斯韦尔、埃尔·塔尔德、哈罗德·伊尼斯、麦克卢汉、库尔特·卢因、卡尔·霍夫兰等人的佳作。大部分名著是新近翻译出版的,部分名著是中文版的修订本,还另附英文全文,以便读者查阅。"译事之艰辛,惟事者知之。"从事这种恢弘迫切而又繁难备至的工作,需要好几代人做出不懈努力,幸赖同道和出版者大力扶持。我们自知学有不逮,力不从心,因此热忱欢迎中青年学人加入译者队伍,我们也将虚心聆听各界读者提出的批评和建议。

展江

2012年11月20日

目　录

译者序　　　　　　　　　　　　　　1
前　言　　　　　　　　　　　　　　7

第一章　起　源　　　　　　　　　　9
第二章　新闻采写原则　　　　　　　16
第三章　新闻首要功能　　　　　　　25
第四章　新闻选择　　　　　　　　　31
第五章　新闻取舍　　　　　　　　　40
第六章　新闻真实性　　　　　　　　50
第七章　新闻获取和编辑　　　　　　60
第八章　报纸个体从业者　　　　　　75
第九章　评论版　　　　　　　　　　81
第十章　评论的职责　　　　　　　　86
第十一章　新闻自由　　　　　　　　92
第十二章　编辑政策　　　　　　　　99
第十三章　编辑结构　　　　　　　　111
第十四章　新闻伦理　　　　　　　　119

The Principles of Journalism	133
Preface	135
Chapter I　The Origins	138
Chapter II　Principles of Production	145
Chapter III　The Primacy of News	155
Chapter IV　The Selection of News	163
Chapter V　The Rejection of News	175
Chapter VI　Truth in The News	188
Chapter VII　Getting and Handling The News	200
Chapter VIII　Personality in The Newspaper	220
Chapter IX　The Editorial Page	227
Chapter X　Editorial Responsibility	234
Chapter XI　The Freedom of The Press	242
Chapter XII　Editorial Policy	250
Chapter XIII　Editorial Construction	266
Chapter XIV　Ethics of Journalism	276
Index	292
索引	297

译者序

19世纪末20世纪初，美国进入了"新式新闻事业"时期，阿道夫·奥克斯（Adolph Ochs）的《纽约时报》奠定了"只报道事实"的客观而公正的新闻理念。美国现代新闻学随着美国"新式新闻事业"的出现而形成，关于新闻学的基本原理、采写原则、编辑学、行业规范及其伦理观、舆论学等分支学科逐渐成形，构筑了整个新闻学的学科体系。舒曼（Edwin L. Shuman）《应用新闻学》（Practical Journalism，1903）、利昂·弗林特（Leon N. Flint）《编辑学》（The Editorial，1920）、菲尔·宾（Phil C. Bing）《乡村周刊》（The Country Weekly，1917）、乔治·佩恩（George Henry Payne）《美国新闻史》（History of Journalism in the United States，1920）、《新闻工作者手册》（Handbook for Newspaper Workers，1921）、《新闻采写原理》（Newspaper Reporting and Correspondence，1919）、《新闻采写教程》（Course in Journalistic Writing，1922）、卡斯珀·约斯特（Casper Salathiel Yost）《新闻学原理》（The Principles of Journalism，1924）和沃尔特·李普曼（Walter Lippmann）《舆论学》（Public Opinion，1922）等著述的出版标志着现代新闻学在西方

的形成。

以美国密苏里大学新闻学院创始人沃特·威廉（Walter Williams，1864—1935）博士、《大陆报》创办人汤姆斯·密勒（Thomas Franklin Millard，1868—1942）等为代表的美国"密苏里帮"从1902年就开始在世界范围推广美国新闻学，促进了世界新闻事业专业化和新闻教育的发展。威廉博士在1914年至1928年期间五次访问中国，对中国新闻界产生了巨大的影响。

20世纪二三十年代，随着西学东渐的深入展开，中国越来越多有胆识的学者、记者和官员赴欧美国家、日本进行学习和访问。一大批曾就读于密苏里大学新闻学院的记者、教育家、官员活跃于20世纪上半叶的中国新闻界、国际传播和外交领域，形成了中国新闻界的"密苏里帮"。其中代表人物有《广州时报》主笔黄宪昭、主管对外新闻的国民党中宣部副部长董显光、《中央日报》社长马星野、《申报》著名记者、复旦大学教授汪英宾、路透社记者赵敏恒、国民党新闻官员沈剑虹、著名报人吴嘉棠、新闻教育家蒋荫恩、梁士纯、谢然之等。接受西方新闻教育的民国报人在创办本土新型报刊的实践中，掀起了新闻学研究的高潮。20世纪二三十年代可谓中国新闻学研究的"黄金"发展期，一系列新闻学著作和译著问世：戈公振《中国报学史》、《新闻学摄要》，蒋国珍《中国新闻发达史》，张静庐《中国的新闻纸》（上海，1928）、《中国的新闻记者》（上海，1928）、《新闻记者与新闻纸》，张九如和周聱青《新闻编辑法》，周孝庵《最新实验新闻学》，徐宝璜《新闻学大意》、《新闻学纲要》（1930）（与胡愈之合著）、《新闻事业》，黄天鹏《现代新闻学》、《新闻文学概论》（1930）、《新闻学刊全集》（上海，1928），任白涛《应用新闻学》（上海，1922），李公凡《基础新闻学》（上海，1931），邵振青《新闻学总论》（上海，1919），王解生《新闻纸改造》（北京，1923），王文萱《新闻概论》，吴定九《新闻事业经营法》（上海，1930），平民大学于1923年在北京出版的《新闻学系级刊》，北平新闻学社于1927—1928年出版发行的《新闻学刊》、《报学杂志》、《新闻学报》。

1997年,中国国务院学位办在文学门类中增设了一个一级学科——新闻传播学,下设两个二级学科:新闻学与传播学。15年过去了,新闻传播学在中国得以长足发展,这得益于中国改革开放以来愈益开放的学术环境,也有赖于新闻研究者孜孜以求的进取精神。新闻学研究者不仅成功借鉴了西方先进的价值理念、职业规范和理论体系,而且在承袭前人的基础上从历史、理论、实务三个向度上继续努力而有所突破和创新。就新闻理论而言,近年来关于新闻价值观、新闻自由、新闻真实性的"时髦词"已经变成了近乎常识的概念,无论对新闻工作者,还是社会大众而言,这是纯粹的福音。然而,综观中国的新闻理论著述,各个概念、各个原则之间缺乏内在联系,零散而不系统的特点表明,中国的新闻学理论研究尚未成熟。理论是活的,在中国目前的语境下,相关研究已到了一个瓶颈,某些学者甚至有对某些理论中的重要概念进行"考据"的倾向。作为同业者,译者甚为担忧:这种倾向会将我们引导何方?

中国近现代新闻事业发端于在华外报,本土报刊带有浓厚的西方的办刊理念。译介和引进西方的新闻理论,不但成为20世纪上半叶中国新闻学者的重要任务之一,而且依然是今天新闻传播学界不可或缺的。不交流,不借鉴,学界难有突破。基于此,我们有责任将前人遗漏的西方新闻学的经典著述翻译成中文。

于1924年出版的《新闻学原理》和同时代的新闻学著述一道,推动了新闻传播学在西方的形成。卡斯珀·约斯特在《新闻学原理》中系统论述了新闻起源、新闻采写原则、新闻选择与取舍、新闻真实性、新闻的获取与编辑等关于新闻学原理的基本问题,某种意义上,它从专业主义的高度为新闻学科的理论体系构筑奠定了基础。

贴切受众的"平民主义"

约斯特《新闻学原理》最突出的特点,便是字里行间散发出强烈的受众观。处在"精英"的位置,约斯特却尽量站在受众的立场上思考。而这种思考无疑是一种伴随着阵痛而主动探索的过程,因为在约斯特的时代,新闻传播学刚刚起步,以约斯特为代表的新闻传播学学者直接从新闻传播主体的身份转换过来,重新闻而轻受众的思想倾向一时还难以去除。但理念的滞后不应成为实践缺失的充分理由,我们仍不得不思考:作为社会的"信息精英",新闻从业者应该奉行何种理念?约氏的回答是,在承认新闻传播主体自律的可能性和有效性的前提下,报纸应该以受众为本,通过引起受众兴趣等手段来实现服务于公众的功能。为什么要以受众为本呢?正如作者所言:"在报纸的生产过程中,自身利益和公众利益不仅是兼容的,而且是统一的。"

有争议的"自由主义"

自由与约束的界限在哪里?这一极具历史争议的问题,在新闻界也是有争议的。在论及言论自由之于自由政府所必需的同时,约斯特指出,暂时限制新闻自由权利的泛用对于社会安全是必要的,他似乎是为自己,也为后人设下了一个矛盾,即产生多大的安全威胁时,新闻自由的去留才可被确定?从约斯特多次引述美国联邦法官的话可以看出,他对美国的新闻自由还是有信心的。由此也不难理解,作为"消极自由"论者的约斯特是从一种建设性而非批判性的眼光看问题。他认为,"新闻自由"须以客观事实为前提,以公众福祉为目的,其使用者必须有"良好的动机"和"公正的目的"。不管怎么说,这有待于实证,非一时一地的思辨所能解决。

坚持原则的"保守主义"

20世纪二三十年代，美国电子媒介的实力正逐步走向鼎盛。包括报刊在内的大众媒介不仅在客观上，也在受众的认识上具有了空前的影响力。在这种磅礴气势和普遍的媒介渗透力面前，约斯特没有跟随大家一道惊呼媒介的强大。他坚持了原有的看法。事实证明，保守的立场使他得以捍卫若干原则。虽然约斯特否认了报纸成为慈善机构的可能性，但他坚持认为：应为受众传递可靠的消息、引导舆论、支持公众权利、谴责政府腐败、改进原则和观念，并运用其力量促进和改善公共福利。换言之，约斯特已经构思了一系列看似模糊但在当时颇为全面的大众媒介的职能说。在他看来，媒介的影响力并没有人们所认为的这么强大，甚至它还有可能是脆弱的：假如它不忠于读者，违背了"以一种普遍方法为读者提供所支付的服务"的话，受众自然就会抛弃它。出于安全及维护公共服务等层面的考虑，坚持原则的选择显然是明智的。

广东外语外贸大学
王 海
2012年9月

前 言

在这本书中,作者试图对新闻学基本原理加以界定和规范。关于此类界定和陈述的需求日益增长,促成了这本著作的问世。新闻学已经在很多专业人士心目中取得认可,其影响力得到认同。新闻事业已经成为现代生活和文明进步的必要条件,其发展亦成为我们这个时代的奇迹之一。它渗透到人类文明的各个层面,而且对人类的思想和成就产生持续影响。然而,新闻事业毕竟是一个新兴的行业,时至今日,整个行业人士才认识到,新闻业不仅是个体求职的普通路径,也是社会精英聚合的实体——"公共领域"。在这个"公共领域"里,个人的权利得以捍卫,个人的诚信得以维系,个人的责任得到认知。基于这样的认识,人们很大程度上把新闻事业作为一个整体来考虑,认为新闻是一种行业,它具备整体的利益和责任,并将其与作为个体职业的新闻业区分开来。由此引发了人们越发努力对以下系列问题达成共识:新闻究竟是什么?新闻应该遵循的标准是什么?新闻对公众应该承担的责任是什么?新闻的目标和理念是什么?

作者衷心希望，这本书某种程度上能够满足读者的这种诉求。由于奠定与本书明确陈述的要素原理相一致的基础似乎是必要的，有良知的记者和大多数从业者能够认知的某些具体准则就成为这样的基石。在试图陈述新闻事业的基本原理的过程中，作者认识到他并没有表达什么新想法，在经验丰富的报人看来，他的陈述近乎陈旧。的确，新奇的事物对于目的的实现可能是无关的。创新的观点可能仅仅是理论的表述。而作为阅历的必要产物，原则不可能是创新的。但是，重视原则的意识，及其运用原则的程度和方式，无论是自觉的还是无意识的，都因人的个性而变化。假如我们要建立良好的新闻业得以估量的标准，我们就有必要从从业者共同的阅历中归纳已经历时验证的必要的行为和实践要素，这些要素符合所有人际交往中被认知的那些公正的基本原则，并且给出了原则的具体形式。没有人可以欣然地全部履行这些原则，但是有人可能从自身的成熟经历及其总体认知出发，收集足够的资料为这样的基础作奠基。假如我撰写的这本书将以某种方式有助于建立新闻业基本原则的体系，那么它的主要目的就实现了。

　　但是，作者希望这次尝试和努力的益处不仅局限于本职领域。没有任何人类的代理机构能像新闻业这样与公众保持着连续、亲密和持久的关系。无论新闻业的影响力是深远的还是肤浅的，也无论是好的方面还是坏的方面，这种影响力的确普遍存在于生活的方方面面。因此，新闻业的产品是公众关注的公共产品，而新闻业本身的思考、指导行业自身并希望借此对行业行为加以评判的标准、新闻业对公众所担负责任的认识、新闻业的宗旨和理念等都应该关系大众利益。我们有必要让公众更好地理解新闻业所面临的困惑，以及践行其功能和实现其理念的过程中某种程度上必须面对的要素。我们有必要更好地理解引导新闻最佳报道的原则，更好地理解新闻的激励作用，更好地理解成千上万未留下名分的记者以付出生命为代价对公众作出的贡献和服务。作者真诚地希望这本书有助于理解新闻业的基本原则。

卡斯珀·约斯特

第一章 起　源

考古学家在探究古代史实时，从未发现远古时代人类的本质与今天有何不同。数万年前的男人们和女人们与现在的男女具有同样的兴趣、愿望、热情、罪恶感和美德，他们为同样的感觉和几近同样的理性而感动。因此，我们可以大胆假定：当该隐（Cain）① 被

---

① 该隐（Cain），圣经人物，亚当和夏娃的长子。根据《创世记》，有一日，亚当和他妻子夏娃同房，夏娃就怀孕了，生了该隐（意为"得"），便说："耶和华使我得了一个男子。"又生了该隐的兄弟亚伯。亚伯是牧羊的，该隐是种地的。有一日，该隐拿地里的出产为贡物献给耶和华，亚伯也将他羊群中头生的羊的脂油献上。耶和华看中了亚伯和他的供物，只是看不中该隐和他的供物。该隐就大大地发怒，变了脸色。耶和华对该隐说："你为什么发怒呢？你为什么变了脸色呢？你若行得好，岂不蒙悦？你若行得不好，罪就伏在门前。它必恋慕你，你却要制伏它。"该隐与他兄弟亚伯说话，二人正在田间，该隐起来打他兄弟亚伯，把他杀了。耶和华对该隐说："你兄弟亚伯在哪里？"他说："我不知道！我难道是看守我兄弟的吗？"耶和华说："你做了什么事呢？你兄弟的血有声音，从地里向我哀告。地开了口，从你手里接受你兄弟的血。现在你必受这地的咒诅。你种地，地不再给你效力，你必流离飘荡在地上。"该隐对耶和华说："我的刑罚太重，过于我所能当的。你如今赶逐我离开这地，以致不见你面。我必流离飘荡在上，凡遇见我的必杀我。"耶和华对他说："凡杀该隐的，必遭报七倍。"耶和华就给该隐立一个记号，免得人遇见他就杀他。于是该隐离开耶和华，住在伊甸东边挪得之地。（本书页下脚注未标明的均为译者注，下不一一标明。）

赶出家，在挪得（Nod）这片土地上寻求住所和妻子时，他不可能完全忘记伊甸的邻里街坊。若干年之后，或许该隐已处在家长制时代，尽管出于明显的原因他可能隐瞒了自己的身份，当他遇见来自伊甸的旅行者时，他还是急切地想获悉来自家乡的信息。毋庸置疑，该隐不仅想了解伊甸地区发生过的事情，他也想知道当时正在发生的事情。他饶有兴趣地了解了较为重要的新闻，同时也探听了最细微的信息。

2　　人们对于了解新闻的热情并非文明进步的表现。上帝为了交流的目的而赋予人类讲话的器官，为接收谈话的目的而赋予人类听的功能，而人的舌头和耳朵总是渴望发挥作用。同时，人类被赋予永无止境的好奇心，人们对人间事和他人的行为充满了持久的兴趣，也对自然万物的运行怀有持续的兴趣，人们还对身边或者远方的每个人的生存环境和他们身上发生的事情抱有始终如一的兴趣。无论在人类历史的任何时期，男人和女人绝对想了解家族、社区、地区或者世界上所发生的事情。同样，人类史上从来不会存在这样的时期——为他们传递好消息或者坏消息的信使不受欢迎。"有好消息从远方来，就如拿凉水给口渴的人喝。"这则谚语充分证明了所罗门时代新闻的价值所在，而导致希腊特洛伊城沦陷的那些信标被当时人们阅读的热情绝不亚于当代人们对现代公告的热情。了解有趣的事情、奇异的事情成为人们渴望阅读新闻的原动力，而这些的确奠定了人类文明和进步的基础。正是由于新闻的不断传播，拓宽了人类的知识，推动了知识在新领域

3　　和活动中的应用。正是由于保禄（Paul）① 在地中海沿岸的布道，才使得基督教教义得以传播；正是马可·波罗从中国旅行回国的消息，开辟了通往东印度群岛的海上航线；正是哥伦布发现新大陆的消息，打开了西半球国家拓殖的航道。而每次科学发现的新

---

① 保禄（Paul，又译保罗），对基督教教义做出了较大贡献，使得基督教不再局限于犹太人范围。

闻都推动了科学的新研究和新发现。但是，假如人类没有接触这样引发其兴趣的报道并在更大的范围内加以传播的话，人类社会就不会出现上述的进步。人类所有的知识以及源于知识的社会进步都来自不倦的好奇心，即人们了解周围事物的愿望，无论邻里街坊的行为、遥远国家的状况，还是苹果落地的原因，都成为人们关注的对象。获悉消息者要告知他人，因为消息的传播与获悉消息同等重要。所以，新闻总是在传播，而且新闻的传播增加了人类的知识库存——有益的、有害的、平庸的、无差别的信息源源不断地添加到人类的知识储库中，人类通过经验对无价值的信息加以筛选和剔除。

"新闻"一词就像其所指事物一样，具有古代语言与生俱来的词根。"新闻"根源于罗盘的几个方向（东西南北）的传言虽广为流传，但是由于缺乏令人信服的事实或者语用方面的证据，只能算作一种误传。新闻源于单词"new"，在词源学发展的奇特时期，语言尚处于形成阶段，当时没有英语语法，"任何单词无论运用于怎样的语法关系，好像都可以承载讲话人的思想"。在英语的发展过程中，"new"是一个古老的单词，一个可以追溯到梵文时代的词汇，而且在几乎每一种欧洲民族语言中都可以找到其对应或相关的单词形式，无论是现在的语言还是历时的语言。梵语中的 *nava* 在拉丁语中就变成 *novus*，在哥特语中就成为 *niujis*，在古撒克逊语种就成为 *niwi*，在盎格鲁—撒克逊语中就成为 *niwe* 或者 *neowe*。它不仅可以用作形容词，而且在中世纪英语的转型期，其屈折形式发生多次编码，这个单词又变成副词，意思未变。作为动词，它的意思等同于"更新"（renew）；作为名词，它用以指代任何新事物。"new"的复数形式是"news"，在古英语的拼写中可以找到类似的名词。例如，在托马斯·莫尔

(Thomas More)① 的原版《乌托邦》(*Utopia*) 中就出现了这样的短语——"不要枉费心机去看新鲜事儿"（not for a vain and curious desire to see news），此处 news 的意思就是新事物。news 究竟何时开始用作现代意义的"新闻"（news）语义来指代新事物，尚不得知。根据《新英语词典》(*The New English Dictionary*) 的释义，在尚存的书写中，该词用于此意的最早记录是在 1423 年，当时苏格兰的詹姆斯一世（James Ⅰ）在《国王书》(*The Kingis Quare*)② 中写道："我带来了王室的好消息。"（I bring the newis that blissful ben.）同样毋庸置疑的权威说法是，该词直到 1500 年之后才被广泛运用，这时它逐渐承传挪威语而形成一个传统词汇——tidings。以 16 世纪威廉·廷代尔（Tyndale）③ 和科威对勒（Coverdale）④ 所译的《圣经》版本为蓝本的权威记录对此作

---

① 托马斯·莫尔（Thomas More，1478—1535），英国律师、政治家。莫尔为欧洲早期空想主义学说的创始人、人文主义者，以《乌托邦》而著称。

② 《国王书》(*The Kingis Quair*) 据说是苏格兰国王詹姆斯一世作于 15 世纪的诗歌。半自传体，描述了国王于 1406 被英格兰俘获和被英格兰国王亨利四世及其继任者亨利五世、亨利六世押往法国途中以及之后被囚禁的过程。《国王书》是苏格兰早期重要的文学作品。

③ 威廉·廷代尔（William Tyndale，1494—1536，又译为廷岱勒、丁道尔、丁铎、廷德尔），16 世纪著名的基督教学者和宗教改革家先驱，被认为是第一位清教徒，英国宗教改革家和《圣经》译者。威廉·廷代尔以其翻译的英文版《圣经》而闻名。他曾长期旅居德国和比利时，深受德国的宗教改革家马丁·路德的影响。他擅长希腊文和希伯来文，其译本《新约全书》、《摩西五书》和《约拿书》等成为后来所有英文版《圣经》的蓝本。在威廉·廷代尔的时代，罗马天主教教廷只使用拉丁文《圣经》，不容许私自翻译，而且只有神职人员可以拥有和诠释《圣经》。威廉·廷代尔却主张应该让普通民众接近和阅读《圣经》，因此他被诬陷为异端。

④ 科威对勒（Myles Coverdale，1488—1569），16 世纪圣经译者。他在牛津大学学习，于 1531 年取得教会法学士学位，于 1514 年在诺里奇成为牧师。他将第一部完整印刷的《圣经》译成英文。他翻译的《圣经》中的《诗篇》（集子）被广泛采用并在全世界产生广泛的影响。

了明证，tidings 一词在《圣经》文本中共出现 25 次，而 news 只出现 1 次；莎士比亚在写作中使用 news 一词达 38 次之多，而使用 tidings 仅有 9 次。根据圣路加（St. Luke）① 的叙述，这就是天使们把 tidings 而非 news 作为人类历史上重大消息报道的标示语的原因："你瞧，我带来了能给所有人快乐的好消息。"（Behold I bring you good tidings of great joy which shall be to all people.）

"新闻"这个词在最终固化为"news"之前，曾经以多种形式出现——neues, niewse, nues, newys, newis, newes。回想该隐遇到来自伊甸园的旅行者的情景，我们可以设想：当他们彼此交换所知的消息时，大家就开始讨论各自社区新近发生的事情，他们都急切地表达自己的看法。毋庸置疑，这是最为普通的新闻传播方式。这种新闻传播方式最具价值的特征在于，无论消息是重要的还是微不足道的，都会引发大家的讨论。讨论往往激发思想，而思想则是一种杠杆，当把这种杠杆放置在真理的支点时，就能够推动人类文明的进步。因此，新闻就成为思想启蒙的食粮。人类社会缺失新闻传播，人们的思想就会贫瘠，除非他们积累起可供思考的丰富资源。即使如此，人们的思想也易于变得陈腐和缺乏灵动，除非人们之间通过讨论社会所发生的事情而联系起来，进而更新知识和思想内容。如果两个人生活在与世隔绝的环境里，与外界无任何联系，那么通常情况下，他们很快就会由于缺乏谈论的新话题而无语。社会人的生活需要交流，需要思维，需要为大脑充料，而且不同时代的新闻都可以为人类提供谈话、讨论、思想和观点的材料。

"新闻"和"观点"曾经是密不可分的两个主体，而且它们还将继续紧密相连。承载新闻和观点的媒介出版物就是新闻事业，这也是一种职业、艺术和商业。它发源于人类本性中压制不

---

① 圣路加（Saint Luke），《圣经·新约》第三部福音书《路加福音》以及《使徒行传》的作者、圣保罗的伙伴。

了的本能，对应于人类普遍和持续的信息诉求，以及人类普遍而持续的追求文明和进步的好奇心，还有对于兴趣和刺激的需求。但是，直到出版媒介发明之后，新闻事业才出现。在字母和拼写阶段之前的很长时间里，出版和新闻传播的唯一途径就是口头传播，偶尔也靠结绳记事，或者借助脚夫和信差留下的篆刻或印记来标示。文字发明之后的几个世纪里，声音仍然是唯一的传播媒介，官方信使和少数有特权使用泥版或者蜡版书版、羊皮纸或者莎草纸者除外。然而，重大的或者特别有趣的新闻，即使在有限的条件下也像长了翅膀一样不胫而走。驿站传递系统在很多国家建立起来，用以快速传递讯息，而集市上口头或者书写告示的信息传播方式引发了现代报纸的雏形——罗马帝国时期的《每日纪闻》(*Acta Diurna*) 和中国《京报》的产生。然而，直到印刷机发明之后，现代意义上的出版途径才得以出现，而且在人们孜孜探求新闻传播的有效途径 100 多年之后，印刷机才开始大规模应用。于是，在德国，有人想到这样的主意：收集当下某些重大事情的记录并以书籍的形式印刷出来，这样的出版物受到人们的欢迎，很快，具备此特征的"新闻信"在英格兰和法兰西的首府出版和发行了。然而，其中的每本新闻信都像其他书籍一样成为一种冒险的个体投机行为，很长时间之后，德国人艾莫尔（Egenolph Emmel）才想出来出版新闻期刊的主意。1615 年，艾莫尔创办了周刊《法兰克福新闻》(*Frankfort Journal*)，他也因此成为"德国报业之父"，尽管这个头衔有时候给予巴黎的勒诺多（Renaudot）① 和伦敦的巴特（Butter）②，但他们数年之后才开始出版报刊。然而，在新闻开始为大众认知之前，正是在法兰克

---

① 泰奥弗拉斯特·勒诺多（T. Renaudot），17 世纪法国医生兼记者，法国新闻之父。勒诺多于 1631 年创办法国第一份周报《公报》(*La Gazette*)。法国文学评论团体创立勒诺多文学奖，从 1926 年起每年秋天颁奖。

② 纳撒尼尔·巴特（Nathaniel Butter），英国出版商。

福，新闻业才奠定了基础，引领着尚不稳定的、尚未达到受人尊重的新闻业达一个世纪之久。在电报系统发明和建立之前，交通设施的发达和印刷机的发明，才为快速和大范围收集新闻提供了条件，报刊才能以低成本大量复制，报刊发行才能够快速和远距离发送，进而把新闻事业引领到一个在人类生活和社会事务中无处不在并发挥重大影响的行业。

在整个世界，没有任何行业可以像报业一样具有如此普遍的影响力、说服力和持久的生命力。每天，报纸进入千家万户，进入人们的办公室，进入生意人的店铺，进入工厂和田间。没有人贫穷得买不起报纸，亦没有人居住在太偏远的地方，以至于根本无从接触报纸。报纸每天都会出现在读者面前，为人们提供社区新闻、国家新闻和世界新闻，报纸还为读者提供好消息、坏消息、重要新闻、相对重要而非完全琐碎的新闻，提供必要的商业新闻、工业新闻、社会新闻和政府新闻，以及即兴的、无价值的娱乐新闻等。报纸的报道内容呈现了一个关于世界及其世事的连续而永久的画面，也提供了关于人类及其行为的画面，描绘了人世间的喜剧、悲剧、罪恶、美德、英雄史诗、献身、进取心、发现、灾难、善行、悲痛和欢乐等变幻莫测而无以诠释的生活万花筒。而同时见报的还有编辑就这些新闻事实配发的评论。这些评论解释了新闻事件所蕴涵的意义，把观点与信息及事实联系起来，进而帮助读者更好地理解自身，更好地评价自我如何作为舆论生成的一分子——"无冕之王"统治着现代世界。这就是新闻业——一种依赖于日常事实的行业，一种反映人类生活万象并呈现每个人的观点的行业。它将整个人类更加紧密地联系在一起，使人们对人类各民族有更加清晰的认识。

第二章　新闻采写原则

9　　　　报纸是人类发明的最复杂、最重要和最具价值的体系之一。报纸的采写首先需要从业者精心研究并倾心致力于这个或许隶属于知识阶层的行业，即报纸是脑力劳动的行业，要求从业者具备成功操作该行业的普通知识和特定知识的积累和储备。但是，报业也是一种生产性的行业，它需要大量技术工人，同时它还是涉及复杂营销和大量销售人员的生意场。营销对这个行业而言是必不可少的，而报纸采写等从业者的工作对这一行业的营销亦是不可或缺的，当从业者和营销者认识到彼此的工作同样是必要的时候，他们之间的协作才能产生最佳效果，而新闻业的运作离开他们的工作就是不完整的。离开完备的商业管理，报纸的运作注定是失败的，正如报纸离开有能力的编辑的管理一样。报纸的这两大部门的任何一方经营不善都会给对方带来不利的影响。然而，两个部门的功能尽管都是创造性的，且服务于同一终极目标，但两者的功能截然不同，它们须各自独立经营，并在同一运作结构中密切配合。

10　　　　报纸的采写和制作过程从根本上讲属于一种生产企业的运作模式，其产品的直接销售是必要的。但它并不是乏味、利他主义色彩浓重的行业，出版的动力、制作和销售的过程是报纸整个制作过程的必要环节。如此看来，报纸的制作好像是纯粹的唯利是图的行业。事实上，无论从哪个角度而言，一张有价值的报纸必须拥有一定量的读者，而且报纸必须拥有永久性的读者。为了获得和保持目标读者，报纸必须具备吸引力和值得读者持续购买的价值。赠送的报纸无须依赖发行量，也不需要赢得读者的尊重。类似的实验已经做过。报纸必须售卖，如果报纸要可持续发展或者具有影响力，它就必须凭借其自身内在的价值被读者购买，就必须成为市场化的商品。而报纸要成为市场化的商品，它必须包含读者或者大部分人愿意购买的品质和内容。

报纸的第一要义是报纸可拿来销售，新闻的第一要义是该行业能够生产可销售的商品。新闻可能报道著名人物的某些事迹，也可能表达高尚的思想，还可能致力于崇高的事业。但是，假如这种产品不具有可销售的属性，那么新闻的一切功能都是无效的。对于一张读者不想阅读的报纸而言，这张报纸形同一张白纸，尽管报纸上还印有文字。报纸决不会卖出去，除非报纸刊登了人们希望阅读的足够多的信息，从而吸引他们购买报纸。另外，报纸可能刊登而且应该刊登大量人们未必想知道而必须知道的、应该知晓的信息，但是报纸只有通过刊登读者想要阅读的信息，才能说服读者购买报纸。"给予人们想要的东西"与"给予人们不应该有的东西"两个概念之间有区别，这一点下文再讨论。这里的关键问题是，确认报纸首先必须成为一种可销售的产品，而报纸为了售卖就必须刊登某种意义上迎合公众愿望的内容。报纸没有销售，就没有读者；没有读者，报纸就没有作用。报纸的立意无论多么高，这条原则都是检验新闻机构成败的标准。

由于报纸某种程度上追求质量和品质，通常情况下，一家报纸的影响力与其读者数量成正比，这多少有些道理。报纸的发行量并非比较和估计不同报纸影响力大小的可靠基础，因为发行量大的报纸可能比不上发行量小的报纸的影响力,其原因在于两者之间在出版性质或者读者性质上存在差别。但是,在所有案例中,无论一家独立出版物的发行量是大还是小,其影响力都随着发行量的上升而增加。有些报纸只是定位于教育、知识和有文化诉求的特殊阶层。于是,这些报纸的发行只是限定于该阶层,而该阶层相对于某个既定地区的整体人口而言只占少数,进而报纸的发行量相对少些。但是,这个阶层通常在社会上、行业内和公共事务方面具有超越其人口比例的影响力,所以当你阅读这样的报刊时,它就具有较大发行量报刊的影响力。所以,在这个阶层内,报刊的读者越多,其影响就越深远。

12 无论报纸办得如何好,如果报纸没有读者,该报纸就一文不值,除非报纸通过吸引读者的内容和良好的销售而说服购买者,否则报纸不可能赢得读者。一位厂商制造的产品毋庸置疑具有价值,是人们日常生活所需,甚至可能成为消费者持续和急需的商品,但是这种产品只有从厂房运出去,通过销售网络进入消费和服务环节,它才能变成消费者急需的商品,其实用价值方显活力。无论商品的价值还是其需求量都无法影响该商品的销售,进而补偿其生产成本。一位尚未建立起销售渠道却绞尽脑汁促销面粉的磨坊主注定是要停产的。尽管如此,没有人敢说面粉不是生活必需品或者不具使用价值。但是,面粉只有经过消费才对生活发挥作用,面粉只有通过销售网络才能被消费,且面粉靠销售的固定环节才能被消费掉。只有在战争或者灾荒等危机时期,面粉才会被分发掉。但实际情况是,个体或者公共慈善机构危机时期的捐赠除外,面粉不可能分送给消费者。即使在这样的情况下,磨坊主照样会被补偿其原本用于销售的面粉。生活中没有其他商品比面粉更加必要了,或许除了面粉之外没有任何产品可以免于人们的批评,人的生活离不开面粉,面粉厂生产的面粉无处不在、无时不在,还有诸多其他客观理由足以说明面粉存在的必要性。

报纸并非人们生活中必不可少的产品。人们不阅读报纸照样生存。确实，多少个年代以来，很多人从来不读报，人们的生活中根本没有报纸。但是，报纸终究演绎为人们的一种需求和本性愿望，报纸变成个体获知信息和公共福利的一种必要工具。面粉毕竟是一种产品，其发送和销售首先是一种企业行为。虽然这并不意味着利润是面粉厂的必要目标。报纸可能具有诸如利他主义或者幕后支持，以至于报社的确忽略了考虑利润因素。但是，不管怎么样，报纸是一种企业组织，它必须遵循企业组织的运作原则，而且报纸如果要完成其经营目标的话，就必须拥有商业能力和实力。报纸印制出来以后，必须进行售卖，而训练有素的员工和商业运作流程对于报纸等媒体的必要性与其他企业运行的意义是同等重要的。

另外，报业一个普遍的实际情况是：一家报纸的公共影响及其通常所讲的公共价值与报纸的商业管理水平之间有着必然的联系。同样真实的情况是，最有影响力的报纸是那些最有经济实力和通过合法渠道最盈利的出版物。报纸的影响力可能不会那么完美，但无论这种影响力是好还是差，它都是建立在读者品质和数量的基础上，建立在发行数量和发行质量之上的。报纸唯有通过售卖，才能取得发行量，而报纸正是通过发行量才将其价值展示给广告商，报纸只有通过来自销售的广告增长而逐渐发达起来。报纸的销售和广告是报业生存的物质基础，而这些报纸的特征在新闻事业的发展中既不能忽略，亦不能轻视，报纸要办得成功，无论其原始立意和目标如何定位，报纸销售和广告都是十分必要的。甚至在个别情况下，人们应该认识到广告本身具有美学和经济学的价值，而这种公共价值使得广告比单纯盈利的新闻业的商业属性更具某种重要性。

商业实力、商业原则和商业方式都是新闻业有效运行的必要条件，但它不能完全被利润所支配和驱使，否则会给整个行业带来灾难或损害。新闻产品的制作不仅是一种企业行为。作为规律，每一家报刊都是建立在所倡导的某种原则之上，旨在支持某种事业，履行公共服务职能或者满足公共需求。在报纸所有的目标中，至少一项目标或者有些目标是为了推动某种观念，无论这种观念的本质是什么，在所有新闻产品制作的开端或者整个过程中，概莫如此。随着这种观念的认知及其运用形式的历时变化，观念的本质、影响公众的基本原则或者旨在推动公共事业进步的公共服务等都不能改变或者放弃，否则会对整个报业带来灭顶之灾。甚至在个别情况下，即使一家报纸或者其他报刊创办于利润至上的经营理念之上，当报纸可能盈利或者在良好经营管理下盈利的时候，其处境也是十分危险的，假如这家报刊的运营处于利润的支配之下，无视新闻业目标和基本原则的话，它注定要停刊。

对于整个人类行为而言，报纸的生存最依赖于永久的公众信任。在所有的人类产品中，报纸对公众的开放程度最高，它完全置于读者的审视之下。正是在这种公共的审视中，报纸才得以存活；正是通过这种审阅的结果，报纸才得以成长或者遭遇萎缩。每天，报纸以日志形式记录世界上发生的事情，揭露世界上发生的丑闻以告世人。报纸的优势和劣势、缺失和魅力通过自身的新闻报道公开展现在每位读者面前，等待着读者对其进行评判、赞誉或者谴责。假如报纸及其报道是令人满意的，报纸就张扬了自己的优势，假如报纸及其报道是糟糕的，报纸同样暴露了自身的缺失。当然，报纸作为人类个体自由表达思想的一种途径，报纸及其所报道的内容不会总是令人满意的，或者总是糟糕透顶的，但无论哪种情况占优势，报纸的优劣都是可辨的。报纸将自身的优势公开表白，并加以标榜，以便读者监督和选择。而无论报纸的定位和目的如何，某种程度上都必须依靠报纸版面来实现，否则这样的定位和目的都是徒劳的。报纸可能具有某种不可告人的动机，或许它邪恶的设计是企图掩盖某种罪恶，但这样的初衷定位和设计却是至关重要的。实际的动机不可能长期隐藏，罪恶的阴谋也不会在众目睽睽之下永久地隐蔽。每一种报刊迟早都会揭露这种不可告人的动机或者阴谋，将之公布于众，报纸如此在公众的评判下生存或者倒闭。

如果报纸的所有者或者掌控者本质定位上不可告人的动机遭到公众的普遍怀疑的话，这家报纸就无法生存，遑论报纸的繁荣发展。美联社常务总经理梅尔维尔·斯通（Melville E. Stone）① 在对报人的一次谈话中讲到，"拥有巨大财产和大企业的人们做过数次尝试：为影响和引导舆论的目的购买并经营报纸，几乎所有的尝试都以失败而告终。贾森·吉尔德（Jay Gould）② 先生曾经拥有纽约的一家报纸，他在经历了短暂而惨淡的经营之后却乐意把报纸贱卖掉。30 年前，塞勒斯·菲尔德（Cyrus Field）③ 先生做出了类似的事情，他购买了一家晚报，以便保护他的铁路公司，并努力经营这家报纸。当然，不久之后他就发现自己并不能正常地运作这家报纸。于是，他想转卖一半的股权给我，并说服我可以用报纸盈利之外的资金来支付。当我问起何人将与我合作经营报纸的时候，他回答说他本人将拥有报纸的另一半股权。这样，我不得不说，假如他想保持报纸的股权的话，哪怕是小股权，我就失去了购买报纸的任何兴趣了。如果一家报纸定位于作为实现不可告人目的之途径的话，它就不会取得成功"。④

---

① 梅尔维尔·斯通（Melville Elijah Stone，1848—1929），美国报纸出版商，《芝加哥每日新闻》（Chicago Daily News）的创办人，重组后美联社的总经理。
② 贾森·吉尔德（Jason Jay Gould，1836—1892），美国著名铁路开发商和投机者。长期以来，贾森·吉尔德被贬为 19 世纪末靠残酷剥削致富的美国资本家的原型。他的成功使其成为美国历史上第九位最富有的人。
③ 塞勒斯·菲尔德（Cyrus West Field，1819—1892），美国商人和金融家。与其他企业家共同创办了大西洋电报公司（the Atlantic Telegraph Company），并于 1858 年铺设了穿越大西洋的第一条电报电缆。
④ The Coming Newspaper，p. 97.——原书注

这段论述被多次明证过，其中的道理是正确的，因为只是通过报纸而不展现其办报宗旨或目的的话，就不可能实现不可告人的目的，而且即使人们努力隐藏报纸的支持来源，报纸迟早都会暴露其来源和背景。报纸所有者肯定首先关心报纸合法出版的发行量和公开的新闻宗旨及其掌控者，而从通常的经验来讲，报纸所有权必须展现在其作品之中。作为规律，成功的报纸往往是那些专业报人创办和发展起来的，他们没有其他的职业和兴趣，大多数这样的成功报纸作为家庭的固定财产持续发展，或者传承到类似致力于该行业的其他人手中。然而，无论报纸如何兴旺或者受到读者尊重，当它们落入所谓的"外来者"手中，被根本不关心报纸生产的人所控制时，报纸就会逐渐衰落或者迅速衰落。并非直接从事出版业的那些人为了私欲而获得了报纸的控制权，他们通常都不能实现报纸所担负的功能，尽管这并不是绝对发生的事情。新闻就好比嫉妒成性的情妇，她要求重金投入，其生产过程中的劳动者亦是如此，由于行业的特殊属性所致，他要经受灾难的惩罚。

　　但是，一家日报不仅每天展现在读者面前，必须依靠自身的品质售卖，而且要全部卖光。报纸属于最短命的产品，或许是唯一短命的产品。今天的新闻就是明天的旧闻，新闻的价值稍纵即逝。报纸的货架上或仓库中不应该有存货。报纸每天必须更新，每天的报纸必须尽力卖掉。而每天的报纸内容必须有所不同。一张报纸必须永葆新颖。报纸必须每天展现在公众面前，并由公众来评判，而公众的评判建立在当天的报道和长期以来报纸的日常报道满足公众喜好并得到公众认可而获取的信任度基础之上。这种信任是日积月累的财富，无论它是经过多长时间培育出来的，无论它保持了多长时间，只要它继续每天接受公众的验证，它就会永存。公众对报纸的信任度丧失的过程比其形成的过程要容易得多，也快得多，而一旦这种信任度丧失的话，它就比起初形成时更加难以恢复。报纸不能背弃这样的原则：培育并保持公众的信任度，绝不能丧失公众对报纸的信任，而且在考绩中要防止报纸发行量下滑引发的公众信任度下降。报纸每天不断面对大众评判的考验，而且每期报纸内容必须证明其满足了公众喜好和尊重读者的权利。假如报纸丧失了其公信力，它就不能生存，也不能发展，报纸必然衰退。因此，与任何其他消费者需求的产品比较而言，报纸在一种更加严厉和持久的审视下坚守自身的公信力，并传播每天的新闻卖点。

基于以上的分析，无论公众给予一家报纸怎样的支持，信息、舆论或者娱乐可能作为其描绘的力量。无论报纸诉求于某个阶层或者大众，也无论报纸质量如何，这家报纸必须每天证明自身的公信力和特定目标读者是否认同其报价。同时，无论报纸读者的特质如何，报纸必须保持读者对它的信任，报纸必须创造和保持其对于读者的良好印象，而无论报纸自身存在什么样的缺点，或者报纸出现失误的频率如何，报纸都必须忠诚于读者，报纸以一种普遍方法为读者提供所支付的服务。假如报纸做不到这一点的话，读者就不会再购买它了。

报纸首先为自身的利益而运行，它不能像风筝的尾巴那样飘摇般地发展。报纸必须为自身的利益而经营，因为正如上文所言，假如报纸要办得成功，对所有者、雇员和读者来讲都有价值，而且报纸要实现其预期的合法新闻目标的话，那么报纸的制作就要投入巨额资金，还要有实现其目标的相关资源和智力的投入。只有当自身利益得以实现而且自身利益可能通过努力得以补偿的情况下，报纸才可能实现其集中目标，无论这种补偿是物质层面的还是精神层面的，或者两者兼有。但是，大量的证据表明，在报纸的生产过程中，自身利益和公众利益不仅是兼容的而且是统一的。新闻事业的基本原则，也可以说基本目标是公共服务，而该领域的公共服务也是一种自我服务。这并非意味着一家报纸必须成为一个慈善机构，相反，它必须提供具体的服务：传递可靠的信息、引导舆论、支持公众权利、谴责政府腐败、改进原则和观念,并运用其力量促进和改善公共福利。假如报纸很好地履行了这些职能的话,它就为赢得公众的尊重、信任和敬仰奠定了坚实的基础,这不仅是新闻业最令人满意的精神回报,而且肯定是报纸最持久的物质财富。

第三章 新闻首要功能

报纸是关于人类本性对新闻的普遍需求的反映和产物。报纸本身不会创造需求。相反，人类的这种需求是永恒存在的，所以报纸就成为人类必要的产品。因此，一家报纸的首要功能就是传递消息。消息的传播是新闻事业的基本功能。除此之外，即使言论这种非常重要的文体也只是报纸的副产品。可以肯定的是，有些期刊只定位于言论，而所刊登的作品也属于新闻，因为它们首先是就新闻事实发表的言论。但这些期刊并非报纸，它们的运行只是履行了新闻的一种独立而从属的功能而已。在新闻业的运行中，消息的地位似乎是至高无上和毋庸置疑的，而实际上这条新闻业的基本准则经常是模糊的，没有正当的陈述来强调其重要性。报纸不时将重心倾向于某种特别的政策或者目的，此种情况下报纸就成为一种实现终极目标的途径，结果导致新闻成为一种相对的附属品。报纸也不时地充当并非新闻作品的"特稿"体裁的附属品，使特稿代替消息而充斥报纸版面。偶尔，人们还假定，成功出版和发行的报纸的首要功能只是娱乐。在这种理念的应用和支配下，报纸所刊登的任何内容，无论是不是新闻作品，都被设定为为读者提供娱乐的作品，娱乐成为报纸的首要职能，而这一切都是以本质上和更大程度上牺牲新闻价值的正确判断为代价的。

实现新闻业的合法目的不容忽视,而这并非仅仅停留在消息发布的表面意义上。消息发布只是辅助性的认识可能的确处于支配地位。但是,无论怎么说,保持新闻业发布消息的首要功能是必要,因为消息发布是整个新闻事业所有功能发挥的必要基础。消息之外特稿的价值也不能予以否定。这些体裁本身可能在提高报纸的品位和作为信息、教育、娱乐的物质力量方面具有明显的优势。但是它们只能作为居于主导地位的消息体裁的补充,而不能代替新闻的位置,也不许超过新闻的分量,进而损害报纸的传播效果。

报纸首先充当消息传播的工具,其次是就新闻事实说话的言论喉舌,除此之外,它当然就没有存在的理由了,因此新闻的生命和兴趣全部集中在消息上。但什么是新闻呢?新闻就像诗歌一样难以准确界定,因为它没有可以想象的边界或者限定。新闻包括自然界和人类无穷无尽的事物。从常识来讲,新闻指最近发生的事情,一点也不难定义。一件新近发生的事情本身不会成为新闻,而关于这起事件的报道就构成了新闻,事情发生后数年才进行报道,这根本不是什么新闻了。迄今尚未报道的有关美洲大陆之发现的事实可能是新闻。鲜为人知的消息构成十足的新闻暴料。事态变化也不是必要的新闻构成。源源不断的报道并非事件的简单记录,而是关于现实状况的反映,这才是新闻。言论不是事态变化,但言论经常被当作新闻报道,而且往往是十分重要和有趣的新闻题材。一个人的所思可能就如其言谈举止一样构成真实的新闻。查理斯·A·达纳(Charles A. Dana)[①]说:"假如报纸不刊登新闻的话,它可能刊登其他任何内容,但那样它就不会非常成功。在我看来,新闻意味着新近发生的一切事情,人们感

---

① 查理斯·A·达纳(Charles A. Dana,1819—1897),美国记者、作家和政府官员。美国内战后,他提倡激进的政治策略。

兴趣的一切事情,而且是其中十分重要、足以吸引和捕捉公众或者部分人注意力的事情"。

新鲜的信息就是新闻,即使信息所指代的事物本身是过去的。阿肯色州神秘的山地人即使在 1896 年才听说罗伯特·爱德华·李(Robert E. Lee)① 投降的消息,这也是可能的。美国内战结束已经 30 年了,但对这位山地人而言,这依然是新闻。人类发现北极之后数个礼拜,世人才了解这件事情。人类发现北极的事实尽管发生在过去,但有关报道依旧是新闻。在电报发明之前,人类的信息传播依赖缓慢的邮差或者人力传送,新闻往往在事件发生几天、几个礼拜,甚至几个月后才能为人们所知晓。几乎将世界各个部分连接在一起的信息传播设备的发展,使得新闻可能在事件发生的同时被报道,在某件事情发生当天,相关的大量新闻已经见诸报端,以至于"新闻"这个词语本身包含了及时性和新鲜性等含义,而及时性某种程度上成为新闻价值的重要判断标准。于是,新闻开始意味着有关事件的独家报道或者记录当天所发生事件的含义,具有新闻要素的过去事情的报道除外。

但是,正如达纳先生所暗示的,我们应该将新闻本身和具有新闻价值意义的消息区别开来。个体几乎与所遇到的每个熟人交换和传递消息,然而,他们所交换的大部分消息对于自身或者亲朋好友的小圈子是没有兴趣的,他们认为有着极其重要意义的消息对于其他人而言却毫无意义或者意义不甚重要。从新闻事业的角度来诠释的话,消息必须具备某种公众感兴趣的品质,即一种公共重要性的衡量标准。正如达纳先生所表达的,消息至少必须具备瞬间捕捉和吸引公众或者足以证明问题实质从而吸引相当一部分读者群体注意力的特质。因此,报纸主编不仅总是面对新闻是什么的问题,而且他还要面对新闻业视角及其本人特定视角下

---

① 罗伯特·爱德华·李(Robert E. Lee, 1807—1870),美国军事家。战后,他积极从事教育事业,曾任华盛顿大学(现名华盛顿与李大学)的校长。

新闻是什么的问题。对于前者,他能够即兴回答,给予完整的定义,即使没有作出精确的界定亦未尝不可;对于后者,他的回答就需要加以判断,也需要直觉,还涉及必须不断实践的辨别力。

这个话题在后面的章节中再讨论。但在认识新闻本质属性的时候,我们不仅要发现新闻无限和复杂的变化,而且要发现其发展的不同阶段,以及繁杂而时常带有喜剧或者悲剧色彩的细节。关于某件事情的新闻可能是一篇完整的报道。值得报道的所有事实都在手上,事实得以陈述,事件得以传播。如果没有后续报道的话,事件很快就会被忘却。大部分通常是相对不重要或者趣味性不强的新闻往往出现这种情况。另外一类新闻是由完整的事态发展的系列报道组成,这类系列报道构成了连续的事件,彼此导致因果关系。系列事件可能突然终止,或者事态发展得越发重要,如此,仅有几行字的"豆腐块"式的报道毋庸置疑就变成充斥整个版面的系列报道的源头。1914年的一天,在巴尔干半岛一个小国家的某个偏僻村庄里,王子被暗杀的消息通过无线电波传遍世界。按照报纸版面的编排原则,在远离事故现场的报纸上,这则消息只是占据了很小的版面。当天发生的很多事情对编辑而言似乎都比这个边远地区发生的悲剧更具新闻价值。实际上,这个暗杀事件本身的重要性相对来讲并不强。如果不是此次暗杀案引发了其他事情的话,它几天内就会被人们忘记,但是由此引发的似乎并不重要的系列后续事件却发展成为新闻业前所未闻的重大新闻,数年来竟然覆盖了世界各大报纸的版面。可以肯定,这是个特例,但是这些各自独立而又相互关联的一连串事情往往起源于一个明显的事态变化或者一件不起眼的事件,而其重要性呈现递进状态。第一次世界大战的案例很好地证明了当天发生的事情可能引起连锁事态变化的可能性。

但是,还有另外一类新闻。这类新闻涉及一件独立事情的全过程,这件事情可能已经完成或者正在进行中。这类新闻记录的是一个连续事件的前后阶段,其中包括整个事态发展中每天的变化和所有环节,而无论这些事情多么重要,其实都是整个事件发展过程中的组成部分,是整个事态发展的不同阶段而已。例如,美国总统大选就是由一连串的竞选活动来完成的,而竞选过程中所有的活动都是为了一个结果,它们有机地组合起来,自始至终都没有分离开来。一场政治或社会运动中产生的新闻属于同一类,其中的事件连续发生而彼此关联,有序展开,旨在服务于一个预期的目标。国会会议产生不同属性和特点的新闻,整个事态包括很多持续发生的事件,有些可能已经完成并取得了效果,有些可能随着时间的流逝而消失,但是整个会议过程呈现了不同的层面和不同的公众利益诉求。

因此,按照新闻业的规律,越重要的新闻越具有多重属性,它们承载了很多连续的新闻故事材料,而每篇报道都可以自成章节,每件事都是整个故事链条中的一个情节。无论故事长短,它们都具有连续性、预期性和不同寻常的、令人吃惊的、吸引人的地方,以及提高和保持触动人类情感和关注度的趣味性。

每天的报纸都会为读者带来创新的内容和不同叙述模式的文章,报纸内容富于变化,从不雷同,没有人能分辨某天的新颖报道可能给将来带来何种意义。但是,报纸通过每天滚动的持续报道脉络,勾勒出我们人生中所谓复杂的万象百态,而且每天的报纸新闻都是生活的一面镜子,通过这面镜子读者可以观察人生和了解人生。

新闻可以细分为两类:娱乐性新闻和信息性新闻。这种细分法只是相对的,因为大量的新闻旨在承载信息,并非娱乐,只有少量的新闻纯粹是娱乐性的,没有什么信息价值。但无论怎样对新闻进行分类,娱乐性新闻和信息性新闻这两种新闻类型是客观存在的,定位于普通读物的报刊以其中一种新闻占据其主导地位,而对于大多数报刊而言,则把两种类型的新闻混合起来。对于信息性新闻为主的报刊来说,无论其内容多么令人满意,多么富有价值,依然可能由于缺乏娱乐性导致报刊缺少了维系公众兴趣和支持的必要吸引力。可以肯定的是,专门致力于信息性新闻的报刊价值毋庸置疑是不完整的，但它们通常都是旨在打造为特定利益群体提供信息服务的出版物，对于报刊所报道领域不予关注的读者而言，这些报刊几乎没有什么吸引力。如果它们不属于指定意义的类别报刊，其发行量就一定局限于某个数量相对小的群体，对这个群体而言，纯粹的信息就成为其主要的阅读内容，因此它们也就成为某一类型的报刊。

想了解"世界上正在发生的事情"是人类的本性，这种由人的本能好奇心所激发的本性是任何个人都不可或缺的。从很大程度上来讲，满足人性这种好奇心的是娱乐性新闻而非信息性新闻。正是新闻激发了人们的兴趣，而实质上它并不具有任何教导意义。新闻所报道的每件事情，无论其多么琐碎或者不重要，它都承载着有关这件事情的信息，而这种信息仅仅是提供娱乐的工具而已。普通人并非为了求得牢固的知识和教导才来阅读报纸，而是为了满足关于当天发生事情的好奇心来读报的。他的眼球被他所感兴趣的新闻所吸引，而这种兴趣则因个体的趣味、品性和交往而有所不同。引起某人兴趣的新闻可能对于另一个人而言根本毫无兴趣，但每个人都在探索和寻求吸引他的新闻，对于大多数人来讲，新闻的吸引力不是学识、知识或者信息等报纸的基本内容，而是娱乐性新闻本身。

因此，娱乐与消遣有别，娱乐的本质内容是新闻认知中不容忽略或者贬低的。这里需要指出的是，新闻事业的基本功能是公共服务，其基本职责是服务于这一基本功能的新闻传播，而新闻传播则通过公共事务和公共事件真相的传递来实现，新闻传播也通过有助于个体日常生活、公民活动及其价值判断的物质和价值理念的信息传递而完成。但是，在新闻传播的过程中，娱乐性新闻为圈定或许并未被具有真正意义的新闻所吸引的读者提供了一个有用的意图。我们从鉴赏的视角来阅读新闻的时候，它就是通向终极目标的有用手段，但它只能是从属的手段，绝非原则性的手段。

第四章 新闻选择

　　新闻报道主要关注公众利益的相关消息。正是记者和出版商关于世事、现状、舆论和行为发展过程的新闻报道某种程度上触动了公众的潜意识，但这并不能创造新闻。通常情况下，只有公众的注意力圈定于某件事情或者某种现状时，才会产生新闻。新闻是事实本身产生的。在报纸诞生之前，有趣的事儿一发生，经由人们的传播即可成为新闻，尽管消息是可信的，然而其传播的范围与引发的公众兴趣大小成正比。假如今天没有报纸和其他传播途径的话，事实就得靠口口相传来报道，某个事实每次经过口头复述的时候，进行复述的人都会在事实的基础上添油加醋，进而降低了消息的可信度，口头传播甚至能达到以讹传讹的地步。我们必须得承认，新闻经常屈从于人类本性的弱点，在口头传播的过程中新闻事实被扭曲或者夸张，但无论这样做是有意识的还是无意识的，这种做法都是对新闻基本原理的背离。

　　新闻的任务是汇集和传播具有重要公共意义或者公众感兴趣的消息，而准确性成为实施这个任务过程中的第一行为准则。新闻承担这种公共服务的功能时，也承担了其传播真理的明确责任。因此，在辨别和选择新闻的操作中，报刊有必要考虑将真实性作为第一要义。这条原则的实际运用并没有像叙说的那样简单,其困难将在本书的独立章节加以关注和阐释。这里只是将此原则与报纸编辑判断和选择新闻的操作联系起来,而且必须将两者联系在一起。

"我应该刊载什么信息?拒绝什么信息?"这样的问题总是摆在编辑面前,而且每天都在翻新。这个问题更多地涉及编辑关于不同新闻卖点或者所表现的相对价值的判断是否合宜。编辑们每天被迫考虑版面的局限性,他有很多适合刊登新闻的栏目,来自各通讯处或新闻代理的新闻数量通常远远超越了编辑所编排和支配的版面。结果,编辑经常被迫拿下很多如果版面允许情况下他会愿意刊登的新闻稿。而报纸版面实际上并非一个常量,而是每天都在变化,甚至每个时辰都有差别,这是由于报刊需求导致了其他新的要求。每期报刊的新闻供给都不同,而且新闻的重要性也不一样。今天的报刊可能刊载的全是新闻,明天报刊的新闻稿可能相对少一些。今天报刊所刊登的大量新闻可能几乎没有什么新闻价值,而明天可能有一大堆"爆料",需要占用更多的栏目来报道。还有,在某个相对平静无事的日子,当天即将结束之际突然发生非常重要的事件,该新闻事件需要占用很大的版面来报道,这样就要求撤掉已经编排好的稿件或者可能已经付印的样版。因此,编辑需要对于新闻事件及其报纸版面的局限性进行调整和再调整,这是个持续不断的过程。而且,记者根据其初衷估计的相对有新闻价值的稿件进行采编,当天所有新闻稿从来不会同时出现在编辑面前。新闻稿是陆续来到编辑们跟前的,像细水长流的小溪一样,而新闻的及时性和媒介设备的局限性也推动编辑以滚动的新闻流而非静态的稿件堆来判断新闻稿。只有报纸的样刊送达编辑们桌上的时候,编辑才能将当天的新闻看成一个整体,此时编辑再从整体的角度用自我的判断来调整新闻版面就来不及了。

尽管在编辑对新闻稿加以判断和选择的过程中存在诸多无法

逃避的实际困难，而且必然存在认同的差异，但新闻的品质很大程度上还是依赖记者和编辑辨别新闻及其新闻价值的能力，无论成功的新闻还是有用的新闻，概莫如此。在这种辨别力高超而且标准较高的时候，新闻业就获得了最为高明的评判，而且最大限度地服务于大众。但是在实际的操作中，我们还要考虑很多其他事情。

新闻选择的第一条原则是公众兴趣的大小。趣味性是报纸选择所刊登新闻的首要质量保证因素，因为正是趣味性本身使得报纸具有吸引力，进而可以售卖。缺乏趣味性的报纸是不稳定的，而公众越是对新闻感兴趣，报纸的销售量越大。报纸之所以值得重复印刷和出版，就是因为它可以售卖。假如报纸不具有可读性，它就失去了任何价值，无论报纸质量怎样提升，其发行量如何提高，都无济于事。公众对于新闻趣味性的需求不容忽视。任何一条独立新闻的价值都是通过其所引发的趣味性的高低或程度来衡量的。但这并非建立判断新闻价值所依赖的唯一基础标准，正如下文所述，这样的标准和判断具有一定的局限性，这只是最初的衡量。

但是，公众对每一条新闻的兴趣在报纸刊登之前究竟该如何衡量和估算呢？"新闻意识"（"新闻鼻"）是所有成功报人必备的品质，这一品质部分源自个人潜意识而部分是由个人辨别事务的经历所导致的本能的鉴赏能力。"新闻意识"是第一位和最可靠的新闻价值判断依据。但是，无论如何，它们都是报人和记者无意识的认知和运用的基本原则。

首先，新闻的趣味性只是大致的判断和评估。我们所有人都特别关注新闻事件最触动我们个人的细节在哪里，影响我们的朋友或所认识的人的新闻细节以及影响我们邻居或者社区的新闻细节是什么。例如在一场火灾的报道中，人们最关心的莫过于住在这栋楼里的是哪些人；其次，人们感兴趣的是隔壁居住的是哪些人；之后，人们关心的是谁居住在同一个社区里以及谁目击了火灾发生的过程。居住得较远的那些人或者没有看到这场火灾的人对此兴趣不大，但是这个城市的居民却有兴趣了解这场火灾的情况，无论居民的兴趣有多大，总比临近城市居民对火灾的兴趣大些。对于非全国范围内发生的任何新闻事件而言，人们的兴趣与他们距离事件现场的远近成反比。总统逝世的消息实际上对于旧金山和华盛顿的居民来说其兴趣是同等的。政府颁布的具有全国意义的任何重要法案的新闻趣味性并非通过相对距离来度量的。有些特定新闻事件在任何地方都足以引起人们的普遍兴趣，以至于它们在到处都有对等的新闻价值。但是对于普通的新闻事件而言，其新闻价值随着人们距离事件现场距离的增加而递减。同样的道理，地方新闻具有自己独特的重要性和特定的优势。的确，很大程度上是共同兴趣使得新闻传播开来。如果报纸失去了对读者及其兴趣应有的尊重和回应的话，那么就没有几家报纸能够生存下来了。而很多报纸将自身限定于地方报道，把提供普通新闻的任务留给其他报纸，这样的报道策略是有益的，也是有利可图的。然而，无论报纸的报道范围如何，无论其收集新闻的网络是否遍布整个世界，它们都不能忽视也不能轻视本土的新闻报道。读者的共同兴趣实际上是整个新闻事业的基石，是整个新闻业环绕的核心，是新闻业得以维系的物质基础。因此，接近性的新闻要素在新闻价值的判断中占据很重的份额。

然而，远方发生的事情也可能引起近地居民的很大兴趣。回顾上个段落火灾的例证，即使房屋的主人不是自己居住在里面，他与租住在这栋楼房子里的那些人同样关注这场火灾事故。假如他居住在千里之外的地方，他的关注可能更加主动。另外一个例子，某个城镇的人们大量投资于一家制造公司的股票，这家公司的工厂设立在较远的一个州或者在国外。那么，这家工厂在火灾中遭到毁坏的消息就会引起当地人们的兴趣和关注，尽管事件本身并没有发生在当地。一个城镇的某个当地名流在远离家乡的某个地方被杀害，这桩谋杀案的消息或许会在这个城镇引起居民的极大兴趣,就好像事件本身发生在当地一样。我们不但对自己社区所发生的事情特别感兴趣,而且对任何地方发生的涉及或牵连我们社区的居民或福利的事情感兴趣。

但巧合的是,我们对于新闻事件的兴趣并非局限于个人或者社区的人脉圈。在最亲近和最直接的人关注我们的同时,我们也想了解世界上其他地方发生的事情。而对于这种兴趣的回应及其鼓励却构筑起新闻业最重要的任务之一。因为我们的兴趣领域越广泛,我们可能从中获得的知识越丰富,我们对世界的理解越深刻,对他人的同情越广博。在对这些新闻进行取舍时,相对接近性或者联系性的新闻原则依然十分重要,正如上文所说,新闻的趣味性随着距离的增加而递减。当然,这条原则之外有很多重要的特例,但无论如何,该原则在进行新闻取舍时都是无法忽视的。最重要的是,我们还要考虑关于报纸出版和发行点所在地区和报纸重点发行或有所发行的特定社区。这个地区的新闻要求特别的考虑,仅次于地方新闻,而且要根据同样的相对价值标准加以判断。整个国家或者部分地区可能作为报纸这样的报道范围,而无论就全国范围还是地方来讲,官方新闻即政府作为国家机器的运行情况是需首要报道的,这比国家任何部分或者国土上任何个体的消息都或多或少具有更高的新闻趣味性。当然,作为规律,关于联邦政府的行动或者建议的新闻对于各加盟国而言具有特别的兴趣,这无需考虑事件发生地距离政府所在位置的远近,但是这个特定地方或者部分利益体还有很多新闻来源需要在各个省区的新闻之间加以区分。一般情况下,最有趣的外国新闻是触及或者影响我们国家事务的新闻,无论政治消息、经济消息或者社会消息,但是我们仍然可能对毫无干系的新闻事件感兴趣,尤其是包含戏剧性新闻要素的消息。

但是,在所有新闻的取舍过程中,无论是地方新闻、地区新闻还是全国性新闻,某种特定的新闻要素原则都会运用其中。这里需要重申的是,我们首先考虑的是对公共兴趣的推测及其评估。而这并非唯一的考虑,出版更多缺乏公共兴趣的新闻是新闻业的职责所在。无论怎样讲,公共兴趣都是整个新闻业所诉求的目标,对于大多数新闻而言,假如报纸要赢得读者支持的话,公共兴趣就是必要的。但是,除了已经讨论的接近性和个人关注之外,新闻吸引大众兴趣的品质何在呢?

最活跃的新闻品质应该叫"人情味",它可能被界定为一种情感的诉求而非理性的鉴赏,一种潜意识的诉求而非思想。这一新闻品质以其所有的不同形式或者对比层次包含了戏剧般人生的全部内容——喜剧和悲剧、磨难和喜悦、痛苦和欢乐、美德和邪恶、富裕和贫穷、建设和毁坏——都可以在当天的新闻中找到,进而追寻人性的同情、怜悯、羡慕和模仿,激起正直者对不公事务的愤慨和谴责,同样经常触及人类的劣根性。例如,趣味性的来源基础可能建立在关于某个人物与对立势力之间一场争斗所引发的普遍吸引力。生活本身就是一场持续不断的抗争,因此这场抗争不仅产生很多新闻,而且比其他任何事物都可能引起普通人更大的兴趣。无论人生竞技是一种技能或力量,还是一种原则或势力,无论它属于物质的、知识的或者精神的层面,其所诉求的事情都能引发人类的兴趣。体育报道极其庞大的读者群体证明了这种注意力的存在,而正是这种人性本能的注意力将其吸引力牵引到职业拳击赛、战争、政治竞选、资本与劳务纠纷、法庭审判、道德和宗教争议等新闻上来。可以肯定的是,有些新闻涉及知识性的理解和鉴赏,但是至今尚未出现达到如此知识或者精神高度的竞争,以至于这场争斗仅仅是一场争斗而已,其中没有任何趣味性的要素。这种本能绝非可以忽视的,尽管有些表现得可能低劣一些。没有争斗,人类就无法进步,而在支撑人类进步的争斗中存在公共兴趣,这也是人类进步的必要条件。

但是,从技术意义上来看,"人类的趣味性"这个字眼很少运用到意义重大的事务上来。它尤其与社会关系中的情感或者引人注意的事务、人性或非人性的次要表现、心灵诉求的事情相关，与仇恨、贪婪、妒忌或欲望有关，它或许仅仅指关于他人的生存状况、活动和行为等的好奇心，无论这是合法的或者非法的。简言之，趣味性指本身蕴涵着很多坏因素或者好因素的事情。这类新闻对于大多数人如此具有吸引力，以至于成为他们对报纸的基本需求内容，报刊很愿意拿这些消息来填满版面，并辅以大字号标题来吸引读者的注意力。当报刊没有刊登关于此类事情的消息时，报刊就急切地搜寻这样的消息，并用有关琐碎事情的夸张和演绎来创造趣味性新闻，而报刊任何部门都不具有如此滥用新闻趣味性判断标准的优势和权力。

但是，从广义和更加局限性的技术层面来讲，人类趣味性指新闻业从中合理地获取强大支持并进而贡献其自身的影响力和公共服务价值的源泉，而公共服务价值则是通过拓宽所提供信息和观点的范围来体现的。人类趣味性直接引发的情感影响具有自身的价值，通常与智力的影响同等重要，有时候它甚至更加重要，因为人类文明的很多巨大进步都是通过信息引发的情绪波而促成的。人类的基本情绪依然是这样引发的，而有良知的记者们的任务就是参照此特征进行新闻选择，分辨良莠，并对必须刊登的、曾经使当天新闻出现色彩的罪恶性事件与正面的指导性和建设性新闻信息进行平衡，以便报刊对社会和文明进步产生总体的持续影响。

这给我们带来了新闻事业的主要功能：新闻报道作为信息传播的过程具有内在的价值，新闻报道把有用的知识信息传播给个体或者公众，这本身就是富有指导性的，进而宣扬了真善美的新闻事件和值得关注的新闻事件，以及此类事件的涵义及其彼此关系所给予的启发。普通读者对于这样的新闻可能有兴趣，也可能没有兴趣，但是行内报纸如果没有提供此类新闻的应有报道，它们就对公众犯下了近似玩忽职守的罪过，而且逃避了通常由法律保护其特殊地位而确立起来的义务。上文已经阐释，从新闻业的基本观点来看，兴趣是新闻的第一要素。除了娱乐而没有其他价值的新闻可能缺乏趣味性。然而，娱乐是诱导和刺激报纸发行量增长的一个新闻要素，因此为了扩大报纸的整个读者群体，报纸的娱乐性是绝对不容忽视的。但是，此类新闻是实现报纸目标的手段，这里所讲的目标就是扩大具有内在价值的新闻信息的报道范围。具备该特性的新闻可能而且经常具有像广泛吸引读者的纯粹娱乐性新闻一样的公共趣味性。的确，此类新闻可能首先具有公共趣味性。因此，兼备趣味性和新闻价值的新闻才是最好的新闻。但是，假如新闻业要实现其对于公众所担负的责任，缺乏公共趣味性但意义重大且具有新闻价值的新闻一直是报纸必需刊登的内容。

赫伯特·斯宾塞（Herbert Spencer）① 说："餐桌谈话证明了，百分之九十的人阅读自己感兴趣或者有趣味的作品，而非指导性的书籍。"这句话所包含的真理不可否认，而无论其目的如何，认知和运用这条原则是新闻事业取得成功的必要条件。但是，这条原则无法改变这样的事实：指导性信息对于十分之九的人与十分之一的人同等必要。绝大多数指导性信息对于维护民主和诸多领域的物质文明与精神文明进步都是必要的，报纸是唯一的知识载体和教导性工具。记录当天发生的事情是报纸的任务，而以足够的版面报道公众即使并不感兴趣而应该知晓的重大新闻也是报纸的职责所在。传递新闻衍生的重大事务的相关信息，并教导受众，这是报纸的职责，即使遭遇公众的冷漠，报纸亦要不断传递信息和教导公众。

因为这是新闻事业的义务之一。尽管读者冷漠，但他们从来不会失去情感。因为至少十分之一的人总是在追求教导性信息，而这十分之一和十分之九的读者群体不仅是可观的，而且通常构成了所在社区最有影响力的因素。因此，从效果上来讲，这个读

---

① 赫伯特·斯宾塞（Herbert Spencer，1820—1903），英国哲学家，被誉为"社会达尔文主义之父"。他的学说把进化论适者生存的观念应用于社会学。

者群体远非十分之一的读者可比，但这还不算全部的效果。对这种新闻不感兴趣的读者就不想阅读这样的新闻，但是他们几乎不能逃脱新闻的影响，尽管新闻对他们的影响是微弱的。为了发现自己希望的新闻，读者至少必须浏览吸引其注意力和集中体现当天报道内容的新闻标题。这些新闻标题都会在瞬间抓取读者的眼球，不管读者是否愿意，他已经从每条新闻标题中获取了新闻所承载的些许信息。假如他在快速浏览新闻标题中认识到自己应该了解的某些重要事情，或者他不想在别人面前显得孤陋寡闻的话，无论他是否对这些事情感兴趣，他都会耐着性子仔细阅读从标题到正文的整个新闻，而且经常会发现自己被不怎么预期看好的报道细节所感染。

但是，编辑的责任和乐趣更多的是培育公众对于新闻本质的兴趣。的确，新闻事业更多情况下正是在公众关注事务的刺激中服务于公众的。例如，为改善市民福利的地方政府很大程度上依赖民意的支持，而这种支持只有在报纸持续的宣传和倡导唤起公众兴趣时才能够获得。尽管公众通常对于各州、国家和世界上的大部分事务都漠然视之，他们对于这些事务的关注程度要低于对个体或者社区事务的关注程度，他们需要不断的信息传递和评论才足以被说服，但他们对于这些事务产生的兴趣具有更加重要的意义。

因此，在新闻报道中，只有当报刊把读者的即时兴趣作为决定报道内容的唯一判断标准的时候，它才能实现自身或者对于公众的义务和责任。另一方面，报纸除非在这样的新闻判断中重点考虑趣味性要素，才能够最好地服务于自身或者公众。换言之，大多数新闻选择必须建立在趣味性的基础上，这样才易于唤起普通读者的关注，而在这个新闻判断的过程中，人的本性、感情、情绪与人类的认知都必须加以考虑和处理，但是，报纸的责任还在于它要刊登很多新闻而无需考虑公众的兴趣。

第五章　新闻取舍

42　　　研究表明，报纸版面的各种限定迫使记者和编辑不断对新闻进行调整，以便符合不同栏目的版面限量。报纸总是有所刊登内容之外更多的新闻。报纸也必定有需要或多或少删减和压缩的内容。报纸不会创造新闻事件，新闻事件也不会考虑报纸的便利而发生——报纸版面紧张的时候，它们就不发生；报纸版面多余时，它们就应时而生。当新闻事件发生时，无论以较大篇幅还是以较小篇幅，报纸必须刊登该新闻事件，并根据报刊和出版物的版面空间对事实记录加以调整。今天报纸删减的消息或内容可能在昨天的版面中找到合适的版位，而今天填满报纸版面的消息和内容可能是昨天完全删掉或者重点压缩的内容。当天早晨报纸接受的消息和内容可能在报纸付印之前及时被拿下了。

　　因此，报纸辨别和取舍新闻的条件每天每时都在变化。但是，报纸首先作出的取舍是压缩次要的或者趣味性不大的新闻及其篇幅，使其适合出版物的版面要求，记者和编辑不必尽力把当天所有的新闻都塞进版面，而他必须刊登的是当天的新鲜事儿，或许这件事会成为最好的新闻。在新闻取舍的过程中，直接负责

43　新闻的编辑必须根据新闻价值进行判断，并以此为规则不断实行

下去。当疑问出现的时候，编辑们要慎重考虑和商议，但是在日报的出版和发行中编辑可能没有时间和机会进行深思熟虑的思考了。在几乎所有的新闻取舍案例中，及时的决定是必要的。在编辑手中通过的持续不断的消息稿流中，他们即兴对稿件的相对重要性或者趣味性进行估计，要么采纳，要么拒绝，要么整版刊登，要么压缩稿件，然而，他们总是在可能利用版面的限制下，和服从突发的、新鲜的、重大新闻对于版面的需求之间的矛盾中，对所有已经编排版面作出重大调整，并且对之前已经编辑的很多消息进行删除或者压缩。

在所有其他生产性企业中，需求和产量之间的关系是相对单一的，或者至少是可以短期加以计算的。而编辑总是面临未知的稿源。每天他开始编排新闻版的时候，他都不了解自己必须编排的新闻稿的情况或者稿量的大小。可以肯定的是，他已经掌握了某些预先告知的事件，而且他已经拥有了某些特定的每日消息的常规来源，但是他不知道这些消息来源中会产生什么样的新闻，也不知道消息来源会对他作出什么样的要求。没有什么预知和先见之明让他能够看透当天或者当时的事情，并提前加以明确计算。大部分新闻都是不可预期的，他们可能以一种稳定的新闻流出现在编辑面前，也可能纷至沓来，闪现在他面前。编辑能够确信的只是自己拥有足够多可以刊登的新闻，而且他必须为最糟糕的情况做好准备。

编辑的任务与其他生产性企业员工的任务区别在于，他完全是在经营短命的产品。在报纸的整个生产过程中，主要的原材料就是新闻稿。在其他所有的物质产品生产过程中，今天没有利用的材料可以用于明天或者留在以后使用。原材料可能是不长久的，就像罐头厂的原料一样，但也不是即刻就腐烂的原料。没有必要浪费原材料，但是今天没有及时刊登的新闻稿通常在明天就成为毫无价值的材料了。而在所有其他物质产品生产过程中，原材料的供给可以通过生产量的控制加以规范化运作。编辑不能规

44

范其稿源的供给。无论稿源多么庞大，他每天必须接纳通过自己建立的来源渠道传递而来的所有的消息稿。他没有采用的所有稿件就是废料，是不可回收的废料。这样的废料并非局限于编辑审阅后拒绝的新闻稿。他不断争辩的不确定性迫使他忍痛割爱般删掉很多当天自己已经接受和"排好版"的消息。通常情况下，每家日报每天编排的消息比其版面所能容纳的内容要多，而且这样的稿源过剩或者过量就是一种浪费。这种浪费某种程度而言却是不可避免的。

　　了解这些状况对于理解日志式新闻业所面对的困难肯定十分有益。报纸必须在当天编排和出版。报纸必须从各种稿源中选取所刊登的内容。报纸必须刊登所面临的所有新闻，但是它无法刊登超过版面空间的内容。因此，关于源源不断的新闻稿源，编辑必然迅速作出应该刊登什么内容不应该刊登什么内容的判断，而某个时候的新闻稿源可能是缓缓的小溪，接下来可能成为暴涨的河水。新闻不仅因为报纸版面的限制或多或少地被删掉，而且已经采纳和编排的新闻也可能由于某种原因频繁地被删掉。某条新闻没有被刊登，一种情况是编辑从新闻的趣闻性和重要性的角度对其价值判断的结果，即在其新闻价值判断的基础上证实了删掉这条新闻的合理性，另一种情况是版面的机械限制迫使编辑将这条新闻与当天刊登的其他新闻加以比较，基于读者对于这条新闻的相对次要的重要性或趣味性将其删掉。

　　一位资深的报人曾经说，"不该刊登什么内容"的判断是测试编辑能力的最高标准。这或许有些夸张，但无论如何，辨认新闻的负面作用与正面作用同等重要。报纸版面的有限性迫使编辑仅仅出于这个原因不断进行新闻价值的判断，而新闻价值判断的基础可能根据每天或者每小时新闻流量的大小而有所不同。通常情况下，微弱的比较优势或许不足以决定某条新闻是否被刊登，但是编辑必须不断地对每条新闻加以判断。"毙掉"一条应该采纳的新闻与采用一条不该用的新闻同等糟糕。但是，这一切都取决于编辑根据持续的版面需求所作出的决定。编辑基于版面的稳定性和版序所作出的决定是必要的。

报纸往往是回应法律的导火索，人们可能相信报纸在民事和刑事诉讼过程中的报道，因为不真实陈述对于当事人的伤害会影响其声誉或者福利。真相是不容诽谤的，但真相并非永远清晰可辨，而且加以证实的途径也并不确定。还有，司法部关于诽谤案的构成要件并没有达成共识。即使报纸关于某件诽谤案的报道是真实的和适当的，诽谤案的报道也无利可图，除非某些独特的公共服务机构为这种冒险行为提供了法律根据，否则当事人不可避免要提起关于诽谤案的诉讼。然而，新闻报道是报纸的职责所在，也是报纸的生存目的所依。报纸在不断的新闻报道中会不自觉地牵涉诽谤，或者报纸所刊登的某些消息使当事人提起了诉讼案。具备公信力的报纸不会有意对某个人加以诽谤，这样的报纸也不会刊登反映某个人正直的报道，除非报纸相信此人的正直行为是真实可信的，而且证明这样的报道具有新闻的某些特征。自我利益和权力两者都要求杜绝意味着蓄意指控的诽谤案发生。因此，编辑的任务就是仔细审核所有的新闻稿，拒绝刊登所有包含由于与事实不符而导致的诽谤性指控，假如事实真相不明，或者删掉了某些可能引起法律诉讼的危险陈述，也可能导致诽谤性指控。铁路系统有个一般原则，运用在这里恰如其分，即"在有疑问的情况下，总是要走安全的线路"，资深编辑经常引用一个警示："你绝对不会由于没有刊登的报道而陷入诽谤诉讼中"①。出于免于诽谤指控安全的考虑，报纸就要求编辑仔细分辨新闻特征，杜绝刊登诽谤性的新闻。

但是，考虑涉及分辨新闻的轻重缓急的顺序也是十分重要的。有人说过，报道人们想知道的消息与报道人们不应该知道的

---

① Joseph B. McCullagh.——原书注

消息之间有差别。而人们不应该知道的消息是什么样的呢？查理斯·A·达纳曾经说："在某些消息来源上应该采取截然不同的处理方法，而报纸应该限制所刊登的新闻数量，有些新闻是不应该刊登的。我不了解如何限制和取舍新闻。我不准备对此分界线保持某种抽象的立场，但我总是认为，无论上帝的意志允许发生何等重要的事情，我都不会过于得意而加以报道。"但是，在实践中，很少有编辑能够根据自己不同目的定位的编辑理念在"适合刊登"的消息与不适合刊登的消息之间加以明确的分辨，他们也很少能够认识到具有公信力的新闻事业与不能刊登的新闻的分水岭。犯罪和罪恶类报道暴露了新闻圈内外一个颇有争议的问题。这就是达纳先生引言中所指出的那类新闻，正是此类新闻应该全部舍弃的观点，使得达纳先生所引用的观点成为整个新闻业的一种经典论调。从原则上来讲，达纳先生的立场是正确的。

犯罪和罪恶类新闻应该刊登。报纸刊登此类新闻不仅是合适的，而且是其自身的一种公共职能。犯罪和罪恶构筑了社会必须不断应对的问题。假如社会要有效地应付这些问题，就必须了解这些问题的本质、内容及其背后的势力和影响。舆论与人类活动的其他领域在犯罪的预防、打击和惩罚方面是同等重要的因素，但是只有在公共事件引发舆论时，某个领域的舆论才能发挥作用。

犯罪和罪恶对社会是一种威胁，而这样的威胁必须由社会创造和保护的代理机构来不断且积极地加以抵制。但是在社会的保护过程中，法律、法庭和警方必须获取公共支持，而这种公共支持只能来自他们对自己必须应对的情况和事实的了解。假如这样的新闻事实遗漏了，人们就被剥夺了了解此类事实的唯一普通而持续的信息来源。

所有的社会进步都依赖于信息的获取和认知。假如我们不知道社会上有罪恶存在，我们如何认识正义存在的必要性？假如我们不知道罪恶是什么，我们如何明白怎样抵御罪恶？假如我们不知道罪恶的程度，我们如何唤起和召集善良的力量？正义只有在睁大眼睛的时候，只有当它看到和评价其对立权力的时候，只有当它急需了解所面临的危险而行动的时候，才是伟大的。压制罪恶性的新闻会蒙蔽认识正确事物的眼睛，而在面对危机的时候就只能用所谓的安全意识来加以欺骗。罪恶总是易于在黑暗中繁殖。罪恶成长于真相的掩盖中。公众对于罪恶活动的忽略导致他们的无知和冷漠，而罪恶就滋生其中。公众的视野必须投放在罪恶之上，这样罪恶的本质、范围和习惯就可以被披露。罪恶性新闻报道是报纸满足公众知晓权的一种责任和服务。

除此之外，公众对于罪恶性事物怀有永久的兴趣。难道这种趣味性有什么不适吗？这是人性的普遍本能。难道人类与生俱来的任何本能的原始设计不是旨在提升我们的身心愉悦和社会福利吗？大量的罪恶滋生于人类本能感官的滥用和误用，或许所有的罪恶都如此，因此我们的本能感官通常是出于善行而发挥作用的判断亦是不真实的。纽曼（Newman）说："人类的部分行为由强有力的本能意识组成。有些本能是善意而持续的，有些本能是罪恶而短暂的；有些本能是猥琐的，有些是高贵的，但它们都是人性中必需的。"我们本能感官的正确运行从来不会引发罪恶；唯有本能感官的滥用才会滋生罪恶。而这种人类本能感官的滥用则是对人性的偏离。我们对犯罪感兴趣，因为犯罪行为是非正常的人类行为，而从普通的社会学角度来看，这种趣味性是一种自我保护。它使得罪恶引人注目，并施加在我们的意识和想象中，迫使我们观察它，认识其错误和危险所在，并不断提醒我们防微杜渐。有关的模仿或者认知的本能随处可能使兴趣成为罪恶对于某个人或者群体的一种影响力，但是通常说来，人类的兴趣导致人们对于罪恶的痛恨和抵触。

假如不是这样的话，善行将永远从地球上消失。因为人类曾经遭遇变态的罪恶及其背离公正的先天的标准、暴力、悲剧和灾难的攻击。人类历史的各个时期都渗透着罪恶的滋生和演绎，罪恶的渊薮像一条溪流，从《圣经》的起源穿越至终点。罪恶始终是诗歌、小说、戏剧和歌剧的主题，而人类历史也充斥着罪恶的行迹。爱德华·吉本（Edward Gibbon）[①] 说："安东尼王国[②]的兴盛表现出历史上罕见的物质进步带来的优越性，而其中并不难发现人类的罪恶、愚蠢和灾难的迹象。"假如人们对于罪恶的兴趣和关注超越了罪恶本身，罪恶很久之前就胜过了善行。相反，新闻的趣味性总是通过揭示罪恶的本质、罪恶对于个体和整个社会的危害、罪恶通常导致的悲哀和惩罚等来限制罪恶发展的。

但有人说，关于犯罪和罪恶类新闻的报道给年轻人带来很坏的影响。已经陈述的原因被否决了，因为除非在罪恶性新闻的叙述中罪恶披上华丽的外衣而显得引人入胜。在人生的早期阶段，每个孩子就发现了这个世界上充满着邪恶和罪责，而他们从少年时期就企图掩藏罪恶存在的尝试从来都没有成功过。相反，各种努力使人们对罪恶着迷，罪恶引起人们更多了解其本质的好奇心。年轻人在某时某地以某种方式获悉了罪恶的本质和范畴，而他们或多或少要了解相关的罪恶信息，这样才能完全装备起来，便于人生的争斗之用。重要的事情是，年轻人应该接受分辨真理和谬误的教育，以便清晰地认识到，正确的事物一度是善行，而罪恶无论怎样掩盖总是邪恶而具破坏性的东西。毋庸置疑，有关犯罪的报道不时引起人们本能的模仿，但通常只有当个体缺乏知识的时候以及在与罪恶相关联或者固有邪恶倾向的地方，对于犯罪行为的模仿才会发生，具备了其中的任何一个条件，犯罪行为

---

① 爱德华·吉本（Edward Gibbon, 1737—1794），英国史学家，著有《罗马帝国衰落史（1776—1788）》[*The History of the Decline and Fall of the Roman Empire (1776—1788)*]。

② 安东尼·派厄斯（Antoninus Pius, 86—161)，罗马帝国国王 [138—161]。

都可能发生,而不管对这样的消息是否进行了报道。作为一般判断,无论年轻人还是成年人都不会由于报刊取消了关于犯罪和罪恶类新闻的合法报道而受益,同时公众将被剥夺其获悉自我管制和自我保护所需信息的权力。

但是,有些关于犯罪和罪恶的消息不应该加以报道,这是毋庸置疑的事实。此类新闻包括从公共福利的角度来看没有意义的新闻和单纯诉求好色之徒的猎奇心态的新闻。从正派的基本趣味性考虑,有些重要的公共新闻的淫秽细节应该被剪辑掉。报纸应该进入家庭,入户的报纸才是读者真正喜爱的报纸,报纸的质量才可以真正地得以检验。报纸的价值及其影响很大程度上依赖于其所激发的国内读者的信任。因此,报纸在精神层面和言论层面都应该是纯洁而正派的。向公众展示和报道当天的新闻事件是报纸的职责所在,而国内外当天所发生的很多事情可能是丑陋的,但丑陋的新闻可以用纯洁而正派的语言来报道,而且丑陋新闻的细节在报道时应该有所删减,记者更不应该为了取得轰动效应和吸引力而对新闻事实进行想象和虚饰,报纸的重要性不应该以过分花哨的手法、过大的版面或者华丽的辞藻进行夸张。的确,这样的新闻尽管是丑陋的,但它们本身十分重要,以至于报纸有必要采用如此的手法并为它们提供版面,而这样做的正当理由应该是从尊重公众兴趣立场和满足公众知情权考虑的新闻价值所致。的确,这样的新闻十分重要,报纸有必要对其报道手法和版面提供法律依据,但是这样做的保障应该以可敬的公众兴趣和公众知晓权为基础。报纸不断刊登有价值的公共训诫内容,以揭露和总结伪君子的伪善,但是报纸提供服务和回绝淫秽报道应该成为报道的动机和控制其报道的手段。只为吸引好色之徒的注意力而将栏目和版面用来报道犯罪和丑闻的做法可能短期内有助于报纸发行量的提升,但是这种做法有损于新闻业的品质,并降低报纸的公信力,进而侵害其最为珍贵的品牌价值。

新闻业提供犯罪和罪恶类新闻报道,旨在揭示其丑态、展示犯罪和丑闻的危害之大，这是新闻事业真正的和必要的服务功能之一。然而，整个新闻事业赖以生存的基础在于分辨提供什么样的服务与不提供什么样的服务、适当的公众兴趣与不当的公众兴趣、合法新闻的价值与纯粹吸引好色之徒好奇心的新闻。简言之，报纸的生存基础是通过自身的新闻理念和判断标准来分辨刊登什么与不刊登什么。报纸不会全部取消这样的新闻，如果这样做的话，其功能就出现缺失。从另外一个方面来讲，报纸不可能沦为不问津正直和善行而一味报道丑闻、罪恶和淫秽，并进而毁坏其公信力的信息贩卖者。

53 　　从很大范围来讲，报纸通过不断揭示社会的阴暗面和丑态而充当着公共道德和伦理维护者的角色。对于大多数人而言，他们害怕自身的行为不断暴露于众甚于对法律威严的恐惧，这便对其正直行为形成了一种更加有力的潜在影响因素。可以肯定的是，有些人则不在乎自己的言谈举止曝光，而畏惧诉诸法律的诉讼结果。的确，还有些人沉浸于报纸对其丑闻的"曝光"中。但是，通常来讲，大部分善男信女害怕损害其名誉和荣光的任何报道，而说到底，这对于所有的人而言是一种防止犯错的有益措施。对于那些缺乏羞辱感的人而言，他们对于法律约束的内心畏惧应该随着量刑的加重而增强。当然，这涉及法律规范的问题。但是，新闻业可能更多地关注犯罪嫌疑人判刑定罪的报道，从而为畏惧法律惩戒的犯法者提供警戒。一项犯罪往往引起记者和编辑足够的兴趣来采编新闻，但是却没有一则案例能够引发公众的浓厚兴趣。法庭诉讼旨在追求辩论的缓慢展开和论证，人们对犯罪的兴趣会逐渐消失，而当定罪无果的时候，报刊的兴趣就会荡然无存。这与兴趣的产生规律一致，但是假如对犯罪的量刑加以更多报道的话，报纸就提供了一次有价值的公共服务。

54 　　刊登新闻是报纸的业务，这一点已经反复论述过，而"压制新闻"则是新闻业最常见的抱怨之一。然而，假如指控被强加了某种邪恶的含义，那么，压制这样的新闻至少有些许理由。已经讨论的分辨事实的所有问题都涉及新闻删减的很多适当原因。由于版面紧张而未能刊登的新闻，或者编辑判断不应该刊登的新闻，要么是因为这条新闻不重要、不合适，要么是这条新闻对读者而言兴趣不大，这是新闻业产生的大多数抱怨的唯一起因，而抱怨者由于自己感兴趣的内容未能见诸报端而失望至极。刊登重要新闻是报纸的职责，在上文提到的新闻要素重要性次序限定内，报纸刊登吸引公众的新闻是自身的兴趣所在。但实际上或者相对来讲，什么是重要的新闻要素和什么是吸引人的新闻要素成为每家报纸编辑在进行独立的新闻判断时必须决定的问题，编辑在作出这种必要的决定时总是面临时间和空间的考虑。然而，这样的判断应该不受外在的或者背后的影响。一般情况下，它应该仅仅建立在新闻价值的概念之上，特别是报纸所服务的目标公众的价值上。而相当部分的新闻对于同类中所有报纸都是十分重要的，或者对于一个国家、地区或社区的所有持相同价值观的人是十分重要的，还有很多新闻的重要性依赖于报道的本质和目的及其读者的品质。换言之，有些新闻对于某一家报纸而言具有新闻价值，而对于另外一家报纸可能没有什么新闻价值可言，或者对于第三家报纸具有相对小的价值。编辑不仅要考虑公众对于新闻的比较兴趣，而且要特别考虑所服务的地方和选区的读者的兴趣和口味。自然，编辑之间由于个体性格、社会交往和观点的差别导致他们对于新闻的判断也存在差异，这样就引起一位编辑拒绝采纳另一位编辑可能刊登的某条消息，或者寥寥几笔简单报道了又一位编辑重点叙述的消息。然而，这些只是不同生活方式产生的个体差异，它们同样对新闻业产生影响，它们就是生活的缩影。但是，无论这些差异如何，大部分编辑都是有良知的人，他们都应该坚守向读者报道真正重要的新闻，以履行其至高无上的神圣职责。

第六章　新闻真实性

所有新闻的基本元素即真实性。假如新闻从根本上来讲都是虚假的，诽谤就会像谎言一样充斥在新闻报道中。因为新闻是已经发生的事实的报道，或者说是现状的记录，假如这些事实没有发生，假如现状并非如此，报道就会失真，而记录失真就不能称其为新闻。杜撰、捏造和谎言可能出现在真正的新闻中，但这只是欺诈行为。这种欺诈行为可能是蓄意的，或者是弯曲和误解事实的结果，但是无论在哪种情况下，满纸谎言的报道只是辞藻的堆积，并非"新闻事实"的叙述或记录。事实是新闻真实性的试金石。

新闻真实性的测量尺度是新闻质量的验证。绝对的真实是任何人际传播过程中都难以获得的效果，无论是口头传播还是文字传播，或者通过书籍、杂志和报纸的传播，除非它只是属于独立的和单纯的事实陈述。一个人告诉另一个人说约翰·史密斯去世了。这个消息是绝对真实的，毋庸置疑或者修正。但是，当告知者开始联系逝者的去世背景时，他的讲述中出现误差的机会就随着细节的扩张而增加了。即使他是逝者去世境况的见证者，他的观察力、知识面和记忆力等层面的限制也会导致他难以绝对准确地叙述每个细节。当他是从别人那里获取信息时，这个困难就越发增大，无论他们多么仔细地进行记录，无论他们多么渴望叙述得真实些。

　　这些困难和人为限制因素在法庭辩论中一直印证着。在法庭上，若干证人用自己的见证来证明同样的事情时，往往出现众口不一的情况，尽管每个证人可能都是绝对诚实的。法庭上的男女证人在誓言中说要讲实话，讲的全是实话，而且他们发誓自己只说实话，从良知上尽力讲实话。然而，作为规律，他们往往不能同等程度地履行陪审团成员和法庭作证的义务和责任。见证事件发生的某两个人、三个人或者四个人关于事情经过的叙述往往不一样，他们的观察点不一样，每个人头脑中关于事情的印象和本质不一样，而且个人不同素质往往使得其中一位观察者或者讲述者的叙述好过另外一位。每个人可能都是值得信赖的，然而几乎没有哪两个人关于事情经过及其细节的讲述完全一致，尽管所有的见证人可能都认同主要事实。尽管其叙述有明显的出入，所有的人可能都在讲实话，但大家出现偏差的程度并不一致。

　　现在，假如关于真相传播的自然限制和障碍在阻止绝对的事实真相、"所有的真相和仅有的真相"方面起到了一定的效果，那么当见证人讲述事情原貌和完全真相的意愿占上风的时候，他们仍然更多地受其习惯、愿望或者目的等有悖于事情真相叙述精准度因素的影响。夸大其辞的习惯是讲述者的一个通病。新闻事实见证者在讲述事情经过时往往希望用重要的或者动人的情节来打动新闻故事的听众，但是他们很少以自己不可告人的私利目的来描述一件事情或者蓄意地加以浮夸，从而给人以错觉。所有这些影响或者部分影响都容易污染真理的源泉。

　　新闻业依赖于分辨新闻的公共重要性和趣味性的职责，那么，假如真理是新闻真实性的试金石的话，新闻真实性的标准就是其质量的检验，正是基于这个检验，新闻业应该被评判而且必须预期进行评判。新闻的绝对真实是一种理想化的境界，获得绝对真实的新闻报道的难度经常不亚于人类个体达到圣贤的难度，但是新闻报道越接近绝对真实，它就越接近完美的境界。在收集和报道新闻时，新闻业必须与人类学机构通力合作，在人性局限性的背景下应对人类学的问题，而人性的局限性确定了新闻真实性这个人们一直面对的困难。

有些记者获取地方新闻，通讯员和新闻通讯社或代理机构则采集外地新闻。报纸首先依赖本报新闻采集者的特性和能力。例如，一位记者被指派"报道"某个特定事件，他的责任就是获取必要的新闻素材并收录到他准备提交给报社或者刊登的新闻稿件中，保证新闻真实和准确的责任主要由这位记者来承担。假如编辑接受了这篇新闻稿，并刊登在报上，那么新闻真实性的责任就转移到报纸或者由报纸承接下来。在地方新闻报道中，编辑多少了解指派记者的情况，假如他有疑问的话，他随时可以对报道的细节进行核查。而且，编辑很大程度上必须依赖的正是记者勘查事实的能力与报道新闻的认真和细心。

对于外地新闻而言，编辑完全依赖通讯员的特性。无论通讯员传递给编辑的是什么样的稿件，无论是直接约定的稿件还是其他途径采集的稿件，编辑都必须假定它是真实的，而他自己则基于稿件所体现的价值对其加以判断来决定是否采用。实际操作中，很少能在允许的时间内验证电报传来的"新闻故事"。然而，报纸还应该对外地通讯员发送的新闻稿负责，就像对于从地方记者采集来的稿件一样负责任，报纸报道的准确性，尤其是报纸由于准确性而赢得的声誉几乎完全依赖于报纸采集新闻的品质。可以肯定的是，编辑复制和校对的过程中还可能出现错误，有疑问的叙述可能被取消。但是，无论其真实性还是准确性都依赖于新闻报道者的品质和能力。

进行新闻报道的男女记者很少见证新闻事件的过程，除非这些事情是可以预期的。假如他们不是见证人，即使不是所有的新闻信息，他们所获得的大部分新闻信息必定也是从其他人那里获取的。在获取新闻信息的过程中，他们必定为克服人类观察和叙述事物的精准的局限性而进行了一番抗争。假如事情是可以预期的而且记者在现场的话，他可能不会看到或者听到事情发生的全过程，他还会依赖其他人提供的信息来拼凑自己亲自观察获得的信息图景。即使他看到或者听到事情的全过程，他仍然是一个社会人，或多或少都会出现误差，这是人类的本性所致。综合考虑新闻的真实性，这些局限和情况都应该公正地加以看待。还有其他出现新闻报道失实的因素。记者一旦获取消息就必须传送到报社，必须尽快写成稿件并进行编排。所有这些程序都可能出现差错，而这些差错可能不会产生严重后果，或者可能产生严重的后果，它们还有可能在出版之前未被编辑发现。

但是，不管怎么说，采写和报道新闻是新闻从业者的任务和职责，除非报道是真实的，否则他们就不能有效地履行这项任务，报纸也不能向公众提供所担负的服务职能。一家报纸无论以集体的还是个体的形式为读者提供服务，它都绝对依赖于所提供新闻信息的准确性。而衡量公众对一家报纸是否忠诚的信任度，就必须不断验证它所报道的新闻是否基本真实。因此，两条刚性的理由促使衡量新闻准确性的标准越来越高。毋庸置疑，一份出版物可以以付出新闻真实性为代价而迎合人类的煽情本性，也可以通过对丁点事实的浮夸将其杜撰成引人入胜的消息稿，还可以通过夸张或者彻头彻尾的谎言来诉求人性的荒诞意识等方法来吸引读者，但是从本来的意义上讲，这样的出版物就不成其为出版物，它所创造的产品也不成其为新闻。因为谎言绝非新闻，杜撰的消息也不是新闻，出版物蓄意和习惯地报道包装的非真实新闻的做法不仅是对公众的欺骗，而且是对新闻事业的冒犯。新闻真实性的衡量标准是新闻业的试金石，而新闻事业凭借这块试金石就能够证明自身或者公众尊敬和信任的价值存在。

然而，有关新闻的真实性需要加以界定。新闻首先是关于新近发生的事实或者情况的报道。假如新闻报道准确地叙述了显著的事件及其具体事实，那么它就呈现了真实，因为新闻主要报道已经发生或者正在发生的事件，同时报道人们易于观察的敏感事情和可能需要通过尝试以其他任何具体事实加以证明的事情。新闻所呈现的真实是叙述的真实，其第一要义并非关注阐释事件，而可能是强调调查事情的起因和目的并报道其他人对于事情的看法，虽然这只是新闻的第二个重要功能。新闻自身阐释事件的功能同样属于新闻事业的领域，在这个新闻功能范畴内，真实性可能采用另外一个定义并引发更大范围的义务和责任。新闻的特殊职责是基本准确地记录事实。当新闻履行这个功能时，它就在告知读者真相，并最大限度地实现了其目标。假如新闻报道没有叙述事情的每个步骤或者每个细节，它就没有讲出事情的真相，就该得到适当的指责。新闻报道能够多大程度地讲述事情的真相可能取决于记者所获得的新闻事实的多少，取决于编辑对于事件相对重要性或者读者兴趣的判断，或者取决于编辑所支配的版面空间。然而，假如他掌握了准确的新闻事实，他们就能够讲述事情的真相。

但是，假如新闻没有公正地报道的话，其真实性诉求就很难实现。新闻应该不偏不倚，这条新闻的基本原则与新闻的真实性同等重要，两者对新闻事业发挥着同等的作用。假如新闻事业旨在为人们提供舆论赖以生成的基础信息，那么记者和编辑对新闻事实的报道就必须十分公正，他们不能戴有色眼镜，他们所报道的事实应该尽量准确。这并非意味着任何类型的话题都会产生新闻，而是事情的两个方面应该给予同等的版面加以报道，或者事情一方面的情况报道了，为平衡报道就应该探索影响事情的另外一方面的信息。关于系列事情的新闻报道要围绕着事情真相展开，不能离题太远。在进行新闻报道之前，相关人员必须做好准备工作。富有公共趣味性或重要性的事情一旦发生，这条新闻所占的版面就依赖于其内在的价值，无论它可能引起什么样的争议。可能的情况还有，有关事情一方面的新闻在日复一日地报道着，另外一方面几乎没有什么值得报道的新闻发生；一方面的情节最终得到持续的报道，无论其处于优势还是劣势，而另一方面的情节却很少得到报道。例如，在一次大罢工中，工会组织发起了事端，引起了公众的注意和争议，而他们作为进攻方通常比作为防御方的行业工人更能出新闻。正是罢工及其罢工中可能出现的任何事情而非争议的内在价值构筑了新闻。

挑起诉讼并非新闻的功能，但是揭示诉讼过程中所发生的触动公众兴趣的事实则是新闻的基本职能。辩论双方的陈述可能都有助于公众的理解或者带来其他方面的帮助，而且公共论坛的辩论被认为是新闻，因为这些辩论与所发生的事情相关，而且可能对公众有所启发。然而，报纸多大程度上允许其栏目成为公共论坛，取决于新闻事件的背景、公众的兴趣程度大小及其实际的公共重要性。报纸可能请求调查并为调查提供特别的证据，以便将隐藏的事实公布于众或者使已经报道的事情更加明朗。但是，所有这些仅仅是报纸在偶然机会才会报道的新闻，报纸可能对公众感兴趣的事情加以调查和评论，也可能不提供这样的辅助性服务，因为报纸的重要功能不会超越其对所发生重要事实的报道范围。过多地阐释或者论证事实并非新闻栏目的主要任务，新闻栏目应尽量公正和准确地呈现事实本身，把观点的表达权留给编辑部或者那些对相关特殊事情的评论可能具有新闻价值的个体或者群体来陈述。评论性文章也可以编排在特定的通讯员的署名报道中。

通常情况下，报纸的任务不只是报道事实，还要努力阐释新闻事实。然而，我们应该这样来理解，"他们的观点只代表个人"。关于事件报道的准确程度依赖于事件的完整性、掌握的事实材料和信息来源的可信度。一件完整的事情可能作为一个整体来观察，与其相关的事实都处于一个限定的范围内。某些特定的信息可以获得，而假如这些信息是通过个人的观察或者权威机构所得，那么有关的报道就像这件事情一样可能是完整的，而且其报道接近绝对的真相。在相似的火灾案例中，假如其间没有可疑的犯罪行为的话，当救火车从视野中消失的时候，这件事情就算结束了。火灾中损失财产的业主的确认、损失的估算、保险的范围等细节按照常规都容易获得。这件事情结束了，重要的事实得以报道，这件事也就再没有什么可说的了。但是，假定事故中有明显的故意纵火迹象的话，单纯这场火灾就并非一个完整的事件，它就成为一个可能引发公众更多兴趣的连续故事，后续的事情比火灾本身更加重要。有关纯粹的火灾事实的报道可能会相当准确，只要事件本身是完整的，但是犯罪事实却给报道带来了很多不确定因素。犯罪证据可能是直接的或者不确定的，或者是直接而可测的，事实越不易接近和证实，新闻采写过程中越倾向于出错，就像法庭更难确定模糊的事实真相一样。新闻采集并非一种尝试，记者是在探寻新闻报道所必要的事实素材，而且他们面临着法庭必须克服的困难，虽然他们没有法庭所具备的提取证据的权力，却拥有法庭没有的避免诽谤指控和错误的权利。

　　上文所述并非为假象辩解，也并非为错误开脱，当报纸出现蓄意的虚假报道时，它是不能得到原谅的，只有无法避免的原因造成的报道失真才可以得到谅解。在此，我们旨在说明，事实并非总是简单明了和随到随取的，相反，新闻事实经常是模糊的，接近和验证新闻事实十分困难。当记者和编辑从不同视觉加以观察的时候，新闻事实经常呈现不同的层面，并因此变得对立。上文论述还说明了，报纸并没有揭示真相的魔杖，但是当真相被掩藏或者蒙蔽的时候，报纸会义无反顾地争取更多的信息和证实事情重要性的事实，就像法庭和政府其他调查机构那样。这样的论述还旨在说明，即使在那些权威的法律机构中，新闻的真实性也是相对的，个别时候才可以接近绝对的真实，但是新闻更多的情况是相对真实。在法律或者新闻中，很少出现"整体是真相，而且只有真相"的事情。而基本真实的事情在日常生活中却是大量存在的，这是由事情的本质所决定的。没有人敢言，即使在动荡的多事之秋历史事实的记录就是完全真实的，尽管史实多年来已经在人们的探究和研究者有意的研究中被赋予了高度的重视、谨慎的观察和详尽的分析，那么，我们如何指望当时的新闻记录永远是完全准确和完整的呢？或者"基本是真实的，而且只是真实的"呢？

然而，报纸应当理解自身的任务并认识其传递信息的职责，它应该将准确性放在职业操守的第一位，并不断追求新闻报道的准确性之目标。那么，新闻报道的准确性达到何种程度算是成功的呢？它能达到何种精确程度呢？有人提出，新闻报道的精确度依赖于"事情的完整性、事实的接近性和信息来源的可靠性"。完整性要素已经进行了简明的论述。作为规律，新闻事实从哪里易于接近、哪里的新闻来源更可靠成为报纸报道准确性的基本要求。"无论在什么地方从事什么行业，每当出现记录事实的良好工具时，现代新闻业就会提供精确的服务。股票交易拥有良好的机器设备，波动价格在自动收录机上闪现，准确地反映可靠的股市行情。总统大选过程中候选人的巡回演讲配有记录设备，随时报道准确的投票数和胜算比率，全国大选的结果通常在大选当晚就可揭晓。在文明社区，死亡、出生、婚嫁和离异都有记录，除了隐藏或者忽略的细节，大家对这些情况知道得一清二楚。在某些行业和政府部门设有记录设备，不同程度地记录了证券、货币和产品、银行结算、不动产交易、工资涨幅等信息。记录器出现在进出口贸易中，因为它们能够直接记录通过海关的人次"①。一般情况下，公共机构官员的正式活动、法庭裁决、立法机关通过或者否决的法案、航运、军事和海军订购活动等诸如此类的事务都可以准确地给予报道。所有接近的、确定的、权威的、完整的事实通常都能以精确的新闻加以报道。可以

---

① Walter Lippman，*Public Opinion*.——原书注

肯定的是，在新闻信息的传递、编辑和编排上都可能出现失误，但是相对而言，这种题材中出现差错的几率是很小的。而这种特征的新闻构筑了新闻业的支柱，其中大部分新闻涵盖了公众需求的有价值的信息。

但是，假如报纸只刊登上述内容，它们会由于可阅读的新闻枯竭而死亡，这就好比人们单凭面包而活命的道理一样。实际上，面包和淡水是人们饮食所必需的，但是仅供应面包和饮水就可能被认为是最严重的惩罚措施之一。人类的福利就像人们的口味一样需要各种调味品，而有些调味品只供娱乐之用。同样丰富的欲望和需求则控制着新闻业的运行。因此，报纸不能局限于记录事实，虽然事实可能难以获悉，有时候可能只能获得部分事实信息，而且事实本身可能并不完整，但报纸必须将报道范畴拓展到其承担的全部责任的无限多样化事务的准确报道上来。在李普曼（Walter Lippman）① 的著作《舆论学》（*Public Opinion*）中，新闻报道的范畴或多或少扩展到缺乏确定性和局限性的广泛领域，而客观事实由于人们对当时无法接近的其他事实的想象和推测而被掩盖起来，报纸希望尽可能精确地报道新闻事实，尽可能完整地呈现当时已经发生的事情真相。这个领域才是新闻业所肩负的最重要而神圣的使命所在，而正是在这个领域，新闻业赢得了最辉煌的成功，新闻业必需不断地在这个领域追求准确性，达到真实地报道每次新闻事实的完美境地。

这再次使我们面对记者的学识、品质和特性养成，及其处理新闻稿件的编辑的岗前培训、品质和特性养成方法等问题。菲利普·悉尼（Philip Sidney）② 很久以前就说过，"有几人能够分辨真相与假象、事实与欺骗呢？"然而，这样的分辨能力就像我们

---

① 李普曼（Walter Lippman，1889—1974），美国政论、专栏作家，著有《政治导言》、《放任与驾驭》、《舆论学》（*Public Opinion*）等。

② 菲利普·悉尼（Philip Sidney，1554—1586），16 世纪英国文学家。

所谓新闻业必需的基本意识——"新闻鼻"——对于优秀记者和编辑的必要性一样。只有通过强调首要的准确性和忠于真相,只有通过强调基于新闻收集和准备之上分辨真相与假象的必要性,新闻报道才能达到其孜孜追求的理想境界——真实性。

第七章　新闻获取和编辑

当然,获取新闻是新闻业的基本任务。事件本身不会考虑报刊报道的便利,它们也不会自我报道。的确,新闻靠自身的优势来传播,事件越重要,消息之舟航行得越快。但是,消息在传播的过程中不可避免地积聚失实和浮夸之报道。报纸不会接受道听途说的谣言式消息,需要调查的不确定的新闻线索除外。从新闻的意识来讲,获取新闻就是径直走近新闻事件,并通过观察和询问尽量确定所发生事实的真实情况,从而取得事实信息。无论国内的事情,还是国外的事情,无论记者还是通讯员,他们都是在报纸的直接控制下进行报道,通讯社采集独家报道而传递给多家报纸刊登,新闻采集的基本原则是相同的。新闻采集要求记者必须到现场去获取第一手的事实信息。

首先,报纸记者是一位事实发掘者。当报社指派他去报道一件事情或者其中的某些事实的时候,他的任务和职责就是获取事实信息。但是,获取新闻信息通常涉及很多方面的事情,绝非追求把一堆材料带回来。这是智能的发挥过程,分辨重要因素与非重要因素、必要因素与非必要因素的意识运作过程;这是一个从各种迹象中推理假设,并据此从隐藏在周围环境或者设计的模糊迹象中得出关键事实的论证过程。假如分辨新闻的功夫到位的话，最不起眼的新闻线索也可能包含着重大新闻。虽然所谓的"新闻鼻"好像是出于本能的，但它不仅仅是直觉。"新闻鼻"是一种心智和思维品行的发挥，它虽然是人们与生俱来的禀赋，但它需要理性的相关推理，而且像其他天然的才能一样，它需要实践和阅历才可以养成。艺术家的才能在于他看到了其他人没有看到的迷人之处；音乐家的才能在于他察觉到了凡夫俗子未能知觉的和谐美；诗人的才能在于他发现了"春江水暖鸭先知"的神秘意境。对于只见树木不见森林的人而言，记者洞察和识别新闻的高超能力就可以在挖掘表象背后的实质性问题的报道中体现出来，而且这也是新闻行业任何部门取得最好业绩所必需的能力。因为从本质上讲新闻事业是一种艺术，一种表达的艺术。即使画家在进行颜色调配时也需要心智的支配，所以如果生活中每天所发生事情的真相的确认和陈述建立在短暂的调查基础上，那么对于这种生活的叙述就必须由懂行的业内人士的直觉判断和理性推理来指导。

　　画家不可能缺乏色彩感，音乐家不可能缺少和谐美的意识，而记者自然不可能缺失新闻意识。但是，仅仅拥有了这种艺术直觉或者禀赋，一个人还不足以成为一名画家、音乐家或者记者。有人认为，诗人是天生的，而非后天生成的，这种说法像很多其他说法一样并不真实。诗人是天生的，而且需要后天的培育。没有生就的诗人。诗人的天赋是与生俱来的，但是名副其实的诗人是在生活、阅历、训练、学习、教育等综合素质的养成和提高过程中造就的。的确，只有通过实践和阅历，这种艺术品质才能得以养成。记者的职业素养概莫如此。没有天生的记者或编辑。新闻从业者具备新闻意识的天赋是必要的，但是他们必须通过培训和锻炼来培育新闻意识，他们必须通过学习、教育和观察来发展这种意识，只有这样，他们才能成为名副其实的记者。"新闻事业需要从业者具备多方面的能力、宽泛的知识和丰富的阅历，以及先天和后天培养的观察和推理事物的能力"①。假如记者要真实和准确地报道新闻的话,他们与生俱来的才能必须在某种程度上与后天获得的能力结合起来,尤其是在他们从事新闻业的初级阶段。品质因素也不能忽略,因为如果新闻的真实性是新闻业试金石的话,那么新闻专业实践显然必须建立在这种职业品质基础上。

上文所说旨在强调记者的品质、禀赋和学识,这些对于提高新闻采集和出版的真实性十分必要,也为所有新闻从业者所敬仰。新闻事业这个层面上的进步和提升很大程度上依赖于新闻采集者和传播者的性格和能力,获取新闻事实和准备新闻报道的基本和首要任务就交给他们了。假如编辑或出版商不考虑产品来源的质量,他们怀有再完美的新闻报道理想亦无济于事。编辑部或者管理办公室无论多么细心、投入多大能量或者智力支持都不能保证报纸质量令人信服,除非在一线进行新闻报道或者撰稿的记者和编辑是可靠的。他们中大多数人能做到如此,就是新闻业的殊勋,也是新闻事业大发展的主要原因之一。新闻年鉴中填满了新闻从业者追求真理的英雄般的事迹和新闻收集者的热心,这些远非其他行业从业者能比,而名不见经传的成千上万名新闻从业者在采访现场和编辑室默默奉献,他们对于新闻业的忠诚、付出的智慧和行动不断推动和维护着"第四等级"的荣光。然而,这里并非轻蔑地说新闻从业者中没有足够可靠的记者和编辑,没有完全胜任行业的从业者。新闻业是一种公共事业的职业,随着公共机构对胜任职工需求的增加,新闻业长期以来对非正式来源的从业者的依赖却在减少。但是,新闻事业对从业者的需求是持续的,它需要更多的从业者。新闻业不但需要大量具备新闻天赋并适于该行业的男女从业者,而且还要求他们接受过基础

---

① From preamble to *Canons of Journalism*, adopted by *the American Society of Newspaper Editors*,April,1923.——原书注

教育、普通的和特别的岗前培训。换言之，新闻业不但需要更多从业者，而且需要具备前期职业实践的从业者。即使见习记者具备了在报纸运作中进行实际操作的优势，他们依然存在的问题是：随着报社工作的日益复杂化和细分化，他们在报社所有部门锻炼的机会在减少，尤其是在都市报纸中。作为从业的实践准备，普通教育和技能教育都是必需的，这不但是环境的要求，同样是为奠定专业的威严、地位和进步的良好、可靠基础而日益增长的需求。

简而言之，新闻学院必然成为新闻机构更加依赖的招募从业者队伍的来源。更加传统的其他行业也经历过同样的路径，行业发展最终必然达到一个临界点，即为了保护行业自身的发展，它将建立某种特定的进入门槛的质量标准。同时，在没有损失的情况下，行业不能不要求获得一定数量的最好资源为自身服务。为了实现这样的要求，我们有必要鼓励从业者为新闻事业奉献的精神，倡导新闻行业是值得尊重的、可为之献身的行业的观念，其直接回报是：这是一个充满着诱惑的行业，它为从业者提供了实现个人业绩和发挥作用的特殊机会。倡导这种观念的最好机构是学校。像其他行业一样，接受教育的准备工作是新闻从业者取得成功的必要条件。报人不是在学校里培养出来的，律师和医生亦如此，但是合适的指导学校可能为准从业者奠定了实用行业知识的基础，告知学员们行业实践的要素并反复灌输行业理念，所有这些都是"新闻事业取得最好效果之必需，在实际操作中就更加必要了。如果事先不能获得的话，在实际操作中就来不及了，即所谓亡羊补牢为时未晚"。新闻学院可能还有助于建立一种职业精神，奠定职业道德的基础，确立年轻从业者心目中的基本行业准则。只有通过实际的锻炼、艰苦的工作和持续的学习，加上与生俱来的天赋，才能造就一名优秀的记者，这些对于其他任何行业从业者的事业成功都是十分必要的，但是从业前的准备教育对于新闻行业的实用性不比其他行业小，新闻业是一个完全值得尊重的行业，它要求从业者接受像其他行业所同样暗示的从业准备教育。

那么，采集准确的基本信息并获取新闻依赖于新闻采集者的品质和性格。首先，取得要报道事件的事实材料和突出的事实细节是记者的任务。在这里，无论怎样强调都从来不过分的事实是：在每个报纸编辑部，事实都是新闻的基本要素。但是，独立的事实材料只不过是新闻报道的框架，新闻报道的构成材料，从业者的精湛技巧与最理性的观察、辨别和区分能力及其对新闻事业的热情和付出的辛勤工作等可能是新闻从业者成功的必要条件。记者正是在采集事实的过程中才发现新闻业的浮夸成分，他们在与采访人物的接触中积累了新闻业最令人神往的阅历，唤起人性本质的某些最可贵的要素。实事求是地讲，尽管其中的大部分经历只是日常最辛苦的工作而已，但他们经历的冒险花絮、克服困难或脱险后的欢呼雀跃却使人难以忘怀。新闻业的艺术在于陈述事实，在于从业者从读者的眼光和兴趣中来准备新闻报道。

两个人对同一事件的报道可能存在着很大的差别，其中一个人的报道可能单调而乏味，另外一个人的报道可能是明快而有趣的。两者的差别可能在于后者具有高超的新闻意识、认识和抓取新闻事件中更吸引人的细节的能力，或者仅仅润色和加工引人注目的事实并进而使之产生相应的趣味性的能力。但是，这可能完全依赖于高超的叙述能力，依赖于清晰、紧凑而连贯的陈述，依赖于恰如其分的词汇选择和运用，依赖于赋予趣味性细节的更加有效的描述。这是因为，尽管获取事实是新闻报道过程的首要任务，而且它经常要求更高层次的行业智力和意识历练，但是收集新闻的制作材料并以新闻敏感性来判断这些材料的价值很大程度上依赖于从中产生的叙事风格。因此，报纸的价值对其呈现新闻的方法的依赖程度并不小，它还依赖于新闻事件叙述中艺术的表达，依赖于新闻被赋予的艺术趣味性。然而，这些是以表达的真相和平衡都未遭遇破坏为前提条件的。

获得新闻是报纸的任务。首先，报纸的基本职能是获取新闻事实。报纸的第二个基本职能是有趣地讲述新闻故事，使读者如身临其境般感受新闻的真实性。报纸的第三个基本职能是审慎地选择与可用版面相关的新闻报道，仔细分辨事件的来龙去脉，根据事件的重要性调整其报道版序，制作适宜的新闻标题，适当地安排新闻的版位，这些形成了报纸的最终编辑流程。以前的章节讨论了新闻选择和调整的话题，这里再次将这些流程罗列出来，旨在说明新闻报道活动中最为重要的步骤，即新闻报道的准备工作。

新闻素材可能完全收集起来了，对新闻事实进行了核准，新闻稿撰写得也很优美，但是除非新闻编辑和美术编辑都是十分称职的，否则上述的很多付出都是徒劳的。了解在何处、何种程度和如何使用蓝铅笔校订原稿，捕捉新闻稿中不准确的陈述，发现可能触及诽谤的断言，认识重大新闻中可能引起歧义的模糊细节，分辨手头的报道与其来源更远的另外一个地方发生的事件之间的关联，迅速抓取一条新闻的意义并撰写正确表达其中蕴涵之意的标题，所有这些都要求从业者具备广博的知识、良好的智力和操作判断的能力。各种主题和风格的消息铺天盖地传递到新闻编辑部，这需要新闻编辑根据报纸的特定需要和版面的特征进行判断和取舍。这些消息的来源和出处成千上万，很多人以各种能力和心智为之付出，其中一些报道采写得粗制滥造，需要改写；有些报道的篇幅拖沓冗长，需要缩写；有些报道只是触及事件的某个侧面，其重要性不强，事件的另外一部分可能更具有新闻价值；有些报道要求扩展到编辑所拥有或者获得的其他相关事实。无论编辑部是什么性质的或者在哪里，说到底它是扬谷去糠而为读者准备精神食粮的地方。如果编辑部不能胜任其工作、效率不高或者软弱无力的话，它制造的产品就是劣质的。无论怎样优秀的报道团队或者什么样的编辑理念都无法克服编辑室效率不高或者效果欠佳所造成的弊端。

假如编辑室像报道组和通信组那样对于新闻的准确性不作要求的话，新闻报道的准确性就很难保持。编辑室的无能或者粗心可能把准确的报道编排得不准确。同样的工作方式和态度还可能丧失一篇优秀报道的生动性、趣味性或者卖点，使得改写的报道中某些层面与事实相去甚远。一位保守的陈述者可能过分夸张事实，或者结构紧凑的新闻故事由于不严谨的编辑而被剥夺了其连贯性和持续性。从另外一个方面来讲，一支精干的编辑队伍可以提高报道的准确性，使得缺乏连贯性的报道富有层次感，强化报道的薄弱层面，可以改正书写错误，经常通过灵巧的结构性改写使得单调的报道富有生机而不失事件的真实性。

报社的文字编辑室在整个报纸的制作过程中是最终的润色环节，其担负的职责至关重要，因为该环节出来的合格产品是整个报纸制作成功的必要条件。虽然文字编辑室的精干员工曾经是匿名的，但他们在整个新闻业中的地位很高。他们不具备新闻采集者执行任务时面临感人新闻故事及其震撼情节的机会，但是千变万化的新闻事件像连续的万花筒画面一样在他们眼前掠过，弥补了他们不直接接触生活的不足。他们经手了大量的新闻稿，他们首先听到重大新闻的"爆料"而激动不已。新闻业没有任何部门或者环节更应该像编辑部那样配备忠于职守、甘于奉献、知识渊博和心智聪慧的员工。编辑室及其编辑工作会诞生自己行业的英雄式人物、天才和艺术家。

在报社编辑室的所有职责中，最重要的任务莫过于制作新闻标题了。制作新闻标题本身就是一种艺术，这需要特殊的表达才能。在美国新闻事业中，新闻标题具有两种基本功能：第一，标示新闻的本质；第二，提高新闻的关注度。在这两种功能发挥作用的过程中，新闻标题还提供了另外的目的——为读者标明编辑对呈现在面前的各种新闻素材重要性或者趣味性的判断。截至19世纪下半叶，美国的新闻标题就只是一个标示——新闻主题的标示。单独一行字通常被认为足够表达最重要的消息。尽管欧洲新闻业宣称的新闻规范比此前的更加保守，但它至今依然坚持这样的观点和行规。美国新闻业的行规形成于唤起受众对新闻兴趣的要求，所以新闻标题的目的不仅在于告知读者所报道的主题，而且是呈现和强调报道的主要特征。新闻标题以言简意赅的形式告知读者信息，它浓缩了新闻事件的主要情节。

　　但是，无论报纸编辑部（室）的体制特征如何，它都面临两个难题。第一，新闻标题越广泛，出现失误的可能性越大。旨在告诉读者新闻事实的标题的放大不能改变基本的事实，而且只有当标题向读者清晰而准确地标示了所承载新闻的本质内容的时候，其宗旨才得以实现。假如标题没有做到这一点，它就不能称之为好标题。但是，很明显，标题越扩展，其陈述和阐释出现失误的机会越多。在一个四行标题中，每行都代表着整个新闻中一个层面的涵义，该四行题就比一个两行题出现失误的几率多一倍。第二，新闻及其标题吸引读者注意力的愿望是标题趋于夸张的持续性诱惑力，这样的标题似乎就比事实更加重要了。标题索引中的内容并非雷人雷语，这就是报纸编辑或者文字编辑克制夸张而值得称道的明证之一。

　　这种体制也产生一种不可预见的非期望的效果，这代表着一个有损于新闻本质属性的严重问题。正如上文所讲，新闻标题的宗旨是表明新闻的本质并引起读者的兴趣。但是，更多的新闻标题旨在告知读者新闻故事，它本身承载了过多的信息，以便满足一目十行的"匆忙"读者的阅读需求。其结果是，很多人从新闻标题中就获悉了消息的内容，或者他们自认为浏览了标题就明白了整个消息的内容，并满足于此。这样，新闻标题的宗旨之一就被亵渎了。新闻标题并非需要细读的新闻故事的文本部分，它只代表着整个新闻故事中某个部分的内容，肤浅读者所诉求的不必要的新闻标题除外。这样随意浏览新闻标题的读报方法在美国十分流行，其结果有损于新闻事业，对于公共利益也带来不利影响。这种做法有损于新闻事业，因为它使得采写和编辑过程中的很多工作都成为徒劳。新闻报道的目的是使读者了解事件的来龙去脉。记者和编辑为采写和编辑新闻而付出的时间和劳动、智力和技术都融于读者面前的报纸所刊登的文章。报纸上的每篇新闻都蕴涵着记者和编辑的心血和付出，他们努力把所收集的事实以详尽的细节描述呈现在读者面前，以便读者更加清晰地了解所发生的事情，或者至少了解已经发生的事实。但是，记者和编辑仔细核对新闻事实以保证新闻的准确性，他们匠心独运地构筑新闻结构以便更加清晰地表达事实，他们精心润色新闻稿以便文笔更加流畅，所有这些对于已经在新闻标题中发现自己要知晓的足够信息的读者而言都是浪费。

　　这种体制对于公共利益不利，因为报纸的公共价值在于它传递了作为舆论基础的信息。假如舆论是理性的，它必定建立在广泛信息聚合的基础之上。读者在新闻标题中获悉的枯燥而单调的信息不能产生理性的舆论。提供信息并非新闻标题的目的所在，相反，引导读者关注包涵所收集信息的报道才是其宗旨。无论怎样扩展，标题只是标明了新闻的主要事实要素，而且仅仅是几个要素。无论标题多么准确地标示其新闻要素，没有任何读者能够从新闻标题中获悉有关新闻事件的清晰而完整的信息。没有任何人能够通过阅读目录索引而了解整本书的内容。书名和目录索引只是告诉读者关于本书的基本特征和大致内容。报纸的新闻标题只是关于所刊登新闻的主题和新闻索引，而有关公共事件和活动的知识信息不能从新闻标题中获悉。但是，假如为了使新闻标题达到吸引读者注意力和引起读者兴趣的效果而在其中融入了过多信息的话，读者就会认为，他不用仔细阅读自己感兴趣的新闻报道的正文而仅仅从标题中就可以获悉足够的相关知识和信息，这样从新闻学的角度来看标题的宗旨就丧失了，而且诱导读者相信，当自己只是浏览新闻标题索引时就获悉了这条新闻的内容。

　　正如上文所言，新闻标题的基本功能就是标明新闻的本质。对于读者而言，浏览了标题就会便于选择和阅读新闻。很少有读者关心和阅读报纸所刊登的所有新闻，而且没有人愿意这样仔细阅读新闻。但是，一位读者通过浏览新闻标题就可能发现本质上吸引人的趣味性新闻，而且假如兴致来了的话，他可以忽略其余所有的新闻而专心阅读自己感兴趣的消息。假如一条新闻标题的制作旨在引起读者关于这条新闻的某种无可厚非的兴趣，对于这位读者而言新闻主题本身的吸引力并不大，那么这条标题就实现了新闻标题的第二大功能。标题不得不扩大自身的趣味性，扩展到增加其服务价值的范围。由于趣味性是报纸发行量的原动力，在更大范围内引发读者的更大兴趣对于提高报纸的发行量非常重要。报纸读者的阅读范围越广泛，报纸的传播效果就越好，如果消息有价值的话，其传播效果就好。因此，通过标题来唤起读者正当的新闻趣味性需求就成为新闻标题当之无愧的功能之一。激发公众对于公共问题的兴趣是新闻事业的基本责任，这是毋庸置疑的。的确，大量新闻的公共价值是通过新闻的这种作用的发挥而创造的，而新闻标题可能有助于引发这种公共兴趣，其作用不可忽视。但是，通过新闻标题来唤起读者对于所有新闻的兴趣的努力，必须建立在这条新闻本质上适合这样做的基础上。通过标题唤起读者对于新闻本身并不具备的兴趣，这样的做法是对读者信任的背叛，同时降低了编辑的判断力，也减弱了读者对报纸上所有新闻标题价值的尊重。记者和编辑对新闻标题的夸张陈述和过分强调没有任何可以原谅的借口或理由。假如读者仅仅浏览标题，他只能得到关于这条新闻的一个错误认知，而假如这位读者阅读了整条新闻的话，他马上就能认识到新闻标题的夸张及其危害了。读者遭遇伤害的案例在其他的报纸中是常见的。

　　同理，新闻标题的准确表达尤其重要。在新闻标题中过分强调某些信息是一种新闻失真，不准确地表达即使最保守的新闻标题都包含的某些事实，成为新闻失真的另外一种情况。尽管并非总是如此，新闻标题的夸张手法通常是蓄意的。非夸张的陈述中存在的不准确细节通常都是无意识导致的失误，源于匆忙的采写

第七章　新闻获取和编辑　**69**

或者编辑，源于浅薄地理解了文字编辑所撰写的新闻稿的含意，源于没有仔细推敲标题中与新闻相符的事实要素，源于标题中单词的误用。经常出现的情况是，仅仅一个单词的误用就可能给予读者关于新闻本质的完全错误的认知。偶尔出现的情况是，标题的陈述与新闻事实截然相反而自相矛盾。编辑在给消息加标题的时候，几乎不会使新闻标题完全背离其作者的初衷。作为规律，质量问题、粗枝大叶或者草率导致的失误都是无意识引起的。在报社的编辑部或者其他部门，再细心也不可能杜绝出错，因此，编辑们制作或润色的标题达到完美表达的程度，其精确度与其引介的新闻正文完全吻合，这种情况也是不可能出现的。读者有资格假定，任何标题都准确地表达了其所引导的新闻的本质内涵，报社有必要建立和维护读者对于这种假定不断得以验证从而形成的对整个报纸的品牌的尊敬，就人力所及范围而言尽可能对此加以彻底验证。新闻标题的真实性与新闻的真实性同等重要。

　　报纸出版的编辑流程涵盖标题的制作、版面中新闻和其他阅读材料的编排和润色等环节。这绝非一种机械的任务。它很大程度上是一种艺术性的工作，置身其中的编辑必须具备建筑师那样的平衡、比例和关联意识。它是一种编辑任务，因为完成这项工作必须了解和掌握事实材料的本质及其比较价值和重要性。正是在这种操作中，很多领域的新闻活动和采集到的不同作品都汇集在编辑部，而且报纸形成了读者每天面对和接受的个性特征。编辑部主任不仅要使读者信任象征报纸脸面和服饰的版面，而且要使他们相信版面是向公众展示报纸生机和活力的报纸的心脏和灵魂，读者瞄一眼版面就能辨认出这是哪家报纸，就像遇见老朋友一样。某张报纸的品牌就如一个人的品性，它应该蕴含深层的含意，而并非留于表面，尽管如此，很多人依然希望报纸有一个清新悦目的面孔和服饰，就像一位绅士的着装，如果他的着装没有引来足够的注意力的话，他宣称自己的品性如何如何的时候就会显得乏力。所有报纸的个体特征或多或少都会受到版面的主观和客观因素的影响。一个引人瞩目的报纸版面不仅能够获取读者的认知，而且毫不夸张地讲，报纸版面也可能成为报纸订阅者满意的缘由之一。无论从哪个角度而言，报纸版面都是报纸品牌的标示之一，这一点绝不亚于品性对于个人的重要性。同理，着装影响个体印象的形成，也影响着个体本身。一位资深作家曾说："着装对于人类行为会产生道德层面的影响。某位绅士如果穿着脏兮兮的靴子、破旧的外套，带着凌乱的领带出现于某种公众场合的时候，他总有可能发现自己会像其着装遭到蔑视一样遭遇相应的敷衍性问候和冷遇。"这段论述对于所有事物都是真实而适用的，相反的事实亦如此，整洁的包装对于纯净的产品而言会大有增色。版面设计良好的报纸，换言之，外观整洁而吸引眼球的报纸，对于读者而言是持续而愉悦的。而且不管多么粗陋，对于那些在报纸出版中作出创造性服务的人而言，好的版面设计也是对自己一种不断的鼓励和慰藉。

但是，版面设计不仅涉及报纸外观，而且涉及新闻编排是否适合读者的阅读方便和新闻展示是否有利于报纸的销售。读者认知报纸价值的一个表现就是熟悉其新闻编排的惯用手段。读者了解在报纸的哪个版位可以找到自己特别需要的信息，而读者对于报纸编排手段的了解是这张报纸稳定喜爱它的读者忠诚于报纸的影响之一。报纸版面编排的促销功能几乎完全局限于街头售卖环节，而且限定于头版的版面设计。头版的确可以称之为报纸的展示窗口。在头版上，报纸展示了其最吸引人的作品和最重要或者最有趣的新闻。从当天所发生的事情中挑选出那些最值得关注或者最能引起受众兴趣的事情，是版面编辑的任务。这项任务涉及迅速并准确地判断新闻价值和读者趣味。因此，为了取悦现有读者的眼球以及吸引报纸潜在购买者的关注和即时兴趣，报纸头版即可成为以新闻稿的质量为标准选择稿件与新闻编排过程中编辑判断和编辑艺术的实验空间。最后，版面设计对于下午截稿的报纸的重要性要超过早上截稿的报纸，前者通常更多地从街头售卖中产生其发行量，因为这种报纸的发行时间更有利于这种促销方法。因此，下午截稿的报纸更重视头版的特稿，报童通常在街头叫卖的气势要大于早报，但是两种报纸的头版对于报纸售卖都会产生影响。

基于此，关于报纸头版的设计需要考虑几个层面的问题，这些问题时常相互冲突。假如头版被认为是报纸的脸面，头版就非常重要；假如报纸作为一个整体赢得了尊重，报纸的外观就值得尊重。报纸外观应该表达其特性，对于一张报纸或者一个人而言，没有任何版位或者部位确实可以胜过脸面所揭示的特性，而更有利于显示其质量或品行了。假如正文及其主题灵魂证明报纸外观没有说谎的话，报纸版面就成为影响其建立与读者永久性关系的因素。报纸头版的功能使报纸的整体外观印象成为编辑部首要的考虑。它旨在通过均衡的新闻编排来持续吸引读者，使整个版面达到赏心悦目的效果而无暇顾及报纸所刊登新闻的质量。当然，质量验证外观是必要的，但是基于这条原则仅仅通过报纸头版的外观设计而取得的印象就没有什么价值可言了。读者喜欢阅读外观看起来整洁、亲和而富有内涵的报纸，而且读者愿意站在版面不带有欺骗性的报纸一边。

然而，假如头版首先被认为是报纸的一个窗口的话，换言之，假如商业影响预先支配了报纸版面设计的话，那么报纸最佳卖点的头版编排就成为编辑们首要考虑的问题了。关于头版功能的这种理论与其他理论是对立的，它并不关注给读者留下深刻印象的报纸特性，而是关心如何赚取读者口袋中的钱。报纸可能具有这种特性，但是报纸版面并无刻意揭示该特性。相反，在报纸版面设计过程中编辑努力收集最骇人的新闻，并冠以最醒目的标题，而且假如这种特性存在的话，它就会如此通过报纸面孔被揭示或者误传。报纸通过耸人听闻的新闻及其标题吸引眼球进而诉求街头售卖来提高发行量的过程中，其精美的外观即刻淹没在阅读者的视觉中。通过这种方式来提高报纸的发行量是毋庸置疑的，但是这种做法并非积极向上的，而且这种做法倾向于怂恿新闻及其标题制作中的过度夸张，进而降低了公众对于整个新闻事业公信力的信任度。

  然而，假如报纸售卖诉求只是版面设计中第二位考虑的要素，而非首先考虑的要素，那么版面作为报纸展示窗口的观点就必须与特性表达的观点一致。由于展示窗口本身可能既是特性的肯定表达，又是报纸公信力和销售量的一种鼓励，为了认识其真相，我们有必要回顾商业展示橱窗的发展情况。长期以来，展示橱窗首先只是展示售卖的不同产品及其品质的地方，众多的顾客拥挤在窗口前。橱窗内摆放着如此众多的商品，顾客们却很少关注橱窗的商品摆放，以至于他们对橱窗及其商品的大致印象只是一堆便宜货，橱窗的细节安排和商品摆放实际上都失去了意义，除非他们花费更多的时间进行仔细观察。在这样的展示橱窗中几乎没有什么吸引或者取悦消费者眼球的商品，商家及其设计者也没有创造相应的可效仿的机制或规则。大部分商业展示橱窗随着消费者对于销售员心理活动的加深理解而消失，而只有在保留着原始商业营销方法的后街或者落后的社区中才能发现。但是，这种类型的展示窗口只出现在很多报纸的头版，编辑如此操作的目的就是在头版上尽可能塞进更多的新闻和信息，每条新闻都设计有加粗的标题，以显示其重要性。报纸头版展示窗口的总体效果是混淆了信息而不是引起读者的关注。即使报纸的影响力和发行量没有因此丧失的话，也因此而减弱了，因为在这样的新闻和信息罗列中没有什么特殊的编排技巧能够以强势的效果来吸引读者的眼球。一个事实以彰显、独立和截然不同的方式被呈现并富有冲击效果，就像森林中一棵不起眼的大树突然间孑然挺立在醒目的地方，此情此景下强势就可能形成。

  因此，随着人们对于这样的展示橱窗的清晰理解，现代商业展示橱窗中为数不多的商品如此富有吸引力，以至于橱窗设计的重心在于吸引消费者眼球，进而销售诉求实质上也增强了，整个橱窗的布局旨在取悦消费者的口味并倡导相应的可效仿的机制和规则。

89　　简而言之，这种营销机制旨在通过展示商品的特性而某种程度上显示其特征，同时促进营销。据说，广为讨论的新闻学基本原则之一是，报纸首先是可以售卖而盈利的。因此，任何有利于增加发行量而不降低报纸公信力的可信手段都被认为是对于报纸基本原则的贡献。从这种观点来看，假如报纸头版作为展示橱窗的理论服从于吸引观察者眼球而给他们留下关于报纸印象的宗旨，并且这种印象能够独立地创造和维持报纸在读者心目中的喜爱和信任，那么该理论就不应该遭受谴责。任何精美的商业展示橱窗的建立对于报纸头版编排的基本原则都是一个教训：其中展示了最可能吸引公众兴趣的同样审慎选择的新闻，同样艺术般均衡组合的文本，而且它同样要避免拥挤的信息。这就是高尚趣味、体面和特性与强烈而持久的销售诉求融合于报纸头版的基本质量所系。

第八章　报纸个体从业者

在本章节的开始我们就应该谈到，消息和评论构筑了新闻事业。消息只是新闻业的两大功能之一，评论本身缺乏构筑新闻业的基本元素。没有评论的报纸或者没有消息的期刊可能会被新闻界所接受，但是两者都不能说报道了新闻领域应该报道的事情。正如上文所论述的那样，评论与消息始终相关。无论何时何地，有趣的新闻报道会激发读者的思想，而如果表达观点的时间和机会具备的话，它就会导致观点的表达。一条消息传递给任何一群男士或者女士，只要他们对这条消息感兴趣，他们接下来就会展开讨论，并提出关于这条消息的本质或者含意的不同观点。如果这条消息很重要，传播它的人就获得了尊重，而他本人关于这条消息的观点就成为大家希望看到的。他不仅被追问有关的细节，而且他还被要求讲解自己对此事的所思所想。在人们相互传播新闻事件的过程中，消息和评论是不可分割的，而且它们总是像孪生兄弟一样形影相伴。

新闻业仅仅作为体现所有人类活动特征的趣味性产品是不够的，除非新闻业在所传播的趣味性信息服务中融合了消息和评论，因为两者都是新闻业所必需的。这种做法几乎在新闻业的开端就被认可，尽管很长时期以来就新闻事实说话的评论的传播受到当局政府或党派的压制，直到争取言论自由和出版自由的斗争取得了胜利，舆论才开始发展成为一种控制和影响人类文明进步的力量。

缺乏自己观点的报纸充其量是一家时事信息的承载者，它只是创造了自身所承载的在公共市场上售卖的有关事件的商业属性，即使事实成为可以售卖的信息。尽管由此提供的公共服务非常重要，而且这就如同新闻的功能一样必要，但不管怎样，新闻业本质上具备商业属性。如此界定的报纸只是一种商品，一种用取之于物质世界的原材料制作而成的无意识的产品而已。像留声机或者收音机一样，它可能收集和传递信息和思想，但是由于它缺乏自身的独立思想而失去了内在活力。正是思想及其表达给了报纸以生命，报纸有了自身独立的言论之后，它才成为一个能够发出自身声音的充满活力的、动人的媒体。报纸有了思想、意愿和宗旨，它所传播的每个单词都能够体现其个性特征。

个性对于一张报纸的重要性就如人的个性对人一样同等重要，人类无法逃避个性的存在，一个人无论怎样普通平常，都不可能没有任何个性特征。的确，正是你自身，即你所意识到的身份认同将你与他人区分开来。这绝非表象或者形式上的品质，尽管报纸的版面和形式也有助于其报道事实。这自然是内因在起作用，即内在的事物在思维、运筹和促进行动，尽管我们可能根据体型和外表来识别一个人，但我们还是不了解其个性特征，除非他通过自身的言行表露其内在的特征，或者他以某种方式表达了自己的思想。个人的外表、举止和着装都不能构筑其个性特征，它们只是内在本性的外在标示而已，而内在本性才是个性特征。

报纸的个性特征亦如此。报纸不可能通过商业属性而创造自身的个性特征。像其他产品一样，报纸可能通过其外观版面来加以识别。报纸的版面与外观、新闻与编排的特点的确可能表现其个性特征，但是它们不能构筑其个性特征。只有报纸评论栏目的观点表达才能表现报纸的灵魂和思想的存在,如果报纸没有评论性栏目,那么它就没有什么个性可言。有人说,消息可能构成报纸的身体,评论则成为其灵魂。假如灵魂不存在了,身体就只是行尸走肉而已。

作为报纸思想和灵魂结晶的个性特征不可避免地向读者揭示了其品质,读者通过阅读、观察和理解报纸持续的报道来了解其办报质量。在揭示其思想时,报纸同时揭示了自身的特征及其知识储备量。报纸的面孔可能成为其表面特征的标示,而评论版才显示了报纸的本质属性。很多人貌似强大,其灵魂却是懦弱的,而充满智慧的头脑经常依存于一个脆弱的身体内。表象可能误导关于事物的认知;但是,无论外表如何,事物内在的个性特征都是通过其自身的表现来揭示的。报纸也是如此。它每天展示自身,以便公众观察和评判,其版面设计可能标示了其特征,或者没有完全反映其特征,但是其特征的真实依存和个性特征的实际表达只有在自身思想的表达中才能体现。

从表面看,报纸或许以其鲜明的个性特征失去了某些东西。实际上,报纸很大程度上以同样的方式报道了很多同样的新闻。尽管存在印刷上的差别,但在过去这样的印刷差别并不明显。普通新闻采集代理公司——通讯社,为很多报纸提供相同的信息,它们的快速发展导致了报纸内容的同质化。辛迪加的增长是造成报纸内容程式化的一个重要影响因素。然而,这几乎成为任何大机械化生产领域中规模经济不可避免的结果。大规模生产过程及其产品易于导致特定的同质化,特定生产线制造的产品或多或少带有标准化的倾向。这归功于生产更加优质的产品、生产成本的减少或者生产规模的扩大所凭借的设计或方法改进。例如,第一批汽车在外观和机械设备上出现五花八门的样式。然而,随着汽车生产经验和技术的积累,明确的制造原则确立起来,汽车工业开始呈现相对统一的机械和设计模式,直到各款汽车之间的差别更多地变成质量而非外观的差别。尽管相当大的外观差别保留下来，以便对汽车类型和技术进行分辨，但是，这种同质化的路径提高了汽车作为一种服务设备的生产价值并便于大规模生产和销售。

  导致报纸制作程式化的另一个影响是扩大了其适用的范围，增加了大机械化的便利和报纸发行领域，为报纸及其读者提供了个别报纸除外其他任何单张报纸都无法提供的更大的新闻服务。面对这些事实，报纸倾向于创建某种外观上的统一性，对此我们不必有过多的惋惜。报纸的个性或者特质并非外表的事情。个性特征本身就可以反映一家报纸的差异化，虽然个性特征可能通过外观加以标示，但是它并非依存于外表。所有的男人都是相像的，他们基本上具有同样的体型，除了极个别男人，所有的男性都有同样的双臂和双腿，以完全相同的标准和方法连接在人体上。借用报纸的术语来讲，所有人的脸型都是与生俱来"编排"好的，五官根据固定而实际上位置和平衡又不断变化的规则组合起来。即使在服从于主观意愿的着装上，所有人也都有着比较趋同的一面。然而，事实尽管如此，谁又敢说人类的个性特征和差异不明显呢！男人之间存在着足够的体型和外表上的差别，借此可以进行识别，这样的差别和识别从外部来看是必要的。而个人揭示其言行和思想的头脑和心灵才是现实生活中识别男人的主要因素。报纸的情况亦如此。影响报纸同质化的倾向绝对不会走向极端，致使所有的报纸完全雷同。报纸之间存在而且永远存在旨在便于识别的外观上的明显差别、品质上的差别、某种程度上反映其个性特征的风格和运行差别、形式差别，以及外观相似性绝对无法改变的个体驱动力的差别。

  但是，这些影响报纸的外观和形体发展的因素与其他的因素还影响着报纸自身内涵的变化。一个客观事实越来越为大家所接受：报纸的进步更多地源自内在活力而非外因。我们经常谈论个人的新闻生涯，有时候带有一种遗憾的口气。毋庸置疑，这种个人从业经历具有价值和吸引力。但是，当天的报纸本身不具有也不可能有个性特征。每份报纸只不过是所指人类个性的表现中介而已。它记录了格里利（Greeley）的言论，或者达纳说过的话。讲话者是人而不是报纸，正是这个人而非报纸在公众心目中留下了印象。报纸所体现的个性特征高于书籍或者小册子的特质。

但是，随着报纸规格和发行量的提高，以及报纸发行范围和领域的拓展，报社有必要组合为类似报业集团的机构，报纸的个体特性进而让位于报纸本身所蕴涵的综合性特质。人们不再谈论格里利或者达纳、雷蒙德（Raymond）说了什么，而是津津乐道《纽约论坛报》（New York Tribune）、《纽约太阳报》（New York Sun）或者《纽约时报》（New York Times）怎么说了。报纸不再由于刊登某个人的言论而引起读者的兴趣。报纸发出了在公众心目中引起共鸣的、揭示报纸自身个性特征和思想的声音。报纸不再仅仅是无意识的表达工具，它实际上变成了一个以自我为中心的自我感知、自我表达的有机体，而根据它所揭示的个性特征及其对于个体留下的印象，这个充满活力的有机体时而为读者所尊敬和爱戴，时而为读者所憎恨和惧怕，时而为读者所蔑视或者仰慕。

很大程度上依存于报纸自身而非个人的个性特征可能产生更重大、更深远和更普遍的舆论影响，而报纸仅仅作为个人表达媒介通常很难获得这样的效果。报纸是具有个性特征的机构，它提出自己的思想并发出自身的声音，其强势和威力给读者留下了深刻的印象，远非某个人的言论所产生的舆论影响能比。《鹰》（Eagle）的编辑约翰·琼斯（John Jones）在自己的人脉圈中并没有神谕般的号召力，他的观点以个人的身份在其人脉圈传播，圈内朋友对其观点的接受程度并不会超过其他人观点的被接受程度。他的才智和学识可能值得尊重，而他只是约翰·琼斯，朋友圈中的一员。但是，当约翰·琼斯代表报纸发言时，其效果就不一样了。约翰·琼斯可能以个人身份表达同样的观点，他们可能明白这种观点实际上是约翰·琼斯的声音，但是当他们在报纸上阅读这种观点时，他们很少能够意识到约翰·琼斯本人。现在正是《鹰》这份报纸在与他们对话，报纸作为与众不同的实体在表达自身的观点，制造自己在读者中的印象，形成自己的影响力。假如报纸的个性特征值得尊重的话，它就赢得了约翰·琼斯不可能拥有的尊重，当众多像约翰·琼斯这样的个体观点不为读者所接受的时候，而报纸自身的观点却会被大家作为结论性观念所接受。的确，约翰·琼斯可能向史密斯传播观点，而史密斯又传播给布朗，不会影响《鹰》的个性特征，因为报纸的个性特征似乎不会受到人事变更的干扰，也不会由于死亡事故而变动。报纸不断补充新鲜血液而充满活力，只要报纸恪守新闻原则，其新鲜的血液没有被玷染，它便会永葆旺盛的生命力。

第九章 评论版

　　报纸具有这样的个性特征——一个与体现人性的个体特征截然不同的客观存在。当然，报纸的个性特征不能独立存在，它从报纸的报道流中汲取生命力，正如每个人从众人那里吸收养分一样。而无论怎么讲，报纸的个性特征是实际存在的，报纸有自身的形态、思维和灵魂。评论版就是表达报纸个性特征及其思想的喉舌，报纸的特点、良知借此得以揭示，其智能也得以测试。

　　由于这种观念，报纸的评论版不可能仅仅被当作"特稿版"，它不可能只是作为新闻业的分支而存在，分析某些被忽略甚至被分流的话题，其价值或重要性在于公开谈论问题。相反，评论版是新闻事业发挥作用的必要条件。从完整的意义上来讲，评论是报纸个性特征表达的必要条件，失去了表达，报纸的个性特征就很难说存在，报纸的个性特征及其表达给予报纸与众不同的特性和活力。而正是评论版表露了报纸的个性特征，揭示了报纸关于所报道事务的思考，并进而揭示了其智能空间、分辨真伪的标准、判断、好恶、偏见和宠爱、情感和抱负、诚实或虚伪，一言以蔽之，报纸个性特征揭示了报纸自身的特征。正是在评论版，报纸向公众发出了自己的声音，它不断地向公众布道、剖析、阐释、倡导、谴责，或者利用公众，而所有这些首先要求通过新闻传播使公众了解所发生的事实，引发和保持公众对公共事务的兴趣，提升公共福利并捍卫公共和私人的公正原则。正是在评论版报纸才彰显其影响舆论的个性特征，并为人民及其自由、民主和文明提供服务，而这是宪法保护报纸言论自由的首要理由。

毋庸置疑，评论版的特征和品质是新闻业头等重要的事务。假如报纸整体上稳固地得到了公众的支持和尊重的话，那么它所揭示的个性特征必然成为验证公众尊重和信任的一种标准。然而，报纸的价值就是通过评论版来测度的断言未免有些言过其实。人们通常并不会因为看中报纸的评论版而购买报纸，无论其评论版办得多么成功。个别评论版成为报纸吸引大量目标读者的主要版面，但是这样的案例实属罕见，而当这种情况发生时，报纸所刊登的消息稿和评论稿之间就会有所失衡。对于多数人而言，任何办得成功的报纸评论版首先有自身的趣味性，但是这样的报纸毕竟占少数。通常情况下，人们购买报纸是为了看消息，他们对于评论的兴趣是第二位的。这符合人类自然和基本的认知顺序。用事实说话有必要先于就事实说话。换言之，一件事情发生在先，之后才有关于事件的评论。在表达思想的机会之前必然存在引发思想的条件。我们人类首先关注的是事件本身，即新闻内容是什么。报纸的首要功能是报道新闻，报纸所刊登的新闻首先要吸引人们购买报纸。因此，从很大程度上来讲，读者通过报纸所提供的新闻服务的范围和品质来估量报纸的价值。

但是，新闻的趣味性刺激读者对于新闻的思考，而旨在了解事实内容及其含意的读者却转向评论版来发现他可能阅读到的此类启发性文章。在这个过程中，读者就从对作品的思考转向了与作品所包含的精神——个性特征的直接交流。他认为，无论自己正在阅读的新闻的信息价值如何，它只不过是事实陈述而已，即时事的记录。但是，当他阅读评论版的文章时，他所阅读的内容就是源自报纸个性特征的思想表达，报纸就成为向他诉说当天版面内容的朋友，就成为他认为自己了解而实际上可能从来都没有具体感知的实体，而且他可能通过持续的交流来获得一种奠定忠诚支持基础的尊重和联谊。这样的感受不可能通过新闻和事实记录而产生。报纸关于时事的记录并不是激励读者敬仰报纸所刊登内容或者部分内容的因素。报纸陈述事实的风格可能吸引眼球，报纸一贯真诚地记录事实，可能培育了读者对于报纸准确报道的信任，而且报纸的公信力可能具有极高的价值。但是，这些都是客观而不具活力的印象，就好像制作某种值钱的产品一样。从另外一个方面来讲，报纸的个性特征正是通过评论版表现出来的，它唤起的情感是人性的本质所在，是创造个体关系和推动心智和头脑的理性思考。报纸的个性特征激励和验证了读者的尊重、信任和爱戴，这是报纸的幸运和可喜之事。对于读者而言，报纸不仅是一张纯粹的报章，它更像一位亲近的朋友和可信的顾问。

但是，报纸的信任和联谊关系是如何建立的呢？显然，这是报纸以同样的品质在真诚、理解和仁爱基础之上整合所有个体人脉关系而构筑起来的。报纸的个性特征与人的个性特征之间并没有本质上的区别。的确，报纸的个性特征是报纸品质而非人性品质的体现。尽管它是合成的，但是它必然产生于人类个性，而且不可避免地呈现了人类本性的形式和特征，包括融合在人性中的善良或者邪恶，或者两者兼有。另外，报纸的个性特征服从于普遍的人类局限性。但是，无论怎么尝试，它都不可能一贯正确，也不可能使本身处于超越人类本性之上的罕见的环境中。它隶属于人类本性的范畴，不可避免地展现了人类本性的各种弱点和强势，所以即使它再努力，它也逃脱不了人类本性的局限性。

我们并不要求也不指望朋友或者顾问多么完美无缺，而且我们没有权利要求或者指望所阅读的报纸像我们给予朋友般的支持那样给力。但是，我们会要求并期望朋友或者顾问真诚、忠实和可信，我们有权利要求并期望我们每天与其交谈的报纸具有人性局限性范围同等的心智和思想的个性特征。为了获得和保持报纸的公信力，我们有必要把报纸当作具有人性般灵验的实体，以便理解其必须具备的品质。这个实体的喉舌及其众所周知的品质赖以形成的工具就是评论版。因此，报纸及其评论版并非只是展示一些可读信息，并非仅仅对所发生的事实加以点评，也不仅仅是阐释新闻、表达或者引导舆论，报纸要揭示其思想和灵魂、心智、感知、是非标准。

整个争论得出的结论是：评论版的主要和基本功能是表达报纸自身的观点，并非便于受众理解的任何个体在版面中的自我表达，而是体现报纸品质和活力的表征。评论可能是一个人或者一个群体的作品，他们可能展示了个人的观点或者编辑们讨论的结论。但是，实际情况是这样的，不管何人发表或者撰写了什么样的言论，这样的言论在报纸付印时都会成为报纸的思想表达。作为一种惯例，读者并不了解一篇评论出自何人之手，或者其结论由什么样的头脑碰撞和共同思考而达成。假如他碰巧明白他很少考虑这种关联，对他而言，评论版就不是某个人或者某群体的声音，而是真正反映现实存在的报纸的声音。这并非幻觉。假如这种声音值得尊敬和信任的话，就给他留下了深刻的印象，因为在评论版没有个体可以撰写富有个性特征的稿件而发出这样的声音。这并非因为写评论性文章都是匿名的。匿名评论实际上减弱了某种观点的分量。在实际操作中，评论性文章不应该匿名。由于是《纽约太阳报》发出的声音，其言论就被读者所认可。

因此，评论版的制作过程涉及报纸个性特征的创造和维持，这是报纸的首要任务。评论将发出报纸的声音，表达报纸的感知和意识，揭示读者心目中报纸值得尊敬的特性和公信力。生活的气息只有吸纳到生命中，生命才能成为有活力的魂灵。这个过程是如何实现的呢？它无需心机或者花招，只要把最具创造性的事物融入其中即可。假如报纸打造的个性特征值得公众尊敬的话，它首先就具备了创造性观点赖以实现的个性品质。没有人能够将自己尚未掌握的观点发表在评论版。可以肯定的是，人们可能经常为自己没有履行的义务而祈祷，每个人都会频繁地出现类似的情况。但是，除非编辑有头脑和意识，除非他本身具有智能、判断、真诚等良好性格所要求的基本品质，否则他就不可能将这些品质付诸报纸，只有在编辑拥有这些品质以后，他才能够把它们灌输到自己负责的其他个性特征中来。无论他欠缺什么，这些品质都会在他所负责的评论版中或多或少被清晰地揭示出来。由于报纸个性特征的大幅度淡化，他能够通过这种渠道使报纸比他本人更突出，但是这不能逃脱报纸制作者的局限性。因此，负责评论版的编辑和员工的个性越明显，他们创造和维持的报纸的个性特征越强，报纸及其个性特征赢得的尊敬越高。当然，这一切的前提条件是他们必须忠诚并全身心投入这项工作，他们有能力进行创新。基于此，评论版不是刚步入新闻业的见习记者或编辑可以掌控的版面，也不是资深的报业才子应付差事的场面。评论版的诉求导向并非固定在对报纸充满信任而思想或者判断力匮乏的不成熟的读者身上，然而这也绝非暗示着它适应老年人，或者适用于对公共事务缺乏整体了解的读者，或者对公共事务关联的新闻事业的职责缺乏理解的读者。报纸评论版的导向是个严肃的任务，评论版不仅是报社中责任最重大的部门，而且对公众而言它也是承担责任最大的版块，应用其中的个性特征和品质应该最容易达到。

第十章 评论的职责

106 　　在单个报纸和新闻业的整体发展过程中,编辑有必要认识评论对公众负有的责任,特别是那些负责评论版的编辑或是向评论版撰稿的作者更应该认识评论的社会责任。这样的断言并非意味着责任感应该成为编辑心目中或者意识中的沉重负担,肩负重任的人不适合评论的岗位。相反,他应该把责任感作为一种特权或快乐而接受它,把它作为一个提供服务和奉献的机会。但是,无论对于这种责任感的态度如何,假如报纸要提供有价值的信息,报纸要实现其反映或者引导舆论的功能,假如报人本身要为报纸和公众提供最好的服务,我们就必须认识到这一点:其关键在于他自己。

　　报纸评论部首先是一个公共部门,尽管公众可能从来没有看到或者了解评论部的编辑。每天,编辑对公众讲述他们关心的相关事务。他并非面对数百位受众讲述新闻故事,正如布道者、演讲者或者政论者一样,他不时地要面向成千上万的读者,年复一年。

107 　　评论的听众并不限定为能够听得到其声音的人们。评论发出的声音和观点到达的范围与报纸的发行量一样是没有限定的,甚至可以说它是没有界限的，因为每一种报纸有很多读者，并非限定于报纸的订阅者中间，在某种特定情况下，该报所发表的评论文章经常被其他报纸所转载，从而到达更大范围的读者。因此，评论版编辑有可能比其他公共演讲者接触和达到更多的受众，他每天都在面向受众讲述新闻故事，而他的言论传播得更直接和更亲切，因为他就像来到家里坐在火炉旁的老朋友，或许正在与主人及其家人谈论着趣事儿。他走进办公室和商业区，向商人、制造商、银行家、销售员、职员和工人宣讲，他深入乡村与农民交谈，大街上穿行的汽车和客车都能感觉到他的存在。一位男士或者女士无论隐居在多么偏远的地方，评论版编辑都可能在他隐居的地方找到听众。报纸的声音无处不在，传播的广泛性、持久性和连续性使得报纸在舆论或者公共意识的创新、引导和表达方面的影响力无与伦比，其他任何机构都望尘莫及。

亚伯拉罕·林肯说："在类似的社区，公众意见无处不在。公众意见存在的地方，所有的事情都不会无果而终；没有公众意见的地方，任何事情都不会成功。结果，吸纳公众意见的人比颁布法规或者宣布决策的人对事务认识得更加深刻。"林肯的用词十分谨慎，我们可以设想，他是有意使用"公众意见"（public sentiment）这个宽泛或者易于理解的词汇来代替"舆论"（public opinion）。按照韦伯斯特（Webster）① 的界定，观点是一种智力的判断。意见包括观点、感觉或者情感，无论哪种占上风，都包含其中。韦伯斯特引用杜格尔德·斯图尔特（Dugald Stewart）②

---

① 诺亚·韦伯斯特（Noah Webster，1758—1843），美国辞典编纂家、课本编写作者、拼写改革倡导者、政论家和编辑，被誉为"美国学术和教育之父"。他于1828年出版了现代《韦氏词典》。

② 杜格尔德·斯图尔特（Dugald Stewart，1753—1828），苏格兰启蒙哲学家和数学家。其父马修·斯图尔特（Matthew Stewart，1715—1785）是爱丁堡大学数学教授［1747—1772］。

的话说:"最优秀的英文作家关于意见(sentiment)一词的用法已经达成共识。在我看来,它表达了人们理性力量和道德情感融合的复杂的意志决定"。从这个意义上来讲,意见是头脑和心灵的混合产物,通常情况下大家所谓的舆论实际上就是公众意见,即融合了感情和思想的成分,这或许是真实的。

但是,无论我们称之为意见还是观点,我们无法否认的事实是,在现代社会,公众意见或者舆论是最具潜在影响力的。决定意见或者舆论导向的人,无论程度如何,他都投入了个人的优势和责任。毋庸置疑,报刊对于舆论形成具有很大的影响力。它比其他任何机构都具更大影响力,这一点是可以断定的,无需担心出现矛盾。这并非因为公众意见或舆论被赋予最高才智或者先见之明。不幸的是,报刊在这些方面的确是低俗的,而是因为它连续而持久地宣扬新闻事实及其思想。新闻本身是舆论生成的一个重要而基本的因素。正是在新闻事实的基础上,所有关于时事的意见或舆论才得以真正形成。但是,作为规律,芸芸众生很少有时间或者倾向性来分析研究新闻事实,从中探寻和理解新闻的含义或者事实之间的关系。一般而言,凡夫俗子过多地忙碌于自身的营生或者个人的趣味中,以至于他们没有过多的时间来关注或者思考公共事件,并作出自己的诠释。有些人花相当长的时间对新闻事实进行研究、思考并提出自己的观点,假如他们没有偏激或者固执己见的话,尤其是当意见来源变成一种可信赖的惯性信息源时,无论仅仅通过习惯或者基于养成的尊重感加以判断,他们的意见就很容易被大家所接受。

所以,报纸每天通过评论版来表达其思想,而报纸正是借此来实现其对于读者的持续性舆论影响,无论读者是否意识到这一点,实际情况的确如此。查理斯·A·达纳说:"报刊是一种强有力的机构。当人们预知的信息不完整时,当人们的推理尚未得出结论时,当人们的意见还没有达成共识时,报刊总会来帮忙。它提出建议、提案和暗示,除非遇到才华出众或者天赋极高的人,一般人都会接受报刊的观点和判断，就像采纳某种公理或者结论一样。报刊经常成为影响人们思想的力量，而报刊对于接受它的人并不提供任何认识和批判。报刊以这种方法形成一种真实而非凡的力量，这种力量总是激励人们担负起严肃的使命感。如此，你征服了一个人的思想，在他不知不觉的情况下，你塑造、引导着他的思想，让他沿着一条自己并不知道的道路前行，而通常情况下，你也不知道这条路通向何方。"

报刊的力量如此巨大，没有人敢妄加滥用。报刊的力量使其担负了巨大的责任，除非报刊认识到了自身的责任并努力为公众利益而履行这样的责任，否则的话，此责任就难以实现。所有报刊的责任依赖于其所有权和办刊方针，但是也特别关乎可信任的编辑履行报纸表达思想的任务。报纸编辑从未亲眼目睹和亲耳聆听受众的行动和诉说的事实，从而阻碍了编辑的认识，但他实际上在面对受众演讲，或许他面对的是庞大的受众群体。于是，他倾向于认为其任务只是要求准备特定数量的文稿来填充特定的版面而已，即为当天的报纸版面准备足够的文字就行了，他的任务仅此而已。这样的态度与编辑用某些值得阅读的文本来填充其所分配版面的责任感并不矛盾，但是与实际上他对正在交谈的、未见面的受众所担负的责任感相对立，除非他认为自己不能履行报纸赋予的面对公众的责任感，也正是为此他不能履行自己对报纸负有的这种责任。正是因为报纸服务于公众，服务于自身，除非报纸认识到这个事实并恪守在心，否则它就不能向公众或者自身提供最好的服务。

每篇评论都是面向公众的演讲或者陈词。任何演讲者都明白，听众通过他所宣讲的内容来评估其学识或者品性。可以肯定，假如他讲话比较流畅，其学识和品性就可以从言辞中加以评估。他理解了这一点，假如有机会的话，他就会进行精心的准备，研究听众并整理其思绪，以便尽其所能为听众留下最好的印象。演讲者将面对听众，通常他可能察觉到其言辞或者个性为听众留下的印象或反映其演讲效果的某些迹象。而报纸编辑看不到受众，而且他很少有机会得到其言论之即时效果的某些反响。但是他毕竟在面对受众演讲，面对的受众群体是任何演讲者的声音都无法达到的范围，而且其学识、品性和报纸的基本个性特征在其日复一日的言论中得到大体的测验。因此，假如他要创造、维持或者加强报纸所具有的由公众心目中的信任和尊重所验证的公信力的话，如果时间允许的话，他每次发表评论文章时，他都会周到地考虑受众及其环境，这一点十分重要。

这是他为报纸的利益而应该担负的职责，但是正如上文所言，他不能履行这样的职责，除非他认识到自己不是在自言自语，也不是在用言论填充某个版面，而是在面向公众讲话。他和自己的报纸以其言论的品性、要领和含义对公众负有真切而明确的责任。这种责任感是重中之重，因为它涉及读者心目中报纸的权力和影响的问题，正如达纳所言："对于报纸所影响的人而言，他不会遭遇暴露或者任何抨击"。很少读者能够觉察到报纸在多大程度上影响着他们的意见。假如报纸所刊登的言论值得阅读，他们就会日复一日地阅读报纸关于公众问题的言论，他们会像自己的观点一样接受报纸的观点，除非报纸关于某个问题的观点与读者的偏好、传统或者判断发生了冲突而引发愤怒。当然，很多人对于新闻事实及其意义提出了真知灼见并习惯于形成自己的结论，他们会像对待其他报刊那样权衡其表达，根据自己的判断标准接受或者拒绝报纸的观点，但这毕竟占少数。然而，他们构成了对舆论产生最大影响的人口要素，而且关于报纸思想的智力、准确和公正的最好测试就是认同和支持这种要素。但是，由于他们有能力而且倾向于进行自我的判断，他们就没有必要托付报纸，因为大多数人沉浸于各自的职业和兴趣中，或者漫不经心，以至于他们不能对新闻事件或者个人意见经由自身的认识过程而提出很多想法。这并不意味着他们缺乏才智。可以肯定的是，多数人的确缺少才智，而其中包括很多高智商者，因为他们的思绪局限于个体直接关注的事务，他们习惯于认同外界思想来源的现成意见，尤其是从当天报纸中采纳既成意见，尽管他们或许无意识这样做。

  报纸实际上承担不起应付或玩闹其表达思想的权力，无论从物质层面还是从道德层面都是如此。如果报纸仅仅满足于肤浅的评论、没有见地的观点、粗制滥造的文摘，那么它就是玩忽职守和对公众信任的背叛。报纸的每位读者都应该曾经验证过这样的感觉，即他发现评论版呈现在自己面前的观点是建立在当时可以接近的最权威信息的基础上，这些评论都是编辑或者编辑部成员尽力创作的最深刻思想的忠实反映的产物。当然，这特别指代关系重大事务的讨论，影响或者可能影响公众关于公共问题态度的地方性或者全局性事务。很多评论并没有这样的内容和特点，即它们并非倾向于以这样或者那样的方式来影响舆论，它们所谈论的话题多少有些趣味性，但是在形成公众意见方面没有重要性或者重要性相对较小。打个比方说，这样的评论就好像"简评"，它自身的价值不仅表现在增添了评论版的吸引力，而且揭示了增强报纸人文特征的个性品质。缺失了这样的小评论，报纸评论版就不完美，它们制作得越成功，报纸就办得越好。

  但是，这并非此处讨论的公共责任所依赖的评论表达的特征。正是在应对公众关注的重大话题或者可能影响公众兴趣的现实问题、涉及公共福利的时事的过程中，报纸践行了施与其自身的公信力，而且报纸以践行的方式揭示了其责任感，至少揭示了报纸履行公众义务的能力。对于报纸的最高级别的评估莫过于评估它为社会带来的影响的范围和品性，而这样的评估整体上适用于整个新闻业。

第十一章　新闻自由

115　　评论版的另外一项职责所涉及的公共义务的严肃性并不亚于其表达舆论的责任，它就是所谓的新闻自由。新闻自由是公民与生俱来的权利之一，维护新闻自由是关系人类福利的关键要素。极力维护新闻自由以促进社会的稳定，这不仅是新闻事业自身的一项严肃职责，而且是人民担负的一项基本责任。的确，新闻自由对新闻事业自身的重要性还不及它对人民的重要性。因为新闻自由的践行是公众利益的基本要求，它是民主保障和进步的必要条件，它是维护其他所有自由权利和构筑人类最珍贵财富的主要需求。这些人类享有的自由权利是经过几代人的奋斗才取得的，其中体现了人类本性所特有的倾向性破坏力。像上述案例那样，在维护已经获得的自由权利方面，新闻自由的威力无与伦比。

　　人们普遍认为，新闻自由是人类与生俱来的基本权利。在美国，从建国伊始，新闻自由作为宪法保护和赋予的基本人权的观点就得到充分的认可，美国宪法规定新闻自由的权利不容侵犯。

116　新闻业是基本法指令重点保护的唯一私营机构，其理由并非为新闻业自身利益而授予其某种特权的愿望，其唯一目的旨在保护人们的权利和自由。库利（Cooley）① 说："在独立革命时期，报刊一直是在民众中间传播自由思想和推动反抗民族压迫准备工作的主要途径，报刊在这方面的指导作用表现得如此之强，以至于遮蔽了它的其他功能。因此，我们可以得出结论：有关公众自由的讨论意味着新闻自由应该得到完全的保护，法律禁止侵害新闻自由，不仅在于新闻审查，而且特别要禁止任何限制性法律或者法律的管理。由此，在美国已经成为惯例的有关公共利益和事务的自由讨论被取缔了，这就等于剥夺了新闻自由作为公民履行权利和保护自由的有利工具或优势。"②

重申一下新闻自由。新闻自由是美国宪法规定和保护的，它并非保护私人利益的法律规范，而是维护人们自由权利的法规。换言之，新闻自由是基本法认定、授予和保障的基本人权，它并非为了报刊的回报或者提升报刊的利益，而是旨在为人民谋福利而制定的法律。这项权利的本质为执法制造了某种似是而非的宪法的局限性，但这种局限性本身对保护社会是必要的。的确，有些人坚持某种局限性，而全然不顾它对于新闻自由权利的侵害。但是，假如这种公民自由的形式是正确的，那么所有的形式都是正确的，而人类的共同经历是，任何类型的公民自由仅仅在其践行有利于笼统利益的程度上维持着。自由除非与法律结合起来，否则就不可避免要自我毁灭。正如克拉伦登（Clarendon）③ 所说："试想，没有法律保护的自由就像手中握有利剑的人要攻击弱于自己的人一样"。这并非意味着简单的法律条款，而是涉及法律的惯例、推理和意识，人类社会各个时期不同政体的国家都

---

① 此处的库利（Cooley）应该指的是查尔斯·霍顿·库利（Charles Horton Cooley，1864—1929），美国社会学家和社会心理学家，美国传播学研究的先驱。
② Constitutional Law.
③ 克拉伦登（Clarendon，1609—1674），伯爵，原名爱德华·海德（Edward Hyde），英格兰政治家和历史学家，查理一世和查理二世的大臣，《英国叛乱史》作者。

颁布了自我保护免于未加限制的自由之侵害的法律。佩利（Paley）① 说："毋庸置疑，在所有情况下，我都希望以自己喜欢的方式行事，但是我在沉思，其他人也将这样做。在争取普遍的自由和自我指导的过程中，我将遇到很多来自对立面和他人干预下违背自身意愿的障碍和困难，以至于我的快乐和自由都将减少，而整个社区屈服于同等法律的支配下。"

新闻自由作为人类自由的另外一种形式，它有必要服从于这样的限制，就像其他权利的保护需要服从于限制滥用自由权利的限制一样。新闻界必须认识到这一点，假如新闻自由本身旨在保护宪法所保护的公共利益，那么人类还有新闻自由之外更值得尊重的其他权利。库利还说："新闻自由或许界定于自由表达和出版公民可能选择的任何言论，如果出版物没有对于公共道德或者个人声誉造成极大的危害，以至于按照普通法的条款，当新闻自由成为一种宪法赋予的权利的时候，诽谤性出版物就要受到审判，新闻自由和出版自由受到保护而免于法律惩罚。"这项权利的意义远非如此，因为真实免于诽谤问责②的原则当时尚未确立。但是，不管怎样，诽谤性出版物受到法律审判之权利的局限性在基本原则和法律中都存在，而且还有其他类似的限制，这些限制作为符合公众利益而无抵触新闻自由之权利的规定被接受。

---

① 此处的佩利（Paley）应该指的是威廉·佩利（William Paley, 1743—1805），英国哲学家和基督教护教学家。

② 在美国的诽谤法规中，真实是最重要的免责要件。新闻报道内容为真实者，可以免除诽谤的责任。建国后，美国法院允许媒体用真实作为民事诽谤的抗辩要件。但有些州规定，媒体被控告诽谤时，除了要证明报道的言论属实外，还要证明新闻工作人员并无不良动机。如果动机不当，即使报道属实，仍然可能构成诽谤。1974年，美国最高法院对诽谤法中的真实举证规定作了重大修正，把真实的举证责任由被告转为原告。即原告必须证明新闻报道的言论错误，才能在诽谤官司中获得胜诉。

然而，法律条款不可能涵盖所有保障新闻正确、公平和公正的约束和规范。不争的事实是，新闻自由受到宪法如此厚重的保护和法律如此宽松的约束，以至于报刊成为一种公共福利代理和旨在明智、公平、正确地为公众谋福利而履行该权利的机构。亚历山大·汉密尔顿（Alexander Hamilton）①说："在我看来，新闻自由尽管反映了政府、行政长官和个人的言行，包括了源自良好动机和公正追求的真相的发布。假如没有得到允许的话，它就排除了游说者和统治者的特权。"这是对践行新闻自由的原则和规范的合理陈述。为了证明新闻自由，就有必要出版事实真相或者我们确实相信的真相。确认新闻真相的困难在本章节已经作了充分的讨论，由于评论的观点很大程度上建立在新闻事实的基础之上，所以同样的困难围绕着评论的表达。但是，在评论的表达中的事实真相应该比新闻报道中的事实陈述得更加仔细，因为评论作者通常具有更多的时间来探究证据，而且他在表达新闻特征借以评估新闻本身的思想和个性特征时，为了所服务的报刊利益和公众利益，他有更大的责任来辨别和报道事实真相。

但是，在践行新闻自由和表达舆论的过程中，仅仅陈述真相还远远不够。它应该追求"从良好的动机到公正的目的"。在所有关于公众人物或者公共事务关联人物的行为的讨论中都预设和暗示了这些动机和目的。但是，这些预设通过真诚的讨论而加以验证，这对于每条独立新闻和整体新闻事业的名声都很重要。对于事实真相而言，关于这种讨论的权利不可能有适当的法律限定，反之，有的是已经提及的约束和下文就要陈述的应对紧急情况的可能性限制。对于言论的表达施加另外的限制不仅危害新闻

---

① 亚历山大·汉密尔顿（Alexander Hamilton, 1757—1804），美国开国元勋之一，宪法的起草人之一，财经专家，美国第一任财政部长。

自由而且危害所有形式的人类自由。法官约瑟夫·斯托里（Story）[①] 说："在一个自由政府的统治下，没有人会怀疑游说公众人物行为和公共措施动向的权利、大胆抨击统治者行为和细心审视政府政策、计划的权利的重要性。这是自由政府的最安全的保证。假如我们保留了这样的权利，舆论必定得以明示，政治性的警惕必然得以灌输，自由而放肆的讨论肯定是有害的。"言论自由对于一个自由政府而言是必要的，而放肆的言谈则是这种权利的滥用，这样就会降低言论自由权利的标准，削弱其影响，危害其安全。新闻自由从来不会受到"良好动机"和"公正目的"的保障，新闻业认识到这一点并逐渐自愿地放弃大部分过去经常发生的肆意谩骂性质的言论，这对于新闻事业来讲应该是件幸事。然而，新闻业应该铭记，言论自由的权利无论怎样不受限制，它都是一种神圣的权利，它本身授予享用这种权利的人一种义务——他们应该为公众目的以体面而适度的方式来运用它，唯有如此，才能够证明维护它的必要性。只有当它致力于维护自由政府的稳定和安全时，它才能够长久地存在；只有当它作为支持所有公民自由权利的工具时，它才可以长期有效地发挥作用。保持新闻自由在利益和权利面前的实用性和纯洁性的责任依赖于新闻业，而新闻业可以成为新闻自由的表达媒介和捍卫者。

在之前的章节中，言及"应对紧急情况的可能性新闻自由限制"。可能的情况是，暂时限制新闻自由权利的泛用对于社会安全是必要的。正如上文已经陈述的那样，言论自由是美国宪法指令和保证的人权，它不仅是保护私人利益的法规，而且是保护人民享有自由权利的举措。假如新闻自由遭遇严重而危险的滥用，这种情形就会危害宪法赋予人民的自由权利并危害自由政府的存在。在这种情况下，对新闻自由的限制就可能是紧迫的。高等法

---

① 约瑟夫·斯托里（Joseph Story, 1779—1845），美国律师、法官，1811—1845年服务于美国高等法院。

院法官韦特（Waite）①曾明确宣称："对符合宪章的自由机构及其成果的保护是新闻自由赖以生存的基础和支柱，因此自由不可能包括实际上有损于这种机构的权利。"我们没有必要认可有意利用这样的断言来证明其合理性的做法。但是，除非符合宪章的自由机构实际上即刻遭遇危害，否则它就不能证明限制言论自由是合理的。这些机构存在的必要性在于，它们服从流行的指令变化，机构本身及其旗下的政府部门应该公开地接受彻底的讨论和批评，这样对于其改进是必要的，因为只有通过这样的程序，政治进步才能成功，政治权利才能得以维护。假如由于条件改变或者条款变化，允许人们谴责他们相信有错的事情，那么无论谴责的权利发展到何种极致，它都应该得到保护。

法官西姆斯（Simms）说："在言论自由泛滥的国家，失误的观点可能是有害的"，在有时间对失误观点进行修正的情况下，事实确实如此。只有当国家处于危急关头，这些失误言论的修正过程不能有效地进行，而且当危言耸听的观点演绎为颠覆自由政府和普通权利的危害性行为时，这种对自由权利的限制可能应该是合理的了。法官霍姆斯（Holmes）②说："我们应该永远保持警惕，反对试图验证我们所厌恶并认为预示着死亡征兆的言论，除非它们急迫地威胁到合法的出版目的时，那么，为了拯救国家就要立即对这样的言论进行核查。"这或许就是限定言论自由和出版自由权利唯一的正当条件，而且只限于即时目的的必要范

---

① 莫里森·雷米克·韦特（Morrison Remick Waite, 1816—1888），美国法官，曾任美国最高法院首席法官（1874—1888）。
② 霍姆斯（Oliver Wendell Holmes, 1841—1935），美国法官，美国现代实用主义法学的创始人。霍姆斯于1866年毕业于哈佛大学法学院，在波士顿从事律师工作，之后他于1870年进入哈佛大学法学院担任讲师、教授，1882年12月担任马萨诸塞州最高法官，1899年起任院长。1902—1932年，霍姆斯担任美国联邦最高法院法官。霍姆斯的学说主要体现在《普通法》（*The Common Law*）（1881）、《法律之路》（*The Path of the Law*）等论著中。

围，过期不再适用。

在新闻自由问题上，新闻业具有两项责任：第一，维护新闻自由的权利免遭任何形式的侵犯，而即时地、紧迫地和明显地危害自由政府和公民自由的行为不属于该项权利保护的范围；第二，考虑到公共福利，我们必须英明而真诚地履行新闻自由权利。

第十二章 编辑政策

　　编辑或者评论版主管肩负的任务就是维持和创新报纸的个性特征,他们的学识和伦理品质会赢得人们的尊重,他们履行报纸所担负的竭尽全力服务公共利益的义务或职责。换言之,他(们)要服务于报纸和公众两个方面。这并不对立,因为作为规律,报纸最好的服务是最大限度地服务于公众。然而,报纸的利益是第一位的,因为物质生存是首要的任务。对于每个人而言,无论其抱负怎样,无论其理想如何,假如他想朝着自己的目标迈进的话,他就首先需要面包。生存途径是生存目的的必要条件,而且必须确立为赖以生存的前提和伴生物。因此,编辑努力保持和提高报纸的物质福利十分必要,因为这不仅涉及其自身的物质利益,而且只要报纸的物质基础奠定了,这样的努力就能贡献于公共服务。大型报纸的建设、某种报纸的创刊本身就是履行新闻事业的正当和合法功能的公共服务,报纸被赋予源自办刊运作的所有的真诚回报,而且可以断言,它首先必须考虑自身利益。没有迹象表明,报纸应该以某种措施牺牲公共利益,或者在履行一种职责的同时有必要兼顾履行其他职责。

　　在办报过程中,报纸有必要确立一种编辑政策。这种政策自身没有必要采用确定的术语来表达,但是它必须使人领会其宗旨和理念。或许,报纸的创办者旨在为某个特定领域提供新闻,而没有其他目的。换言之,他可能在出版这家报纸的过程中没有特定的目标。他可能没有想到利用报纸来提高某个集团、阶级的利益或者地位,或者推广某个明确的计划或公共行为准则。不管怎么说,一个可以感知的编辑政策是必要的。因为不管一家报纸的宗旨和愿望如何带有局限性,仅仅作为一张报纸,如果它要保持成功的话,报纸的出版都会涉及导致公众认可的公共信息和公众观察、批评、判断标准。假如这种认可要获得和维持的话,就必须对报纸自身的个性特征和效果进行研究。除非报纸对这些品质进行了思考并有了编辑理念,否则报纸的报道就是没有价值的;除非报纸的编辑理念建立在某些公众所理解和接受的原则基础之上,否则报纸就失去了指导原则或者宗旨,进而其报道就缺乏效果。被新闻事业赋予的创造力所鼓舞的人就会创办一家报纸,但是,与此决定同时,假如他们没有像通常所要求的那样来制定编辑理念的话,他们就会遇到问题:报纸到底属于哪种类型?报纸的服务宗旨是什么?而不管这些问题的答案如何,他们都被迫制定报纸的政策、目标及其实现目标的途径。假如第一个问题的答案仅仅是"一家好报纸",第二个问题的答案是"报道新闻",他即刻就会面临这样的困惑:构筑一家好报纸的因素是什么?报纸如何才能成为优秀的报纸?这样,他就不可避免地考虑采纳一些报刊的标准做法。

  一旦报纸进入运作的过程,报纸与生活和事实产生接触与联系,报纸对万花筒般的新闻必须做出反映,报纸设定为时事信息传播者和舆论领袖的义务等方面的事情不仅要求报纸持续应用这些要素或标准,而且要求报纸根据这些编辑政策对当天发生的各种事实、状况和话题不断调整。报纸的办刊政策只能抽象为基本的原则,这决定了报纸的特征,揭示了报纸作为信息传播者和事实阐释者的品质,而且以一种普遍的方法表明了其宗旨和理念。

这些原则是固定的，它们可能在报纸的成长经历中，或者通过其背后的精神变化而发展，进而演化为远远超越其原始概念的东西。它们或许在品质和行为上退化，进而阻碍报纸的发展，除非它们原本就不具操作性。但是，除了这些作为永久性政策的指导原则之外，每天发生的事情不断生产需要评论的新闻，而这些观点的表达则是通过报纸的编辑政策加以明示的。

因此，报纸的编辑政策就是观点及其表达不断调整的过程，其调整是为了或多或少地与报纸运作的固定原则一致，适应不同的事实和话题。换言之，报纸的编辑政策就是有关生活万象的公开表达形式——评论的相对固定原则的运用。其导向不像溪流中漂曳着的小船的航标，它面对的境况是不断变化的，有的地方是激流，有的地方是缓流的涟漪，而有时候缓流变得急促，其中有沙洲，也有可见的或掩藏水中而需避开的礁石和残树沉根，但是，假如这条船是坚固的，向导是警觉的，那么这次航行就是安全的，而航向则是不断变化的。然而，向导具有双重的责任：他使航行有价值，同时对船主有利；他保护委托给他的乘客的生命安全和货物安全，保证航行的安全和所有人的利益。他不能按照自己的主观臆断行事；他不能采取不必要的冒险行为；他不能忽视或者玩弄雇主的利益，而假如自己是船主的话，他不能糟蹋自身的利益；他不能忽略其权利，也不能危害上次货运的安全。他的任务和责任是掌握行船的航向，并将货物运至港口。其任务涉及不断的观察和瞭望，稳定掌舵，其责任感和义务感使得背离自身利益的脱离岗位的行为不可能发生。

报纸的编辑政策遵循同样的道理。鉴于报纸一贯诚实的宗旨原则，其向导只能紧握方向盘掌控航向，并密切关注当天发生的各种事件及其进展情况。但是，报纸舵手所担负的双重责任不能忘却。假如报纸要办下去的话，其物质利益必须维系，同时报纸的珍贵财富——公民的物质和精神利益必须加以维护和保障。他不能危害或者牺牲两种利益中的任何一个，他也不能顾此失彼，有所偏颇。两种利益是不可分的，背叛了公众就是背叛了报纸。既忠诚于报纸又忠诚于人民的指导原则对于评论十分必要。

但是，航船不可能置航标于不顾而驶向岸边。正如林肯所言，报纸的编辑政策就如同人的双腿一样重要，健壮的双腿适于人远行，而合理的编辑政策则是报纸成功运行的有力保障。编辑不可能在读者面前喧嚣报纸的利润或者成功。他可能比读者先知先觉，但是他从来不会脱离读者。假如他要引领报纸取得更大的成功，他们必须走很长的路，而且其引领方式必须以读者所能理解的词语来表达。假如编辑要维系其与读者之间的信用关系的话，他就必须尊重读者的意见、情感、偏见和热情。新闻应该保持独立性，但是它不能独立得远离其所服务的公众，从而失去公众的支持并损失服务公众的机会。换言之，除非与所信任的对象建立信用关系，否则一家信用机构就不能运行起来。

威廉姆斯（Talcott Williams）[①] 博士说："这种信用关系承载着记者服务的义务及其对公众肩负的责任感。用一种不太恰当的说法，编辑从来都不会像一位吹鼓手那样按照既定的套路引领着队伍前行而不能有所变动。显然，当他从吹奏者和打鼓者面前走过时手中指挥棒的即时旋转都随着已经谱写好的曲调而挥动，从类似大报的轰动性新闻到乡村周报传来的天籁般笛音都是如此。但是，偶然发生的实情是，记者们会从行进的队伍中出列而转向

[①] 威廉姆斯（Talcott Williams，1849—1928），美国记者和教育家。威廉姆斯是基督教公理会传教士的儿子。他于1873年毕业于阿默斯特。之后，他受聘于《纽约世界报》(The New York World)，同时担任《纽约太阳报》(The New York Sun) 和《旧金山纪事报》(San Francisco Chronicle) 的通讯员，还担任斯普林菲尔德（马萨诸塞州）《共和党人》(Republican) 的评论作者。威廉姆斯担任《费城新闻报》(Philadelphia Press) 的编辑达30年之久，直到1912年他成为约瑟夫·普利策捐建的哥伦比亚大学新闻系的系主任。他还担任《国际新百科全书》(New International Encyclopedia) 的编辑。1913年，他获任美国新闻学教师协会主席 (the American Conference of Teachers of Journalism)。

街边。很多独立记者都会发生类似的情况,他不再当记者了,而成为自己及其出版商羡慕已久的举足轻重式的人物——小册子作者,他自己支付印刷费用,而不管人们是否认可其出版物。一位记者不会无视这一点。假如人们离开了其所任职的报纸,某天他可能发表有关世界历史的最佳出版物,其中充满了曾经令人惬笑的最有智慧的观点,但该出版物并非报纸。相反,这是作者和创造者以高昂代价出版的日志式书刊,这种出版形式使得其保存不可能,其展现形式极其昂贵,其未来一定是被忘却。"①

这种情况的真实性毋庸置疑。但是,从另外一个方面来讲,记者不可能坐等人民呼声并洗耳恭听,而不敢讲话。与报纸所服务大众的观点保持一致是一回事,而回应这种观点是另外一回事。报纸不能太超前于公众的思维或者淡忘公众,它也不能沦为应声虫的水平。实质上,报纸的观点必须在其提出相关问题的时候就形成并加以表达,而且在公众有充足的时间或者机会对时事形成自己的观点之前,报纸必须不断声明其观点,无论是暂时的结论还是定论。实际的情况往往是,报纸评论不伤害观点的直接表达,直到公众反映的态势出现某些迹象,但这样是为了抑制公众的建议并很大程度上使其依赖报刊的指导,而这应是报刊提供的功能。与新闻学的基本原则不一致,这是一种谨慎而非胆怯的说法。然而,有时候信息不完整或者过于冲突,富有启发意义的观点就可以应运而成,而明确的信息就会等待了解了更多的和更清晰的知识以后才可以获悉。也会出现这样的境况,由于编辑判断的范围太接近甚至是平衡的状态,以至于他们很难决定哪些是正确的或者是最好的信息。在这样的环境下,仔细而审慎的思考是明智而非胆怯的做法。公众有权利对编辑所做的事情做出明智的判断和最清晰的界定,而且公众对于一家报纸的尊重及其观点

---

① *The Newspaper Man*.——原书注

的影响正是建立在这种判断的特征和品质之上。在任何环境下，"怒发冲冠"而成的观点或者"不太成熟"的观点都不是新闻业所需要的好评论。

但是，在公众意见表达之前这些例外的评论相对来讲是不寻常的，而且他们这样操作只是为了延迟原始而独立的判断。在这里，这样的判断并非实用或者合适。通常情况下，编辑必须对所面临的事件和问题形成自己的观点，无需参考公众对于这些事件或话题的任何现存的或者预测性认识，其观点形成更多的是从所经历的公共意识的表达及其发展态势的不断接触和研究的认识中衍生而来。因此，如果他要适当地履行新闻事业的这项重要功能并影响舆论导向的话，他必须在公众的舆论出现之前提前形成自己的观点，而且他总是能做到这一点。为此，他有必要不断冒着公众可能拒绝听从其观点的风险。但是，假如他从阅历中学到了知识并从中增强了敏锐的洞察力，估计了公众的感受和某个既定问题的相关愿望，那么，这样的冒险就不算太大。然而，经常发生的情况是，他可能发表了与公众意识对立的观点，而且他想证明其独立、真诚，他要履行作为公共福利的向导和保护者的职责，那么他就准备为捍卫其深信不疑的观点并反对世俗偏见、激情或失误而斗争，直到他取得胜利或者以失败而终。公众会频繁地被其情绪和无知而误导，或者被与其实际的福利对立的有意识或者无意识的影响所误导，因此公众亟须捍卫自身信念的权利。

因此，编辑应该考虑读者的知识及其对于公共问题的习惯性态度、立场、口味和本质。通常情况下，假如编辑希望读者与自己保持一致并领导他们沿着自己遵循的路径来认识事物的话，他就应该努力与读者保持一致，而其行业和服务的基本条件要求他把读者纳入自己设定的路径，这些十分重要。同时，他必须相信自己对读者的兴趣、需要和情感的了解，保持自己及其所服务的报纸与读者的联系，以及对读者的同情。因此，编辑保持自己对于整体的编辑政策的赞成和支持非常重要，即使编辑也可能经常发现编辑政策走向了其所希望和感受的某些细节的反面，他们亦要遵循报纸的编辑政策。

　　的确，假如加以测试的话，报纸的论点不可能一直取悦于所有的读者，或者假如报纸的论点具备了某种特质并因此具有某种价值的话，报纸也不可能一时取悦于所有的读者。报纸发表的评论不可能足够明确和肯定，以至于它所产生的某种威力必然引起某些当事人或多或少的厌恶。然而，不管读者群体可能在整体上多么相似和一致，报纸试图取悦每个读者的做法实际上不会取悦任何人，这肯定是新闻业的一条规律，它就像个人的生活规律一样。从另外一个方面来看，报纸不取悦任何人的尝试通常也不会奏效，比较可靠的路径是在公众支持和公共服务的必需义务所创造的限定范围内取悦某个人。换言之，假如报纸要尊重自我并获得公众尊重的话，报纸的观点应该基于自身对事实的认识和研究的开展或者认知的基础上，而且与其关于公正的概念一致。但是，报纸在达到自己对于公正的判断中，它不得不铭记自己是一家报纸，而非一个小册子，在表达自己观点的过程中它与公众是一种信用关系，它表达观点的目的并非宣扬某个人的意见，它亦非以宣扬而取悦读者，而是以正确的方法激发读者兴趣、满足读者的知晓权和引导读者。

　　这个过程涉及公众感觉、公众兴趣和公众需求所限定的思想表达的独立性。在观点形成和表达的过程中，独立性是新闻业的基本品质。这与政治层面的所谓"独立报纸"之间没有什么联系，因为独立性排斥哪怕是最密切的党派利益。从这个联系来看，报纸的独立性意味着形成和出版符合某个人公正理念的固有权利，而不考虑这种理念是否正确，无论它是公正的还是偏激的。有些迷恋党派精神的老实人，他们不能想象政治上正确而没有其政党标记的事情会怎样。假如这是他们的自愿理念的话，他们在表达上就不缺乏个体的独立性。但是，新闻业随着人的变化

132

133

而改变。只要政党存在，就永远有政党偏见，只要引起重大观点分歧的话题存在，政党及其政治偏见就永远存在，因为一个人可能在其他领域有着远比政治领域更大的偏见。但是，即使在政治意识上存在直白的偏见，新闻从业者在判断上也已经多少有些分辨力，他们倾向于衡量人物并测量其个体品质。过去，新闻事业的这种发展态势引发了被大家广泛赞成的党派意识的真正消失，并促进了"独立"报纸的新闻报道。这并非通过有些人想象的所谓"中立"手段来实现，也不是通过与政党及其目标的对立来实现，但是这种脱离政党利益的做法允许报纸对于所有问题发表独立的见解，而无需考虑政党利益。假如在某个特定的环境下，支持和信任被验证，而至少从理论上讲，其判断建立在特殊境况的价值概念之上，而非基于政党利益，那么，政党的宗旨或者行为就不会遇到最强烈的抑制。简言之，限制意义上的独立新闻事业呼吁政党约束之外影响公共利益的每个问题或者判断真伪的权利和责任。

　　自然，这种态势不利于政党的团结或者联盟。在一个民主的政府中，政党显然有必要提出有关政党和公务员的新闻职责的问题。独立新闻业是否比政党新闻业更好地推动了公共福利呢？新闻业自身的发展态势就是一个肯定的答案。因为新闻业在日益增强其职业意识——人民的利益和权利是新闻业的终极关注，政党的生存和权利只能通过其对公共福利的贡献来验证，而无论这些政党多么值得称赞，它们必须旨在实现其终极目标。只要政党实际上成为人民的代表，反映人民的意愿，并忠诚而有效地代表人民的利益服务于政府事务，它们就能够实现其终极追求，而因此导致的结果是一种进步。所以，这种认识可能减弱了个体与政府的联系，但它需要对于政党地位及其通过执政代表的言行而表达的行为进行分辨性考虑。换言之，这种发展态势迫使人们对公共问题和公共行为的观察越来越多地从有关公共利益的个体特征方面进行，而非完全从政党利益相关的问题出发加以考察。当然，它的影响效果和表现程度各异，但是它使得哪怕最具政党色彩的报纸都不再盲目地沦为政论报刊，以至于充当政党喉舌的报纸实际上已消亡。相反，它呼吁独立思想和观点表达，创造了大量宣称其完全脱离政党控制或者负有政党义务的独立报纸。

  这种认知是在人们将新闻作为公共服务行业这一认识的发展过程中所形成的，一种自然而不可避免的衍生物，新闻业要有效地服务社会，它的新闻报道和观点表达就必须建立在真实的基础之上，而欺骗人民甚至为政党的终极目标而服务则等同于对真理的背叛。因此，这是新闻业在伦理、政治和专业化层面的进步。像所有的行业进步一样，新闻业自身认识到，在不影响从业者的前提下，为了新闻业的独立，它需要预言家和领军人物，它也认识到上述情况的原因和公众需求。伦敦《泰晤士报》(Times) 的约翰·撒迪厄斯·德莱恩 (John Thaddeus Delane)① 就是这样的人物。1852 年，德比勋爵 (Lord Derby)② 和格雷勋爵 (Lord Grey)③ 受到德莱恩对于他们对英国政府有关路易斯·拿破仑 (Louis Napoleon) 政策的批评的奉承，两人都极力诋毁他，尽管

---

① 约翰·撒迪厄斯·德莱恩 (John Thaddeus Delane, 1817—1879)，英国记者，担任伦敦《泰晤士报》记者达 36 年之久。

② 第十四世德比伯爵爱德华·杰弗里·史密斯·斯坦利 (Edward George Geoffrey Smith-Stanley, 14th Earl of Derby, 1799—1869)，英国保守党领袖。他在 1752 年 12 月—1855 年 2 月之间三次出任英国首相。

③ 亨利·乔治·格雷 (Henry Grey, 3rd Earl Grey, 1802—1894)，英国政治家。1826—1845 年为下院议员，后在上院成为自由党领袖。在其父任首相期间，他曾任殖民副大臣［1830—1833］，梅尔本子爵内阁期间任陆军大臣［1835—1839］，约翰·罗素内阁期间再任陆军和殖民大臣［1846—1852］，成为第一位在当时条件下最大范围内推行殖民地自治政策的英国大臣，他力图使英国本土与殖民地之间发展自由贸易，主要在加拿大获得成功。他支持加拿大总督埃尔金伯爵（第八）的政策，在 19 世纪 40 年代末期，英国终于承认加拿大的地方自治。他曾为新西兰制定一部宪法，又企图把囚犯转移到开普敦殖民地，但都不了了之。1852 年辞职以后再未担任公职。

他们隶属不同政党。德比勋爵说:"假如在这些日子里,报刊极力鼓吹政客的影响,它们应该铭记自身并没有摆脱相应的政客职责。"对此,德莱恩在《泰晤士报》的一篇评论中进行了答复,他认识到新闻的责任,而否定新闻"像那些政府大臣一样局限于同样的范畴、职责和义务。"

他说:"(美国)两大党的目标和责任是不断分化的,通常情况下是各自独立的,有时候其提案正好对立起来。报纸从接受政党附庸位置的那一刻起,其体面和自由就受到了约束。为了完全独立地履行其职责并最大限度地发挥其公共产品的优势,报刊不能与当今的政客建立联系或者进入他们的圈子,也不能把其长久的利益拱手相让并服务于任何政府的短命执政党。报刊的第一职责就是最快速和最准确地获取新近所发生的事实信息,并不断地报道这些事实信息使其成为民族和国家的共同财产。报刊通过及时的新闻报道而生存,无论什么样的事实信息载入报刊的栏目,都会成为我们时代的历史和知识的组成部分。报刊每天都在诉求介于当今和未来之间有关事件的预期性舆论的启示力量,并将其调查结果传播到世界各个角落。报刊的责任就是发表言论,政客却应该保持沉默。我们有义务说出所发现的真相,无需担心其结果会庇护不公正或压制言论的行为,我们应该即刻将事实真相传递给世人加以评判……这或许适合于政客遮盖"自由照耀世界"的目的……尽管其初衷是阴暗的或者其行为是肮脏的,政府必须以表面的尊重和礼仪来对待其他政府,同时,外交家在外事活动中彼此以礼相待,但幸运的是,报刊没有这样的约束和羁绊,报刊能够揭露某位著名人物心灵深处卑劣的想法,或者握有权杖的手上沾满着杀戮的血腥味。记者与历史学家肩负着同样的职责——首先在于探索事实真相,并向读者展示真相。虽然事实真相距离政客近在咫尺,而他们却不希望公众了解这些事实真相……更不用说让那些由于不能否认甚至不敢掩饰罪行而祈祷的人们明白事情的真相了。我们曾经在另外一所学校接受培训,我们不能回避的事实是：我们不能大胆地宣告自由思想，尽管我们不愿接受的职责是告诉德比勋爵，他已经堕落到了其声言领导的政党工具的地步了，我们还应该告知格雷勋爵他已成为其要统治的政党的祸患。"①

  这就是现在总体上统领独立新闻业的精神及原则，就像很久之前统治德莱恩时期的原则一样。但是，在这些原则的实施过程中，我们永远不要忘记，报纸自身像政客一样肩负着重大责任。尽管新闻自由和言论自由现在不受任何法律限制，但新闻业有义务履行其职责。公共福利往往像维护另外一种财产时那样有效，无论怎么讲，新闻业都具有在其影响范围内尽力保护、保存和提升公共福利的庄严义务。新闻学宣告保持独立性并享有宪法赋予的言论自由的权利，而这并不能保证新闻业不会做出有损于公共利益的胡作非为之事。新闻的持续责任是监督关系人民福利的事件及其进程，考虑并讨论关涉或者影响人民利益的问题，指出其中的失误，抨击虚假或者不力的公共服务，揭露任何部门的严重危害公信力的行为而无论它被标榜得如何好，谴责错误并支持公正，而所有这一切都建立在分辨真善美与假恶丑的个人观点之上。这样的判断并非一贯正确，我们不能说这样的认识就没有失误。相反，它服从于影响整个人类的判断的多变性和脆弱性。但是，它毕竟是所有舆论实质上赖以建立的信息来源，很大程度上来讲，不管舆论如何变化，为舆论的声音及其发展提供指导成为新闻业特殊而公认的功能。

  因此推理，新闻业的责任就是思考舆论的影响，进而考虑对于公共福利的影响，而正如之前所言，所有这些都在于个人。与履行这种责任相一致，假如他们漠视真相和公正、公平而理智的判断的话，新闻业就不允许个人的偏激或者仇视的观点表达。法

---

① Cook，*Delane of the Times.* ——原书注

律、命令和政府行为作为公共福利的必需条件，关于政府代理的对立批判应该以事实和关于真伪的忠实观点为依据。法律代理者被授予尊重新闻事业的权利，正如人们长久以来验证了这样的尊重感一样，因为唯有这样的尊重程度，人们才相信他们能够有效地服务公众。不加区别地和不公正地攻击他们，易于降低他们在公众心目中的地位，进而降低其公共服务的质量。拥有最大限度的舆论支持是政府行为中最重要的因素，而且舆论应该建立在政府行为的成绩之上，无论是普通的还是特殊的成绩。实际上，舆论控制着民主政府的特征，舆论某种程度上以真实而准确的信息传播及其公正的良好影响改善了政府管理。关于个人或者政府行为的错误和误导的信息，以及不公正的动机或者观点，不仅有危害公共福利的影响，而且当其是蓄意而为的时候就成为没有价值的新闻了，为此它们都将遭到贬损。在所有的环境下，确认和分辨真相的困难已经在本章节得到充分的讨论，而在有关公众人物或者措施的讨论中，哪些是公平的而哪些是不公平的还不十分清晰，这很大程度上在于人们没有感觉和认识到永久区分两种判断的综合尺度。但是，有人可能贸然断定，所有涉及观点表达的新闻报道的合理性测试就是基于知识和真诚的理念。这种知识和真诚的明证是公众对新闻的公信力和信任感的验证和保证。

第十三章 编辑结构

现在，让我们从总的编辑政策转向特殊的编辑方法，即编辑政策得以表达的手段。可以肯定的是，新闻有或者说应该有某种编辑政策，它涉及新闻收集的方法、新闻报道的准备和新闻的发布，但是此阶段运用的编辑政策的原则已经在对应的章节中进行了讨论。在这里，我们编辑认为政策是评论版在观点表达过程中所揭示的规律。

有人说，评论版是报纸个性特征的思想和灵魂之所在，评论是"报纸个性特征的表达，进而揭示其特性、认知的意识和标准"的语言。评论的地位和功能的概念界定使其成为报纸中威严而重要的部分，假如报纸必须创造其个性特征，并维持通过公众支持及其舆论和行动影响的基础——报纸思想和心智的质量——而赢得的优势和尊敬的话，我们就必须认识到评论及其评论版的这种威严和重要性。一家新闻机构在表达其鲜活的个性思想时，其思想不必要与机构内形成这种思想表达的个人的思想确切地一致起来。如果两者一致的话，这种思想毋庸置疑表达得更好、更真诚而令人印象深刻。的确，假如报纸真诚而生动的个性特征要产生深刻的印象，报纸的个性思想与表达这种思想的记者和编辑的思想的一致性在很大程度上就必须存在。但是，无论怎么说，报纸对公众的关系与编辑对公众的关系两者之间是有所差别的。编辑作为个体不同于其他个体，他作为个人的公共职责与其同事是分离的，他的公共职责不比其他人的大。他在个人人脉圈内所说的话和做的事通常都无关公共事务。他可能在个人圈子里自由地发表自己的观点，或许其言论像其他任何人的评论一样有些许效果。但是，当他投入报纸个性思想表达的工作时，他就发出了超越其自身的更大声音，他在以重大的、显著的和明确的责任感来评论这些事务，而这是他必须认识和敬畏的义不容辞的责任。在他践行有关报纸个性特征的过程中，他通常有必要限制、修改或者扩充自己可能所持有的观点，尤其是当他作为负责编辑导向组成员之一来表达自己不完全认同的观点的情况下。

由于报纸的公共关系和公共职责，一家报纸不会总是无所顾忌地讲出个体的话，它可能纯粹为了保持公共福利的方便而这样做，只是用个体可能自由表达的防范性词语来表达，或者以活泼而富有生气的方式公布个体或许根本不愿意说的话，这是报纸的责任。我们这里想表达的观点是，报纸的个性特征必须被客观地看作具有与创造和保持其个性特征的某个人的个性截然不同的趣味、责任、义务、职责、权利和优势，而报纸的个性特征往往超越个人特征。报纸的个性特征或许具有与时代的任何个人无关的一种持久性，它或许具有由于其显著的特征和品质而确立的声誉，而报纸有必要或者有愿望保护和维持这种特征和品质，不管背后的个体力量如何变化。综上所述，归结为一点，一位编辑更多地考虑的是编辑的导向和指导，以及编辑的撰写，并非个体的观点，他们的义务并非仅仅是竭尽所能做好工作，而是尊重所服务的新闻机构的权利及其所履行的责任，进而表达该新闻机构的个性可能得以维持的公众思想，而新闻机构与众不同的个性是持续的、值得公众认知和信任的。

因此，报纸的经历被看重，因为无论报纸在读者心目中的地位和感受如何，这一切都起源于报纸过去的所作所为。有时候，报纸可能有决定改变原则、政策和流程的合理理由，因为它们已经陈旧得跟不上时代的步伐了，报纸为扭转其下滑趋势，有必要对此加以改变，或者这样的变化是希望之中的，恰好是报纸扩展其实用范畴的正确的决定。然而，这些都是充分考虑和理解报纸的义务和所涉及的风险而蓄意进行的调整。他们指的是报纸运行过程中可能遇到的危机，假如报纸曾经遇到了这样的危机或风险的话，也并非经常遭遇的危机或风险。而如果社会上缺少这种改变的需求，人们就会假定，就报纸所体现的个性特征而言，报纸的过去值得尊重，它需要持续发展。报纸的成长、扩展和进步就没有障碍，因为报纸就如同人，"他们可能置之死地而后生，拾阶而上，走向辉煌"，而一家优秀报纸的过去就是为报纸的现在和未来的获利而积累财富。

　　勉强承认以上陈述是真实的。那么，假如报纸仍然处于这个界定阶段的话，报纸为维护和增强个性特征或者创造个性特征而必需的评论原则是什么呢？首先，评论作为报纸思想的表达，它有必要成为思想的产物。用华丽辞藻而思想浅薄或者没有承载读者所需内涵的言辞来填满被分配的栏目或者版面，这是一位评论作者很容易操作的事情。假如评论版没有读者喜欢阅读的言论，那么这可能是因为评论"缺乏内涵，缺乏关联"，也可能因为它们没有趣味性，不能满足读者的知情权和引导舆论，还可能因为评论写得思想贫乏而无实际思想可以传播给读者。假如评论版缺乏可读性，那么这就是编辑的失误，而非读者之过。假如评论版值得阅读的话，它总是深受读者喜爱的。但可以肯定的是，报纸评论版并非受到所有读者的喜爱。报纸中没有任何版面的文章曾经得到所有读者的喜爱。但是，值得阅读的评论将有很多读者来阅读。假如评论受到大多数读者的格外喜爱的话，那么这样的评论读者就构筑成为某个社区最有见识进而最具影响力的要素。与这种读者的数量相符，报纸能够为发行范围的读者传播其思想、特征、个性,并进而留下其直接影响。新闻具有培育和发展拥护者和支持者的优势,这个优势是其他任何优势无与伦比的。报纸的拥护者和支持者关注报纸及其言论,因为报纸评论了解真相,报纸了解他们的想法及其真诚,进而相信他们,没有任何财产具有如此大的价值。但是,除非报纸每天都发出自己的声音,刊登最诚恳、最忠实而富有思想性的评论,它才能培育这样的支持者和拥护者群体。

显而易见,这样的思想必须建立在知识的基础之上。尽管大部分学校里学到的知识或者过去积累的特殊学问都是必要的基础,但基础的构筑不仅需要这些,还特别需要了解关于当今的环境和条件、个人和群体、问题和现状等层面的情况。这样的知识只有通过对事件及其起源和本质、态势的不断观察和研究才能获得。有责任心的编辑必须是一位勤勉的读者。他从很多新闻来源中采集信息材料,他并不满足于与自己观点吻合的论点或者偏好。他想获得事情的真相,他会权衡和分析事实直到真相大白。他也不能满足于了解当时公众感兴趣或者重要事务的相关信息。今天似乎不值得一提的事情或者状况可能明天就会发展成为一个大话题。无论世界上正在发生什么事情,特别是在他采集新闻的活动区域,只要影响或者可能影响公共兴趣或者公共福利的事情,都值得他关注,尽管这件事情可能永远不会证明他的评论。

这并不意味着,一位编辑应该在头脑中想着这些细节。在头脑中塞满这些资料信息可能很容易,但是它们会占用思维空间,有用的信息空间就所剩无几了。"活字典"经常充当着一种适用性办公设备,但是它通常情况下只具有参考性的价值。编辑必须保持的所有内容就是一个主题的要点,这能够唤起他回忆信息线索或者脉络的印象。一般而言,当探讨细节时,有关事物的细节信息都是可以获取的。为此,很少有人愿意满脑子装着琐事缛节般的信息。当一个人只见树木不见森林时,他就很难获得对于评论判断至关重要的、有关整个问题的客观认识。考虑周详而形成的公平表达的评论观点的巨大价值在于，它是客观的，它是从外围观察事物的产物，这样的观察视觉或多或少都是难能可贵的，所观察事物的所有可见部分都显示了与整体的关系，恰似某航班上的一位乘客在俯瞰某一座城市，他看到的是整个城市的鸟瞰图，同时他的眼睛分辨了这座城市的地形走向。基于某件事情或者某个问题的单独层面的分析意见看起来如此接近事实真相，以至于这样的看法妨碍了其他层面的观点或者所有层面的观点，由于认识视觉的狭隘很容易失之偏颇，并因此产生误导。人们不可能永远从纯粹客观的视觉来认识问题，因为视野存在缺陷，并且证明这种观点的所有必需事实都不在手边。但无论怎么说，这对于最好的和最合理的判断都是必要的，而编辑总是站在而且应该站在比其他观察者更好的角度来获取这样的观点。即使他的目的是带有党派倾向的，但无论从任何意义上来讲，除非他了解所反对的和所支持的立场或观念，否则他都不可能做出自己的最佳评论。

而思想和知识的价值很大程度上依赖于其形成和表达的方式。一位编辑从来担负不起这样的后果：他忘记了自己所谈话的对象不仅是一支庞大的受众群体，而且他还要面对所有类型和条件的男人和女人，以及如其所希望的不同文化和不同教育背景的年轻人。假如评论版的阅读范围总是达到了所希望的广度，假如它在圈内的威力只有通过广泛的阅读量才可以得到发挥的话，那么，报纸的思想就要尽可能用读者普遍理解的词语来表达，突破当今优美的英语词汇理解的局限性。同时，假如这种思想及其背后的个性特征要得到尊重的话，就有必要用能够以自身的语用选词水准来证明其尊重的语言来包装。这不但意味着良好的文稿，而且是优秀的文稿，即普通读者无需查词典就能够清晰理解的词语所表达的思想。普通人心目中的文稿可能只赢得少数人的掌声，并提升作者的荣誉度，但是它不会提高其影响力所依赖的基础——大众对于评论版的兴趣和依恋。

人们总是假定：读者具有丰富的学识来理解用通俗易通的英语表达的清晰的陈述。评论版不能根据低能者的见识或者文盲的无知而调整。但是，我们不能总是假定，无论读者的学识如何，他都需要被告知任何评论话题的主题，除非他阅读了全部的新闻报道或者他是一位见多识广的人，他没有缺失信息的任何借口。假如拥有这种知识或者信息存在疑问的话，那么在读者理解观点的情况下评论的主题就应该制作得像有关思想那样清晰。换言之，评论应该处于这样的境况下：它本身承载着充足的信息来启示读者对于讨论主题的认识。而缺乏观点论证的言论陈述不是大家所希望看到的，除非你可以预测观点的论证已经为大家所熟知。随着教育事业的进步和人们对于公共事务的兴趣增强，人们越发不愿意接受既定的观点，且更加倾向于排斥没有逻辑论证的教条式主观判断。他们需要评论观点的论证，或者说其中很多人想这样，而且他们被授予知晓论点推理和论证的权利。在论证合理的情况下，揭示结论得以完成的论证过程的评论以及结论本身都是最具说服力的表达形式。而这样的讨论不仅对于读者提高认识问题的能力有益，而且是一种关于报纸精神的证明，更是报纸具有独立思考实力而为读者留下初次真实印象的明证，也是报纸期盼的一种声誉。

评论表达的另外一个必要条件即评论必须是真诚的。真诚的观点只能建立在真相的基础之上，或者至少建立在对其前述事实真相的信任基础上。当然，真相的绝对判断或多或少总是困难的，尤其是与时事相关的事实真相，而关于真实的事物是什么的评估在很大程度上归属于个人判断的事情，就像关于该事物的含义和意味的认识一样。然而，公众的权利认知很大程度上正是依赖评论对于真相的判断及其观点的判断上面。因此，真诚的评论表达涉及事实的真实陈述，这一点好像是编辑，也是观点真实性的基础所在。对于评论的真诚和真实的特征来讲，两者可能同时有误，其中之一不可能总是正确的。报纸只能希望其评论是真诚而真实的，并劝服其读者信服报纸评论大部分时候是正确的。但是，评论的真诚和真实只是近义词的关联，两者是说服读者信任报纸评论的必要条件，也是建立和维持报纸公信力的必要条件，进而又是报纸的物质和精神福利的必要条件。

但是，这种影响还需要更多的思考。报纸希望像获得读者的思想那样赢取读者的心。思想或者理性的尊重是报纸获得最高声誉的必要条件，但是这种尊重不会主动生成，也缺乏可靠的忠诚度，除非报纸建立了某种程度的接近或者触及读者喜爱的联系。为了达到这样的目的，报纸评论应该渗透人类的情感因素。这并不是说，报纸应该情绪化，而是说报纸应该认识到人性本质对于其个性特征的培育和提升是必要的，除非情感与思想激活了这些人性品质，否则它们就不能得以充分的表达。换言之，报纸在思考所报道事物的同时还必须有所感触，假如报纸要被读者视为朋友和顾问，它必须将情感融入其思想和评论中。可以肯定的是，情感必须受到推理的约束。感触总是比思考容易些，而且没有什么比不能加以控制的情感对于公众兴趣或者报纸的实际趣味危害更大。的确，很多评论更多的是情绪的表达而非理性的诉求，如果报纸及其评论旨在表达灵魂深处真诚而强劲的声音，而且它对于公众思想和意识产生的强烈印象十分重要，那么报纸在万不得已的情况下没有必要诉诸情感，除非它为了谴责极端的情感表达。唤起情感和适宜诉诸情感的环境下产生的观点可能用辩论的技巧加以装饰，但是，假如观点的论证充满了教条式的说教而非排斥情感因素的话，它就缺乏了能够引发读者回应的生气和活力。作为"冷漠的循规蹈矩"的观点表达媒介，报纸及其评论就可能沦为"华而不实的摆设"。而且，正是通过诉诸情感，与伦理和利他主义关联的人类最高理性和服从于心灵导向和守护的最高尚的精神愿望和理想才能得以表达。简言之，报纸的个性特征必须具备灵魂和理智，而且假如它要与所代表和呈现的人性一致，假如它要成为人类的合适的伴侣和有影响力的指导者的话，作为"他者",它要敢于揭露某个人或者事物。没有其他任何领域比新闻的操作具有更强大的实用性和公共服务性。当条件有保障时,新闻及其运行可以唤醒人们心灵深处的情感并促进他们积极向上。除非报纸具备自身的灵魂,即报纸具备包涵心灵和控制头脑的灵魂,它曾经回应人类所遭遇的苦难、人类良好的愿望和人类行为,否则,它就不能有效地发挥其威力。

第十四章　新闻伦理

　　每天报纸以这种或者那种方式记录的事实都或多或少地涉及伦理话题。报纸所呈现的犯罪场面经常超越了伦理规则所要求的观察范畴，因为报纸报道这样违反常态的犯罪行为，旨在捕捉和获取公众的注意力。这是通过引发公众的趣味性和好奇心来构筑所谓反常的、另类的新闻重要成分的惯用方法。相反，厌世者尽管触犯了道德准则和放弃了研究报纸的巨大责任，但是他们依然表明了其在人类行为上的反常行为，自人类文明以来他们一向如此。从几个世纪以前所形成的人类行为标准来看，绝大多数人某种程度上都不能远离吸引大众注意力的新闻，也不能拒绝将它们作为文明社会中人际关系的必需。但是，每天的新闻可能也包含令人眼花缭乱或者不同寻常的有关伦理原则的评述，它们记录了提升伦理原则的活动，而这样的原则通过公共法案为自身匹配了有价值的公共新闻。

　　换言之，报纸评述涵盖了包括违反伦理原则现象的相当宽泛的内容，无论报纸评述是否定的还是肯定的，它本身通常是伦理原则和行为进步的一个重要的影响因素。作为该原则此种程度上的说明者，报纸平素尤其要服从这样的原则。报纸生存于公开的环境下,而且它必须生活在这样的环境下。无论报纸做什么,好的或者坏的举动,它都要暴露在公众及其批判的视野中,因为它正是依靠公众的揭露才得以生存。报纸不可能有自身的私生活。报纸通过被揭露而维系生存,它不可能隐藏自身。当然,从某个方面来讲它的动机可能是富有建设性的,但是其行动每天都在舆论评判面前得到证明。因此,报纸的伦理行为不断涉及自身创造的循环过程,伦理成为新闻业实践的一个特别重要的方面,而伦理对新闻事业经营管理的重要性也不可小觑。

由于新闻事业应对的几乎都是与人际关系相关的事务,而且它具有持续性和连贯性报道相关公共事务的义务,所以它的基本原则很大程度上是一个涉及伦理本质的问题。通过本章节的论述,伦理的思考就得到彰显,因为它们是不可逃避的话题,但是在考虑新闻活动的特别伦理标准时,我们似乎就给有关新闻原则的讨论画上了句号。

很可能发生的情况是,很多记者手中握有关于报纸及其活动应承担责任的指南,但是他们一旦在职业生涯中取得了成功和荣誉之后,他们就会将这些报纸指南束之高阁,他们不再考虑诸如伦理这样的话题,在头脑中再也不会形成与自己工作相关的哪怕单独一条明确的伦理准则。然而,记者很可能按照应有的伦理原则的要求从事报业活动。毋庸置疑,成千上万的人都不曾听说过《十戒》(*The Ten Commandments*),但是他们却像那些熟悉和看穿了其指令的人一样完全遵循这些准则。无论他是否意识到这一点,每个人都会受到某些道德准则的影响。他们可能或高或低、或宽泛或严格地受到限制,他们可能一直或者时断时续地拿这些准则支配自己的行动,但是从某个方面或者某种程度上来看,道德对人们的影响通过其行动得以表达,尽管他们可能没有意识到这样的准则就像某些明确形成的事物一样存在着。换言之,道德准则的影响一旦为人们所接受并付诸实践,它就会对人们的行为产生比知识更加深远的影响。在伦理学诞生之前,尚未出现任何明确的词汇来命名伦理原则，但可能在任何道德准则形成或者被采纳之前的几个世纪，这些伦理原则就在发挥作用。但是，无论怎么讲，人们都有必要建立这样的准则，以便认识可能用来指导人们履行其义务并从法律或社会途径谴责其未履行义务的公平尺度。有些人认识到这些道德准则不仅是判断人类行为的基本是非标准，而且成为他们必需的行为规范，而道德准则一旦被这些人采纳和运用的话，其影响力就扩散到那些未有这种认识的人群。他们只是发现，为了维持其所控制的某种社会立场，他们有必要某种程度上与其行为原则一致起来。不具备道德领袖施与公众概念影响的那些人，从来不会取得道德上的进步，而这样的概念或多或少体现在明确界定的人类指导性规则中。同时值得提及的是，没有道德进步相伴的物质进步从来不会长久。因为物质发展的程度越高，社会状态和社会关系就越复杂，人们对用以指导社会关系的道德准则的需求就越强烈。

　　通常情况下，不同群体的人们具有像大众一样共同的兴趣。这种群体中的任何个体可能都具有自己关于公平概念及其实践的独特认识，或者他可能不具备公平的概念，在其行为中根本不考虑有关公平的理念。由于没有认识到关涉整体利益的公平标准，每个人都在个性本质的支配下行事。假如他的个人标准过高，他有关共同利益的行为就遵循高标准；假如他的个人标准过低，他在相关的行为中就遵循同样低的标准。其他指导人们行为的关于公正的个人认识可能不存在，影响具有低标准公正愿望或者高标准基本条件的人的途径亦不存在。但是，低标准比高标准在群体中的应用对于其声誉具有更加深远的意义，这一点与人性的本质习惯表现一致。多数人的行为可能无可指责，正所谓法不责众，但整个群体必然遭受少数人不良行为带来的谴责。然而，少数人的多数行为并非蓄意或偏好所致，而是缺乏对原则的更好掌握，或者缺乏对原则的思考所致。在关于行为标准认知缺失的情况下，一个人很可能受控于其个人的公正理念，或者由于个性特征所推动的愿望导致他缺乏这样的概念，或者他根本没有思考伦理及其差异。只有这个群体为所有成员建立了指导个人行为的标准时，个人行为与整体关系的判断可能才有明确的尺度，借助这样的尺度，漠视或忽略这些原则可能会发现他的缺失所在，而大多数同类者才可以通过这样的感觉而倾向于改进自己的标准与大家保持一致。正是基于这样的考虑，专业人员和其他群体才有必要建立伦理准则，以保护、提升和改善群体利益，至少保护了该群体的个体成员的利益。

但是，直到个体提出有关伦理原则的想法并形成自身的指导标准时，才会出现这样的案例，而且基于此培育吸引同领域其他人的注意力并进行思考的具体准则。"通常情况下，这是一个缓慢的发展过程，直到人们认识到这样一个与众不同的群体利益的存在，而且认识到它对于个体利益而言十分必要的时候，它才得以形成。作为大众和个体进步的途径，这个群体利益必须得以保持和提高，道德准则成为敏感的和急切的问题。"换言之，我们首先要认识到，大家都是一个团队的成员，而且正是基于团队的集体利益和目标这个团体才得以建立。假如这个共同利益要得到改进，那么共同的标准和目的就是改进的必要途径。假如一个群体要实现整体的物质或者道德上的进步，它就必须首先把自身看作一个单元，然后朝着这个既定的程序迈进。或许，新闻业从不缺乏对报纸的伦理责任进行严肃思考的代表性人物，很多编辑已经通过创造某种指导自己所任职的个体报纸的准则而对此问题作出了形式上和行为上的考虑。例如，很久之前当乔治·W·蔡尔兹（George W. Childs）出版《费城公共纪事报》（*Philadelphia*

Public Ledger）① 时，其善于经营的编辑威廉·V·麦基恩（William V. McKean）采纳了几乎整个新闻业的伦理规范要求作为其报纸的编辑伦理体系。这个编辑伦理体系如下：

  永远公正而坦率地对待公众。
  报纸要想赢得读者的信任和尊敬，它就必须为读者提供值得信任的信息和咨询。而误导读者则是一件非常严重的事情。
  留有余地地陈述你的报道胜过言过其实。
  保证每次报道的真实性，尤其是批评性报道。
  犯罪嫌疑人与罪犯之间有着本质上的区别。
  温和地对待弱势和无助的违法者。
  判断事物之前仔细理解事物的两面性，铭记任何事物都存在两面性。假如你试图做出决定，你必须了解事物正反两

---

① 根据［美］埃德温·埃默里、迈克尔·埃默里著《美国新闻史》（新华出版社1982年版）第169页有关《费城公共纪事报》的论述，"本杰明·戴的两位印刷商朋友威廉·M·斯温和阿鲁纳·S·艾贝尔看到，尽管他们曾对戴提出过令人悲观的劝告，但《纽约太阳报》却仍然办得兴旺，于是，他们在1836年3月与合伙人阿扎赖亚·H·西蒙斯一起创办《费城公共纪事报》，这无异于他们彻底承认了过去的错误。"［美］埃德温·埃默里、迈克尔·埃默里著《美国新闻史》（新华出版社2001年版）第122页的论述为，"本杰明·戴的印刷商朋友威廉·M·斯温和阿鲁纳·S·艾贝尔看到，尽管他们曾对戴提出过消极的建议，《太阳报》还是办得很兴旺。但是，到他们于1836年3月与合伙人阿扎赖亚·H·西蒙斯（Azariah H. Simmons）一起创办《费城公共纪事报》时，才彻底承认了自己的错误。"布莱雅（Willard Grosvenor Bleyer）著《美国新闻事业史》（*Main Currents in the History of American Journalism*）第195—179页的论述，《费城公共纪事报》于1836年3月25日由《纽约太阳报》的三位合伙创办人威廉·M·斯温（William Swain）、阿鲁纳·S·艾贝尔（A.S. Abell）和阿扎赖亚·H·西蒙斯（Azariah H. Simmons）创办，是费城第一家成功创办的便士报，乔治·W·蔡尔兹（George W. Childs）后来担任《费城公共纪事报》的出版商。

方面的情况。

当你只是听说某件事情的时候，千万不要说你知道这件事情。

绝不要听信道听途说的传闻而贸然行动。谣言只是考问时的附表而已。

仔细核对事实，准确地报道事实。准确地报道事实好于快速报道事实，因为快速报道事实经常出差错。报道延误是糟糕的事情，而报道失实更加糟糕。

走出去收集第一手的原始信息，假如你不能收集到这样的信息，那么你就要争取最接近事实真相的信息。

记者的职能就是收集事实和记录事实，依据事实发表评论是编辑的职责。

用事实和论证来讲述新闻故事，不要用华丽的辞藻撰写新闻。

不要过分自信。记住，你总是有可能出错。

所有的人都有评价法庭诉讼和审判的平等权利。

绝不要对大众的激动情绪煽风点火。

没有什么比习惯性地漠视法律会对公共事务产生更加伤风败俗的影响。

支持当局维持公共秩序的稳定，通过法律途径来纠正错误。假如法律有缺陷，废除法律不如修正法律。

严格的法律约束总是存在。强加于人而产生最大危害的执法是失败的执法。

在美国社区没有必要也没有理由制订平民的法律。

尽管坏人很多，但是你要记住，与成千上万的民众相比较，他们就是微乎其微的。

公共福利的诉求高于任何党派的呼声。

雅致而清新的文风总是所希望的，但是绝不要让修辞代替清晰、直白而强劲的表达。

浅显易懂的词语对于学识不高的人是必要的，而平朴的文字对于有学识的人同样是适用的。①

以上准则包含了很少的共识和令人敬仰的哲理，它只是揭示了个体准则创造者心目中一种强烈的公正和公平概念的伦理原则。尽管它比之前的伦理原则具备更多的情感色彩而缺乏理性的思考，但是它依然是沃伦·哈丁（Warren G. Harding）②在自己创办的报纸中所采纳的准则：

> 记住，每个问题都有两个方面，要将这两个方面都反映出来。
> 要可信。
> 要挖掘事实。错误必不可免，但是要努力做到准确。我宁愿有一篇非常准确的报道，而不愿有100篇有一半错误的报道。
> 要正派、公正、宽容。
> 要支持人——而不是打击他们。每个人身上都有好的一面，将这好的一面引发出来，永远不要无谓地伤害别人的感情。
> 报道政治聚会时，要搜集事实，并如实地报道，而不要按你自己希望的那样去报道。
> 对所有党派一视同仁。如果有什么党派需要评论，我们

---

① *Payne's History of Journalism in the United States.* ——原书注
② 沃伦·哈丁（Warren Gamaliel Harding，1865—1923），美国第 29 届总统 [1921—1923]。沃伦·哈丁是来自俄亥俄州的共和党人，他是一位有影响力的自办报纸的出版商。他曾在俄亥俄州任职 [1899—1903]，担任俄亥俄州第 28 任副州长 [1904—1906]，1915—1921 年担任美国参议员。他还是美国第一位竞选总统的报纸出版商。沃伦·哈丁制定了《马里恩（印第安纳）星报》编辑部信条。

会在社论栏目中进行评论。

对待所有宗教事务都要尊敬。

如有可能,永远不要忽视一个无辜的妇女或孩子对自己亲属的错误或不幸的倾诉。不要等被要求才去这样做,而要主动去做。

而最重要的,要干净。永远不要让一个脏词或未被确证的报道付印。

我希望这张报纸能这样做,这样它才能走入千家万户,而不伤害任何一个孩子的天真无邪。

在惠廉士(Walter Williams)① 创造的"记者信条"中,我们发现了一个关于新闻伦理原则的精美表述:

我相信新闻事业的专业性。

我相信,公共报刊是公信力的载体,以最大的责任感来衡量报刊及其相关的报道都是值得公众信任的,较少接受公众服务是对这种信任的背叛。

我相信,清晰的思维和陈述、准确和公正是好新闻的基本原则。

我相信,一位记者应该采写他心目中认为真实的新闻。

我相信,除非考虑社会福利的因素,压制新闻的任何理由都是不可原谅的。

我相信,没有任何人像记者那样具有绅士般风度而敢于撰写自己不愿意说的事情;通过某人自己的钱袋来贿赂就像通过另外一个人的钱袋来贿赂一样是不可避免的;个体的责任可能是无法回避的,他要为通过另外一个人的教导或者回

---

① 惠廉士(Walter Williams,1864—1935),美国来华记者、教育家。

报而辩护。

我相信，新闻、评论和广告栏目应该为读者提供同样最大的利益；有益的、清晰的事实报道应该是最重要的独立标准之一；新闻业是否良性发展的最好评估手段是它提供的公共服务。

我相信，最成功的新闻事业和称得上最成功的新闻业从不惧怕备受尊敬和享有荣耀光环。她坚定地保持独立，不为傲慢的观点或者权势的贪婪所改变；她提供建设性的信息，宽容而不放纵，自我控制力强，富有耐心，总是尊重读者而从不惧怕读者；她很快就对不公平的事物充满了愤慨；她不为殊荣的诱惑或者民众的哗然所动摇；新闻业力争给予每个人，以及法律和政党的薪金、人类兄弟般的情谊认知所创造的机会；新闻业充满着爱国激情，同时真诚地促进国际良好祝愿和世界友谊。这些都是当今世界充满人性的新闻业所必需的。

这些例子足以表明伦理观念和个体记者的伦理理念。没有人能够说清楚为专门指导特定的报纸而创造了多少类似的规则，但是我们完全可以断定，对报纸方向负责并在新闻实践中对伦理行为话题作出思想贡献的大多数记者都意识到了这样的原则，而且他们努力运用这些原则。正如上文所言，很多记者在不自觉地运用这些原则，因为他们属于这种人，他们不会做出相反的举动。

但是，作为个体并运用于个体企业行为的原则陈述不会影响整个行业，除了其运用在其他方面的影响。换言之，正是示范的影响局限于为其人脉圈留下印象，而且它很少揭示激励自身的特定原则。个体标准曾经保持着个性，而且总是因个性的变化而变化。所有人都认可的共同标准只有通过集体的考虑和行动才能够建立起来，进而明确宣告共同遵守的伦理原则，既把这个伦理原则作为公正的指导又作为公正的标准。通常情况下，这种运用于新闻职业的规则于1923年被美国报纸编辑协会（the American

Society of Newspaper Editors，简称为 ASNE)① 所采纳，被命名为《新闻记者规约》(Canons of Journalism)②，其条款如下：

绪　言

第一修正案保护言论自由不被任何法律剥夺，保证了人们通过媒体表达言论的宪法权利，并因此赋予报纸工作者一项特别的使命。所以新闻工作对其从业者，除了行业和知识的要求外，还要针对新闻工作者的特殊使命对其追求正直品质的情况有所要求。为此目的，美国报纸编辑协会制定本原则声明，作为职业表现和工作道德的最高标准。

第一条

责任。搜集和传播新闻与意见的最初目的是服务大众利益，将情况通知他们，使他们能对当时的情况作出判断。为个人私利或不值得的目的滥用自己专业工作者的力量的报人，将辜负公众的信任。美国新闻媒体是自由的，这不仅是为了告知大众，或作为一个争辩的论坛，也是为了能对社会中的力量，包括政府各级官员的行为，进行独立的检查。

第二条

新闻自由。新闻自由属于人民。必须保护新闻自由不受来自任何公共或私人集团的侵蚀与破坏。新闻记者

---

① "美国报纸编辑协会"现更名为"美国报业编辑协会"（American Society of News Editors，ASNE)。协会每年举行一次年会。协会设有杰出写作奖、"杰西·拉文索尔"奖、大众新闻服务摄影奖等奖项，奖励优秀的新闻编辑工作者。
② 这些规则由美国报纸编辑协会伦理标准委员会主席和纽约《环球》主编赖特（H. J. Wright）制定。这些规则自 1922 年开始作为《新闻记者规约》被采用，1975 年被修改并重新命名为《原则声明》。

必须时时警惕，关注公共事务是否在公开场合下讨论解决。他们必须同任何利用新闻媒体为自己牟私利的企图进行勇敢的斗争。

第三条

独立性。新闻记者必须避免任何表面或实质上的不适当、表面或实质上的利益冲突。他们既不应该收受任何东西，也不应该参加任何看起来有可能伤害他们正直性的活动。

（一）提高有悖于公众福利的任何私利的做法，无论出于何种理由，都是真正的新闻事业所不容许的。如果没有公众关注其来源或者用事实证明其新闻价值的形式和实质的呼声，源自私人的所谓新闻就不应该报道。

（二）故意背离真相的偏袒性评论严重侵犯了美国新闻事业的优良品质；新闻栏目的这种做法就是对新闻行业基本原则的颠覆。

第四条

真实与准确。来自读者的良好信任是优秀新闻的基础。应该不惜一切努力保证新闻的准确、没有偏见、平衡表达各方意见。社论、分析文章和评论，在准确性上应该与报道中的事实做同样的要求。严重的事实错误和疏忽产生的错误，都应该做最快的和突出的更正。

（一）从真诚信任的每个角度来考虑，报纸都不得不遵从真实性的原则。在所控制的范围内，假如报纸没有掌握这些基本品质而作出不完整或者不准确报道的话，它就无法得到谅解。

（二）标题凌驾于文章的内容之上，标题是否得当应该由此得到充分的印证。

第五条

公正。公正并不意味着新闻媒体不应该进行质问，或者不应该发社论表示意见。但是，它却要求媒体在新闻报道和媒体意见之间为读者划出一个清晰的界线。其中有观点和个人意见的文章应被明确标识出来。

第六条

正义性。尊重规则，公平对待双方或各方。报纸不应该报道影响声誉或者道德品质的被告无机会申辩的非官方指控，正当的操作要求在司法程序之外给予所有的严重指控案例以申辩机会。

（一）报纸不应该在缺乏有别于公众好奇心的公共权力的确定证据的情况下而侵犯私人权力或者感受。

（二）无论错误的原始状态如何，报纸对自身出现的有关事实或者观点的错误而进行即时和完整的修正，这是报纸的特权，也是报纸的职责。

第七条

正派。报纸不能逃避虚假的罪责。假如报纸一边宣称高尚的道德宗旨，另一边却为在犯罪和罪恶的细节中发现的卑鄙行为提供刺激和鼓励，那么它刊登的内容就不是崇尚真善美的。由于新闻业缺乏实施其准则的权威，这里所代表的新闻业只能表达这样的愿望：蓄意怂恿邪恶的理念将面对公众的强烈抵制或者遭到绝大多数专业人士的谴责。

这些准则是为了保持、保护和加强联结美国新闻工作者和美国人民的信任和尊敬，这种联结对确保这个国家的创始人委托给美国新闻工作者和美国人民的言论自由事关重大。

这里集中体现了以前章节已经讨论的新闻学基本原理，而且从最宽泛的意义上论述了这些原理中直接相关伦理行为的特殊运用。这些准则构筑了新闻业实践中普遍的公正标准，而且这些标准得到最大发行量和影响力的报纸中掌管编辑业务的群体的赞同。因此，人们可能假定他们表达了新闻业中普遍运用的伦理基本原则本质上的共识。

但是，在新闻事业中宣布原则是一回事，而运用这些原则是另外一回事，实际上在所有行业中都是如此，在所有人生中亦都如此，相信这些原则是一回事，将其基本原理付诸行动是另外一回事。除了可能被迫受到的惩罚之外，公式化的公平准则只不过是公正的要点，它只是表示了有意认知并极力遵守这些准则的所有人的指导标准，它也是无意遵守这些准则的人评估其过失的标准。每个人都必须根据自己对于这些准则的解释及其相关认知来运用此标准。因此，即使在那些希望公正做事的人当中，某种程度上也存在关于遵守准则及其特征的认识差别。人们的头脑和感知不可能由于某些准则或者法律而标准化。

道德标准的发展和明确陈述依旧是超越各个领域人类为之努力的个人奋斗的道德进步之必要，因为直到公正的原则设计出来并形成了轮廓，人们才可能对于公正为何物有普遍的了解。但是，道德标准一旦形成，并作为公正的普遍评价尺度为人们所接受，它们就会由于共同的赞成而变成影响和指导公众迅速成长的深厚力量。

新闻业合乎规律的发展是现代社会的奇迹之一。这种进步是值得人类引以为自豪的。假如没有热爱新闻事业的记者们所满意的道德水准进步，新闻业的发展就不可能实现。像其他所有职业一样，在新闻业不难发现例外的情况，但是整体而言，在公正的认知、新闻业的服务特征、新闻业的责任和义务的认识、新闻业日益重视揭示真相、新闻业更多探讨的公平性，以及在新闻业对公众利益作出的更大和深远意义的贡献等方面，新闻事业已经取得了进步，而且还将持续进步。与一种行业相伴而生的共识拓宽

166 　了新闻领域的视野，加强了整个行业巩固其立场和福利的愿望，促进了旨在提高公众利益的共同话题和行为的系列研究。新闻事业的准则是这种进步的成果之一，而它本身则是新闻事业这个最崇高行业道德进步的显著标示，同时新闻准则是人类物质和道德进步的伟大而强势的代表以及未来进步的保证。

The Principles of Journalism

Preface

In this book the writer has attempted to formulate and define the fundamental principles of journalism. The work is the result of a conviction that there is a growing need for such a statement and definition. Journalism has taken its place among the great professions. Its influence is universally recognized. It has become a necessity of modern life and modern progress. Its development is one of the wonders of our age. It pervades all civilization and makes a constant impress upon human thought and achievement everywhere. Yet it is in fact so new that it is only now beginning to realize within itself that it is not a mere aggregation of individuals pursuing a common vocation, but an entity, whose rights must be guarded, whose integrity must be maintained, and whose responsibilities must be recognized, by its individual parts. This realization naturally leads to a larger consideration of journalism as a whole, to thought about it as a profession, having collective interest and duties, distinguished from journalism as an individual calling, and out of this comes an increasing endeavor to arrive at a common understanding of what journalism really is, what are the standards by which it should be governed, what are its obligations in relation to the public, what are its aims and ideals.

It is the hope of the Writer that this book may contribute in some degree to such an understanding. For it would seem to be essential that a foundation be laid in an agreement upon elemental principles definitely stated, something concrete upon which conscientious journalism—and most of its practitioners are conscientious—can plant its feet. In this effort to state the primary principles of journalism the author realizes that he presents nothing that is new to thoughtful and experienced newspaper men. Novelty, indeed, would be foreign to the purpose. Anything new would be mere theory. Principles, being necessarily the product of experience, cannot be new. But the consciousness of underlying principles, and the degree and manner of their application, whether conscious or unconscious, vary with individual character, and if standards are to be established by which good journalism may be measured, it is necessary to draw from the common experience the essential elements of conduct and practice that have been proven by time and that are in accord with those principles of right that are recognized in all human association, and give concrete form to them. No one man may accomplish this to the satisfaction of all, but one man may assemble, from his own mature experience, and his conception of the general experience, sufficient material to make a start on such a foundation, and if this work will help in any manner to that construction its main purpose will be served.

But it is the hope of the writer that the interest in this effort will not be confined to his profession. There is no human agency that is in such constant, intimate and persistent contact with the public as that of journalism. Its influence, whether profound or superficial, whether good or bad, is universal, pervading every avenue of life. Its conduct, therefore, is a matter of public concern, and what journalism thinks of itself, the standards by which it guides itself and by which it wishes to be judged, its conception of its responsibilities to the public, its aims and ideals, should all be matters of general interest. There is need for a better public understanding of the difficulties that journalism encounters, and must of necessity encounter to a degree, in the exercise of its function and the realization of its ideals. There is a need for a better understanding of the principles which direct its best expression, a better understanding of its aspirations, and a better understanding of the devotion to the public service that is shown by tens of thousands of journalists who live and die unknown. It is the earnest wish of the writer that this book may be helpful to such an understanding.

C. S. Y.

Chapter I
The Origins

The archeologists, who dig farther and farther into antiquity, have never found that human nature in the remotest ages was different from that of to-day. The men and women of ten thousand years ago had the same interests, the same desires, the same passions, the same vices and virtues, they were moved by the same instincts and much the same reasonings, as the men and women of the present. It is therefore safe to assume that when Cain left home to acquire a residence and a wife in the land of Nod he did not wholly forget those he left behind in the neighborhood of Eden, and that when, in years long after, a patriarchal century perhaps, he met a traveler from that region, he was eager for news from home, although, for obvious reasons, he may have concealed his identity. Doubtless he wanted to know not only what had happened in the country about Eden but what was happening at the moment, and he absorbed with relish the smallest details of information, as well as those of larger importance.

The passion for news is not a development of civilization. Man is provided with organs of speech for the purpose of communication, with organs of hearing for the receipt of communications, and both tongue and ears have always been eager to function. Man is also endowed with unfailing curiosity which creates a continuous interest in the affairs, the conduct and the acts of others, a continuous interest in the processes and events of nature, a continuous interest in events and circumstances of every character, whether near or far removed. There never has been a time when men, and women, did not want to know what was going on in the family, in the community, in the region, in the world. There never was a time when the bearer of good news, or the bearer of bad news, about others, was unwelcome; never a time when news was not a commodity of constant exchange. "As cold waters to a thirsty soul, so is good news from a far country," says the author of Proverbs, bearing eloquent testimony to the value put upon news so long ago as the days of Solomon, and no modern bulletins are more eagerly read than were those beacons that heralded to Greece the fall of Troy.

This interest in events, this curiosity about things, which is the source of passion for news, is, indeed, the foundation of civilization and human progress. It is this which constantly enlarges the bounds of human knowledge and spurs that knowledge into new activities in new fields. It was the news that Paul spread through the Mediterranean provinces that established Christianity. It was the news that Marco Polo brought back from Cathay that started a search for a water route to the East Indies. It was the news of the discovery by Columbus that prompted the voyages which opened the Western Hemisphere to settlement. The news of every discovery by science has inspired science to new researches and new discoveries. But there would have been no such results if there had not been the everreceptive soil of human interest to receive their reports and to spread them in ever-widening circles. All knowledge, and all advancements growing out of knowledge, come from man's insatiable curiosity, his desire to know about things, whether it is the conduct of his neighbors, the nature of distant countries, or the reason of an apple's fall to the ground. He who learns tells, for the disposition to communicate is as strong as the disposition to hear. So news is disseminated, and always the process has been in operation, adding knowledge, good, bad, and indifferent, indiscriminately, to the human store, to be sifted through human experience for the rejection of the worthless.

News! The word, like the thing it names, has its roots in the remotest antiquity of language. The theory, widely circulated, that it was derived from the points of the compass (N. E. W. S.) is a fantastic notion without respectable foundation in fact or in usage. It comes from the word "new", through one of those curious developments of etymology which were common in the days when the language was in its formative stages, when there was no English grammar, and when "it appeared as if any word whatever might be used in any grammatical relation where it conveyed the idea of the speaker." "New" is one of the oldest words in the language, one of the number that are traced directly to the Sanscrit, and it is to be found in related form in nearly every European tongue, living or dead. The *nava* of the Sanscrit became the *novus* of the Latin, the *niuiis* of the Gothic, the *niwi* of the old Saxon, the *niwe* or *neowe* of the Anglo-Saxon. It was not only an adjective, but when shorn of its inflections in the transitions of the Middle English period the same word became an adverb, with the same meaning as newly; a verb, equivalent to renew; and a noun, applicable to anything new. In its plural form, news, it is found as such a noun in the older English writings. For example, in More's *Utopia*, in the original, appeared the phrase, "not for a vain and curious desire to see news," meaning new things. When it began to be applied to new events in the modern sense of news is not definitely known. The earliest use of the word in that sense in extant writings, according to the New English Dictionary, was in 1423, when James I of Scotland wrote in the "Kingis Quare," "I bring the newis that blissful ben." The same unimpeachable authority says it did not come into common use until after 1500, when it began gradually to supersede the older "tidings," a word of Norse descent, in popular favor. This is clearly shown in the fact that while in the "authorized version" of the Bible, drawn largely from the sixteenth century texts of Tyndale and Coverdale, the word "tidings" appears twenty-five times and "news" but once, Shakespeare uses "news" thirty-eight times and "tidings" only nine. That is why it was as "tidings," rather than as "news," that the greatest news in the world's history was announced, according to St. Luke, by the angels in "Behold I bring you good tidings of great joy which shall be to all people." The word "news" took the various forms of *neues*, *niewse*, *nues*, *newys*, *newis*, *newes* before it was finally fixed as "news".

Recurring to the imaginary meeting of Cain and the traveler from Eden we may presume that when they exchanged the news they possessed they fell to discussing the events reported, each expressing individual opinions about them. This, it is needless to say, is a universal accompaniment of news. And it is one of its most valuable attributes that, whether it is important or trivial, it arouses discussion. Discussion promotes thought, and thought is the lever that, when placed upon the fulcrum of truth, raises humanity. News is ever food for thought, and without it the mind must starve unless it holds within itself material for contemplation, and even that is likely to grow stale and lacking in substance for the mind unless refreshed by contact with events. Two persons living in complete isolation, without any communication with the world about them, will soon. as a rule, grow silent through sheer lack of new subjects for conversation. Life demands something to talk about, something to think about, something, however small, to exercise the mind upon, and news through all ages has supplied this material for conversation, for discussion, for thought, for opinion.

News and views! Ever they have been inextricably associated, and ever they must continue to be. The publication of news and views is journalism, a profession, an art and a business, developed out of the irrepressible instincts of human nature, responding to a universal and insistent desire for information, a universal and insistent curiosity that seeks enlightenment, a universal and insistent demand for the stimulation and satisfaction of interest. But journalism could not come into existence until facilities of publication had been created. For ages, before the syllabic and alphabetic stage of writing, the only means of publication, the only means of disseminating news, was by word of mouth, save, on occasion, by signals from hilltops, or by understood symbols carried by messengers which reached their highest form in pictographs. For ages after the invention of letters the voice was still the only means of communication except for official messages and for the favored few who could use the tablets of clay or wax, the parchment or papyrus scripts, Yet news of great importance or particular interest had wings even under those restricted conditions. Systems of runners were developed in many countries for the rapid transmission of intelligence, and spoken or written proclamations in the market places contributed to the spread of information that authority desired to communicate, developing faint promises of the newspaper in the Acta Diurna of Imperial Rome and the so-called "gazette" of Pekin. It was not, however, until the invention of printing that the means of publication in the modern sense was created, and it was still more than a hundred years after the presses began to work before anybody seems to have thought of them as an aid in the dissemination of news. Then, in Germany, some one conceived the idea of collecting accounts of certain important events of the time and printing them in a book. The publication received popular approval, and soon news books of this character began to issue from the capitals of England and France. Each one of these, however, was an individual venture like any other book. it was still a long time before a periodical news publication was thought of by a German, Egenolph Emmel, who in 1615 started the Frankfort *Journal*, and became the father of journalism, though that title is sometimes also given to Butter of London and Renaudot of Paris, who began periodical publication of newspapers some years later. It was in Frankfort, however, that journalism was founded, to lead a precarious and unrespected existence for another century before its value began to be recognized, and still anuther before the invention and establishment of the telegraph, the growth of transportation facilities, and the development of printing machinery, supplied the means for the extensive and rapid collection of news from everywhere, for rapid printing at low cost, and for quick and far distribution, and ushered in the era of journalism as an omnipresent and respected influence in the life and affairs of man.

There is no influence in the world so ubiquitous, so persuasive, so persistent as the newspaper. Each day it goes into the home, into the office, into the shop, into the factory, into the fields. No man is so poor or so remote that it does not touch him. And each day it lays before its reader the news of the community, of the country, of the whole earth, news that is good, news that is bad, news that is important, news that is relatively if not wholly trivial, news that is essential to the conduct of business, of industry, of society, and of government, news that has no value save in the momentary entertainment it affords, It presents a continuous, never-ending moving picture of the world and its occurrences, of mankind and its conduct, depicting comedy, tragedy, vice, virtue, heroism, devotion, enterprise, discovery, calamity, beneficence, sorrow and joy—human life in all its kaleidoscopic and inexplicable changes. And accompanying all this is editorial comment upon the news, interpreting the meaning of events, associating views with information, opinions with fact, and thereby aiding the reader to a better understanding and to an opinion of his own which becomes an element in the creation of public opinion, that "sovereign mistress of effects" which rules the modern world. Such is journalism, a profession that exists upon the events of the day, that mirrors all life and presents it to the view of every individual, thereby bringing all mankind to a closer unity and to a clearer conception of its kinship.

Chapter II
Principles of Production

The newspaper is one of the most complex, as it is one of the most important and valuable, of human institutions. Its production requires primarily the extensive and intensive study and labor of a profession which may be classed among the learned, in that it is a vocation of the mind which demands an accumulated store of general and special knowledge for its successful practice. But it is also a manufacturing enterprise to which a score of skilled crafts are essential, and a business which involves extensive buying and complicated salesmanship. The business is indispensable to the profession, and the profession is indispensable to the business, and their association is most effective when each recognizes that the other is equally necessary, and that the work of journalism is not complete without the labors of both. A newspaper without competent business management fails, just as surely as one without competent editorial management. Superexcellence in neither can compensate for inadequacy in the other. And yet the two functions, though both creative, both contributing to the same end, are distinct and different and must operate separately, but in contact, within the same body.

The production of a newspaper is fundamentally a manufacturing enterprise in which the direct sale of the product is essential. It matters not how disinterested, how altruistic, the motives inspiring the publication, the process of manufacture and sale is as necessary to their accomplishment as if its purposes were purely mercenary. For a newspaper to be of value in any way it must have readers, and it must have continuous readers. To obtain and retain such readers it must have elements of attractiveness and worth that justify payment for it, and continuous payment. A newspaper that is given away can acquire neither dependable circulation nor respect. The experiment has been tried. It must be sold, if it is to have any standing or influence. and it must be bought for its intrinsic value. It must be a marketable product. To be a marketable product it must contain what the people, or a number of them, are willing to pay for.

The first essential of a newspaper is that it be salable. The first essential of journalism is that it produce a salable commodity. It may create something of the highest character, it may express the loftiest ideals, it may be devoted to the noblest of causes, but if the product is not salable it is utterly futile. For a newspaper that is not read is no better than a blank sheet, though it contain letters of gold. And a newspaper is never salable unless it furnishes enough of what people desire to induce them to buy. It may in addition, and should, contain much for which they have no desire but which they need and which they ought to have, but it is only through that which they want that purchase can be persuaded. There is a difference between "giving the people what they want" and giving them what they ought not to have, that will be discussed later. The point here to be impressed is the principle that a newspaper must be, first of all, a salable product, and that to be salable it must, to a certain extent, respond to a public desire. No sale, no reader; no reader, no effect. This is the formula of failure in journalistic enterprise, however high its motives.

And while it is to be qualified in some degree, it is none the less true that the influence of a newspaper is, generally speaking, in proportion to the number of its readers. Circulation is not a reliable basis for estimating the comparative influence of different newspapers, for one of large circulation may have less influence than one of smaller circulation, because of differences in the character of the publications or the character of their readers. But in every case, whether the circulation is relatively large or small, the influence of each individual publication increases with the increase of its circulation. There are newspapers that are designed to appeal only to a class distinguished by education, intelligence and culture. Their circulation then is practically limited to that class, which in relation to the whole population of any given region, is comparatively small. But this class as a rule has an influence, in society, in business and in public affairs, quite out of proportion to its numbers, and so the journal which it reads has a similar influence of a larger nature. But even within this class it still remains true that the larger the number of its readers the more extensive is the impression made by such a journal.

However fine in itself, a newspaper is worthless unless it has readers, and it cannot obtain readers unless it persuades buyers through the character of its contents, and through selling activities. A miller produces a commodity of universal necessity and of unquestionable value, a commodity for which there is a continuous and large demand, but it appeases no hunger, sustains no life, until it goes out from the mill and into service by distribution through sale. But neither value nor demand will effect sale of itself to an extent that will repay the labor of production. A miller who does not establish means for the sale of his flour and actively endeavor to promote sale is practically certain to cease production. Yet no one can say that flour is not wholesome, nor necessary to life. But it is only through consumption that it contributes to life; it cannot be consumed until it is distributed, and it cannot be distributed, as a permanent process, save by sale. It can be given away in emergency, but the fact remains that it is not, and never has been, given away, except as a public or private philanthropy in time of need, and even then the miller is usually compensated-he sells his product just the same. There is no product so essential to life as flour, and perhaps none so free from criticism, yet its production is everywhere and at all times a business enterprise, and for many practical reasons it must be so.

The newspaper is a manufactured product that is not essential to life. Existence is possible without it. Many do exist without it, and for ages all people lived with no newspaper to aid them. But it responds to a need and a desire of human nature, and it has become a necessary agency of public welfare and of private information. No less than flour its production and distribution is fundamentally a business enterprise. That does not mean that profit is an essential object. It may have such altruistic or ulterior support that profit indeed is a negligible consideration. But none the less it is a business enterprise, that must be conducted on business principles and with business ability and energy if it is to accomplish whatever purpose it may have. It has to be manufactured and it has to be sold, and the training, talents and processes of business are as essential to these operations as they are to the conduct of any other business.

Moreover, it is generally true that there is a direct relation between the public influence, and usually the public value, of a newspaper and the capacity of its business management. It is usually true that the most influential papers are those that are the most prosperous, those, indeed, whose publication is most profitable in a legitimate way. That influence may not always be wholly good, but good or bad, it is based upon the number and character of its readers, upon the quantity and quality of its circulation; and it is through sales that that circulation is acquired, it is through that circulation that value is given to its advertising space, and it is through its advertising growing out of paper sales that a newspaper draws its prosperity. Sales and advertising are the products of business ability and activity, and these qualities can neither be ignored nor depreciated in the consideration of journalism, to the success of which, whatever the nature of its primary purposes, they are essential. Incidentally, it should be realized and recognized that advertising in itself has aesthetic and economic public values that make it something vastly more important than a mere income-producing feature of journalism.

But while business ability, business principles and business methods are essential to effective journalism, it cannot be wholly dominated by the desire for profit without injury or disaster. Journalistic production is not simply a business enterprise. As a rule, every journal is established mainly to advocate certain principles, to support a certain cause, to perform a public service or supply a public need. These purposes, all of them, some of them, or at least one of them, are the impelling motives, whatever their merit, of all or practically all beginnings in journalistic production; and while the identity of such motives or the form of their application may change with time and experience, the nature of them-the basic principles of public impression or public service for public advancement-can not be altered or abandoned without peril to the enterprise. Rarely, if ever, is a newspaper or other journal established with the idea of profit foremost, and while profit may come, often does come, under competent business management, and it is highly advantageous if it does come, it will almost certainly disappear if it is permitted to become the dominant motive of production and overrides the basic principle of journalistic purpose.

For of all human undertakings a newspaper is most dependent upon sustained public confidence for its existence. And of all human productions the newspaper is most open to public scrutiny. It is by that scrutiny, indeed, that it lives, and it is through the results of that scrutiny that it grows or withers. Each day the newspaper, in its diurnal form, is exposed naked to the world. Itself, complete, with all its faults and virtues, its weakness and its strength, it is spread before every reader, to be approved or condemned upon its open face. If it is good it shows itself, if it is bad it reveals itself. Naturally, being essentially an expression of human personalities, it is never either all good or all bad, but, whichever may predominate, it is discernible. It lays its goods upon the counter, labeled, for the reader's inspection and selection. Whatever purposes it may have, it must express them somehow on its pages or it is utterly futile. It may have ulterior motives, it may, perchance, have sinister designs that it attempts to disguise, but such a policy is invariably fatal. Actual motives cannot be long concealed nor evil designs disguised in the full glare of publicity to which it is constantly exposed. Sooner or later, every newspaper, every journal, must reveal itself for what it really is, and survive or perish on the public verdict.

Nor can a newspaper survive, much less prosper, if there is a widespread suspicion of ulterior motives based upon the nature of ownership or control. "Repeated efforts have been made by men of great wealth and having large interests to buy and conduct newspapers for the purpose of affecting public opinion," said Melville E. Stone, long general manager of the Associated Press, in a talk to newspapermen, "but in almost every instance these efforts have failed. Mr. Jay Gould once owned a daily newspaper in New York, and after a short and inglorious career with it, was glad to sell for a greatly reduced price. Something like thirty years ago Mr. Cyrus Field bought an evening paper to protect his railway interests, and made an attempt to run it. Of course. it was not long before he discovered he could not make the thing work. He then offered to sell me a half interest with the understanding that I should pay for it out of the paper's earnings. I asked who would be associated with me, and he replied that he would keep the other half himself. I was forced to say that without any desire to be offensive I could not buy into the paper at all if he were to remain in it, even with a minority. A newspaper cannot *succeed if it is to be made the means toward an ulterior end.* "①

The proof of this assertion has been repeatedly and expensively proven, and it is true because it is not possible to forward ulterior purposes through newspaper control without revealing them, and, sooner or later, revealing their source, if effort has been made to conceal that source. Newspaper ownership must be primarily concerned in publication for the legitimate and open purpose of journalism, and its control, it would seem from the general experience, must show in its creation. As a rule successful papers have been established and developed by men having no other interests and no other occupation, and most of such have continued as family properties or passed into the hands of others of like singleness of interest, Where, however, such a newspaper, no matter how prosperous or respected, has fallen into what may be termed alien hands, into a control that is not primarily and directly concerned in the production of a newspaper, it has slowly or swiftly declined. Acquirement of control of a newspaper. to forward private ends, by those who are not directly engaged in the work of publication, has usually if not invariably failed to accomplish the purpose. Journalism is a jealous mistress and demands the concentration of the capital involved, as well as the labors in the production, for its own sake, under penalty of disaster.

But a daily newspaper is not only exposed to the world naked every day; it must be sold upon its merits each day, and fully sold. It is the most perishable of manufactured products, perhaps the only one that is literally ephemeral. Born to-day it is dead to-

---

① *The Coming Newspaper*, p. 97.

morrow, its value gone. There can be no stocks on shelves or in warehouses for the newspaper. Each day it must be created anew. and each day must endeavor to sell the entire output. Each day, too, it must be created different. A newspaper must be eternally new. It must submit itself daily to the public judgment on the basis of what that day presents, plus the public confidence it has acquired through continuously and daily justifying its title to public favor. That confidence is an accumulative asset, yet no matter how long it has been developing nor how long it has been maintained, it is permanent only so long as it continues to be justified each day. It can be lost more easily and more quickly than acquired, and once lost it is more difficult to restore than to obtain in the beginning. It cannot betray that confidence without losing it, and it cannot decline in general merit without reduction of sales. It is constantly, daily, before the bar of popular judgment, and must justify with each issue its right to public favor and esteem. If it does not it can neither grow nor stand still; it must decline. It is, therefore, ever confronted with the necessity of holding its own and of disposing each day of that day's creation, under a more searching and continuous scrutiny than is given to any other human production by its consumers.

It follows that whatever the basis of the public support given to a newspaper, whether information, opinion or entertainment predominates as its drawing power, whether it appeals to a class or to the mass, whether its quality is high or low, it must daily justify itself and its price to its particular readers. And whatever the character of its readers it must keep faith with them; it must create and maintain the impression that whatever its faults or however frequent its mistakes it is honest with them, that it is giving in a general way the service for which they pay. If it does not they will cease to buy.

It is essential that a newspaper be conducted for its own interest; it cannot prosper as the tail to any kite. It is necessary that it be conducted for its own interest, because, as has been said, the production of a newspaper requires the concentration of the capital, the brains and the energy involved upon that one purpose, if it is to be made a thing of value to its owners, to its employed creators, and to its readers, and if it is to accomplish whatever aim of legitimate journalism it desires to achieve. For such concentration is possible only where self-interest is complete, and where self-interest may find compensation for its efforts, whether material or moral compensation, or both. But there is abundant ground for the conviction that in newspaper production self-interest and the public interest are not only compatible but identical. For the fundamental principle, as well as the fundamental aim, of journalism must be the public service, and public service in that field of endeavor is also self-service. That does not mean that a newspaper must be an eleemosynary institution, but that it must render concrete service in the supply of reliable information. in the development of intelligent opinion, in the support of public rights, in the condemnation of public wrongs, in the advancement of principles and ideals, and in the use of its power to promote and advance the public welfare generally. In so doing, if it does it well, it lays the most solid foundations for public respect, public confidence and public affection, which are not only the most satisfactory spiritual awards of journalism, but the most certain and the most durable of its material assets.

Chapter III
The Primacy of News

The newspaper is a response to a universal demand and need of human nature for news. It did not create that demand. On the contrary the demand has always existed, and the newspaper is its necessary and inevitable product. Therefore the primary function of a newspaper is the publication of news. News is the essential foundation of journalism. All else, even opinion, important as it is, is accessory. There are, to be sure, journals which deal only with opinion, and their production is in the field of journalism, because it is of necessity based upon news; but they are not newspapers, and they exercise but a single, and secondary, function of journalism. The primary position of news in the operation of journalism would seem to be so obvious as to need no assertion, but the fact that the principle is often obscured warrants the statement of its primacy with emphasis. Not infrequently concentration on particular policies or purposes, for which the newspaper is a means to an end, results in a relative subordination of the news. Not infrequently attachment to "features" that are not news leads to a preponderance of features at the expense of news. Occasionally it is assumed that mere entertainment is the first requisite of successful newspaper publication, and in the application of that theory anything that is presumed to be entertaining to the readers, whether news or not, becomes of first importance, at the sacrifice of correct judgment of the relative value of news in its larger and essential sense.

The importance of legitimate purposes, over and above the mere publication of the news. is not to be disparaged. Accomplishments to which the publication of the news is but contributory indeed may be the dominating consideration. But none the less it is essential to maintain the primacy of the news, because it is the necessary foundation of all accomplishment in the field of journalism. Nor should the value of features that are outside the realm of news be denied. They may have merits in themselves that add considerably to the moral as well as the material weight of the newspaper, as a medium of information, education and entertainment. But it is only as supplementary to the news that they are of advantage. They cannot take the place of news. nor can they be permitted to overbalance the news without loss to the effectiveness of the paper.

Except as a vehicle for the dissemination of news, and, secondarily, of opinion based upon the news, the newspaper, of course, has no excuse for existence, and the life and the interest of journalism therefore centers upon the news. But what is news? It is as difficult to define with precision as is poetry, because it has no conceivable boundaries or limitations. It encompasses all humanity and all nature and partakes of their infinite variety. While in a general sense it refers to recent events, occurrences, happenings, it is by no means confined to them. An event in itself is not news. It is the report of the event that constitutes news, and that report may not be made until years after the occurrence. It is none the less news. Hitherto unreported facts in connection with the discovery of America would be news. It is sufficient that it be fresh information. Nor is an occurrence essential. A crop report is not an account of events but of conditions. Yet it is news. Opinions are not occurrences. yet opinions are often news, and news of the greatest importance and interest. What a man thinks may be as truly news as what he does. "If the newspaper has not the news," says Charles A. Dana,① "it may have everything else yet it will be comparatively unsuccessful, and by news I mean everything that occurs, everything which is of human interest, and which is of sufficient importance to arrest and absorb the attention of the public or any considerable part of it."

Whatever is new in the way of information is news even though the event or the matter to which it refers be old in itself. The mythical mountaineer of Arkansas who first heard of Lee's surrender in 1896 is a fanciful illustration. It was more than thirty years after the event but it was news to him. It was weeks after the discovery of the North Pole before the world knew anything about it. The fact was old but the report was news. In the days before the telegraph, when communication depended upon

---

① *The Art of Newspaper Making.*

slowly moving mails or personal conveyance, news was usually days, weeks or even months behind the events. The development of facilities for the transmission of information that puts nearly every part of the world in practically instantaneous communication with every other part, makes it possible for news to be synchronous with events, and so large a proportion of published news relates to matters occurring the day of publication or the day before publication that the term "news" has taken to itself the sense of immediate freshness, and this immediacy becomes to some extent a test of value, News has thus come to mean almost exclusively reports of the events or conditions of the current day, reports of past events as matters of news becoming exceptional.

But, as Mr. Dana intimates, there is a distinction to be made between news *per se* and news in the journalistic sense. The individual exchanges news with almost every acquaintance he meets. Most of it, however, is of no interest save to themselves or to a small circle of their friends. It may be of great importance to them but of no importance or interest to others. News, in the interpretation of journalism, must have a certain public interest, a measure of public importance; it must be something, as Mr. Dana expresses it, that will arrest and absorb, for a moment at least, the attention of the public, or a part of it sufficiently large to justify consideration. Therefore there is always before the editor not only the question, what is news, which he answers instinctively, without any need for precise definition, even if that could be accomplished; but also the question, what is news from the standpoint of journalism, and in particular from the standpoint of his journal, and to answer this requires the exercise of judgment as well as of instinct, involving a discrimination which must be constantly exercised.

This is a matter for later discussion, but in the consideration of the nature of news one finds not merely infinite and intricate variety, but varied stages of development, with numerous and often dramatic or tragic ramifications. The news of an event may be complete in a single report. All the facts worth presenting are at hand. They are stated, and the event is dismissed. If it has no sequel it passes into oblivion. A large proportion of news, usually of relative unimportance or interest, is of this character Another class of news is composed of reports of occurrences that are complete in themselves, but which form a succession of events, each leading to another. The series may suddenly end, or it may develop importance progressively, an item of a few lines becoming an unsuspected herald of one that fills pages. On a day in 1914 a report went out, over the wires of the world, of the assassination of a prince in an obscure village of a petty Balkan state. In newspapers far from the scene it was given little space, as a rule. There were many events of that day that seemed more important to their editors than this remote tragedy. In itself it was, in fact, of little relative importance. If it had not been for other events to which it led it would have been forgotten in a few days; but the succeeding events, all growing out of this seemingly unimportant item, developed the greatest news that journalism has ever reported, and filled the pages of newspapers the world over for many tragic years. This, to be sure, is an extraordinary example, but such successions of separate but related events of growing importance, starting with one apparently, or actually, small, are frequent, and the one of the World War serves well to illustrate the possibilities that lie in the chonicles of each day's occurrences.

But there is still another class of news which involves processes of a single event which may or may not arrive at completion. The news in this class records successive stages of a progressive event, in which every occurrence and all occurrences from day to day, however important in themselves, are but parts of the whole, steps of a continuing process. An election, for example, is an event which completes a long process of developing events in the course of the campaign, all contributing to a single result and never separated from the end to be reached. A political or social reform movement furnishes news of the same nature, continuous and inseparable, which progresses, or endeavors to progress, to a desired end. A session of congress produces news of a processional nature in which there are many continuing currents of events, currents which may attain completion in achievement or which may disappear in the sands, but which in the process present varied aspects and varied appeals to public interest.

Much news, therefore, and, as a rule, the more important news, is of a serial character, carrying many continued stories of fact, each report a new chapter, each incident a link in a chain. Whether long stories or short they have the attraction of continuity, of expectation, often of surprise, promoting and sustaining interest in the degree in which they touch human emotion and concern.

Each edition of a newspaper is a new creation. And each day's creation is different from that of any other day. Each day brings new material with which to create, material of different pattern, ever varied, never quite the same, and no man can tell what the creation of one day may mean to the future. But through all run threads of continuity which bind each day to every other, making a connected narrative of that complex thing that we call human life, and daily presenting a mirror to life in which it may see itself and know itself.

News, again, may be divided into two classes, one under the head of entertainment, the other under that of information. Such a division can hardly be made absolute, for while there is much news that conveys information without entertainment, there is little news, if any, that is wholly without information. But none the less the two classes exist, governed by the predominance of the one quality or the other, and in a journal designed for general reading, as most journals are, both qualities are of necessity combined. For in formation without entertainment, however desirable and however valuable, is generally lacking in that attractiveness which is essential to sustained public interest and support. There are, to be sure, journals devoted exclusively to the publication of information and their value is not to be questioned, but they are usually class publications, created to supply information to certain special interests and having no attraction to readers not concerned in the particular field so covered. If they are not class journals in the sense indicated their circulation is and must be limited to the comparatively small number of people to whom information unalloyed is the chief object of reading, and thus they also become class journals of a sort.

Human nature, prompted by that instinctive curiosity which no human being wholly lacks, wants to know "what is going on." In very large measure the response to that curiosity is entertainment rather than information. It is news that excites interest but does not edify in any material degree, if at all. It is true that the report of every event, however trivial or unimportant it may be, conveys information as to that event, but it is information that is merely a vehicle for entertainment. The average man, or woman, does not deliberately read a newspaper for instruction or for solid knowledge, but primarily for the satisfaction of curiosity as to the occurrences of the day. His eye is caught and held by that which attracts his interest, and that interest is governed by individual taste, character and association. That which is of absorbing interest to one is of no interest at all to another, but each seeks and finds that which appeals to him, and for the majority the attraction is not learning or knowledge or information in the substantial sense but entertainment.

Therefore the matter of entertainment, which should be distinguished from amusement, is one that cannot be ignored or properly depreciated in the consideration of news. Yet the newspaper would serve no constructive purpose if it confined itself to entertainment. If, as is here asserted, the primary function of journalism is public service, then the primary duty of journalism is the publication of news that contributes to public service, through the dissemination of actual knowledge of public affairs, of public events, and the principles and motives which actuate them; and through the distribution of information of substance and value which is helpful to the individual in his daily life and in his judgment and activities as a citizen. But, in this dissemination, news whose chief interest is entertainment serves a useful purpose in drawing readers who would not be otherwise attracted to the news of real significance. Used with discrimination it is valuable as a means to an end, but it is a subordinate, not a principal.

Chapter IV
The Selection of News

Journalism deals primarily with news of public interest. It is reporter and publisher of news of events, of conditions, and of processes in the development of public opinion and action, that has somehow touched the public consciousness. It does not create news. Ordinarily it does not seek news until a measure of public attention has been drawn to an event or condition. News is created by the events themselves. Before newspapers existed every occurrence of interest became news as soon as it was known to one who could tell about it, however confidentially, and it was spread in proportion to the degree of public interest it excited. If there were no newspapers to-day, events would be reported in some way, by word of mouth from one person to another if no other form of communication existed, and each repetition would add something to the report, decreasing its reliability with the square of the distance, so to speak. Journalism, it is to be admitted, often yields to that weakness of human nature, and distorts or exaggerates news in the telling, but this is a violation, whether it is done consciously or unconsciously, of an elemental principle of journalism.

The task of journalism is to gather and disseminate news that is of public importance, or that has a sufficient measure of public interest, and accuracy is the first principle of action in the performance of that task. In assuming that function of public service it also assumes a definite responsibility for the truth of that which it presents. In the exercise of discrimination in the selection and treatment of news for publication it is, therefore, essential to consider truth as the first requisite. The application of that principle is by no means as easy as its statement, and its difficulties will receive attention in a separate chapter. It is mentioned here merely to link it, as it must be linked, with the operation of editorial judgment in the choice of news to be published.

The problem always before the editor, and renewed afresh each day, is, What shall I print, and what reject? This involves much more than a judgment as to propriety or as to relative values of the various items presented on their merits. Each day he is obliged to consider limitations of space. He has so many columnsavailable for news. The news that comes to him from his various reporting agencies usually far exceeds the space at his disposal. In consequence he is often obliged to reject much that he would print if the room at his command would permit it. And this space is an unstable quantity. It varies from day to day, and not infrequently from hour to hour, as other requirements of publication alter in their needs. And the supply of news is as variable in its volume and importance. To-day may be filled with news; to-morrow comparatively newsless. To-day may furnish a great quantity of news, none of which is of much importance; to-morrow may bring a rush of big news commanding many columns for its presentation. Or, again, a relatively uneventful day may proceed to near its end when news of great importance suddenly demands large space for its telling, requiring the rejection of much that is in type or that has been printed perhaps in earlier editions. There is, therefore, a continuous process of selection and rejection, of adjustment and readjustment to events and to mechanical restrictions.

Moreover, the editor never has before him at one time all the news of the day from which to pick and choose in accordance with his deliberate estimate of relative values. It is coming to him in a flowing stream, and the necessities of time and the limitations of mechanical facilities compel the exercise of his judgment upon a moving current instead of upon a static mass. He cannot see the news of the day as a whole until the printed paper comes to his desk, and then it is too late to exercise his judgment from the viewpoint of the whole.

But notwithstanding these inescapable difficulties under which editorial judgment labors there is and must be discrimination in the selection of news, and it is largely upon the quality of that discrimination that journalism depends, both for its success and for its usefulness. Where that discrimination is wise and its standards high journalism attains its loftiest elevation and contributes most to public serviee. But in the exercise of it there are many things to be considered.

The first principle of selection is the measure of public interest. Interest is the essential quality in the major part of the news chosen for publication, for it is interest and interest alone that makes a newspaper attractive and therefore salable, A newspaper that is uninteresting is unsalable and the greater the public interest in the news it presents the larger its sales. Unless a newspaper is sold, it is worth while to repeat, it is not read, and if it is not read it is of no value for any purpose, howsoever elevated, that prompts its publication. The appetite of the public for news that appeals to its interest cannot be ignored. And the value of any single item of news is to be measured by the degree and extent of the interest it is likely to arouse. That is not the sole test upon which judgment should be founded, as will be shown, and it is subject to limitations, but it is the primary test.

But how is the degree of public interest in an item to be gauged or estimated in advance of publication? The "news sense" is a necessary quality in every successful newspaper man. It is an intuitive appreciation that is partly instinctive and partly the result of experience in discrimination. It is his first and surest dependence. But nevertheless there are elemental principles which he consciously recognizes and applies.

First of all, interest is measured by proximity. We, all of us, are particularly concerned in that which touches us personally, that which affects our friends or acquaintances, that which affects our neighborhood or community. In the case of a fire, for example, the persons most concerned are those who dwell in the building; next in degree of interest are those who live next door and after them those who live in the same block or who see the fire. Those who live farther away or did not see it have still less interest, but all who live in the city where it occurs have a livelier interest in this fire, whatever its magnitude, than have those who live in a neighboring city. Interest in any event that is not national in its scope decreases with the distance from the scene of the event. The death of a President is of practically as much interest in San Francisco as in Washington. The interest in any important act of government that is of national significance is not to be measured by relative proximity. There are certain events, too, that make such an appeal to human interest everywhere that they have an equal news value everywhere. But in the ordinary run of events news value decreases with distance. It follows that local news has a peculiar importance of its own and a certain precedence. Indeed it is largely by community interest that journalism is sustained. Without due respect for, and response to, that interest, comparatively few newspapers could exist, and many of them helpfully and profitably limit themselves to the local field, leaving to others the task of supplying general news. These others, however, cannot exclude local news. Whatever their scope, however world—wide their field, and their newsgathering facilities, they cannot ignore nor depreciate the home news. Community interest is the basis of virtually all journalism, the hub around which journalism revolves, the bread upon the table of journalism's subsistence. The factor of proximity, therefore, has large weight in the judgment of news values.

Local interest, however, may be manifest in an event occurring at a distance. Recurring to the illustration of the fire in the preceding paragraph, the man who owned the house, if not himself dwelling therein, would be as much concerned in the event as those who inhabited the building. And that concern would be as active if he lived a thousand miles away. The people of a certain town, to present another illustration, have invested heavily in the stock of a manufacturing company whose plant is in a distant state, or possibly in a foreign country. The destruction of that plant would be news of local interest, though the event itself would not be local. A prominent citizen of a town is murdered at some place far away from home. The news of the crime is perhaps of as much interest in that town as if the event itself had occurred there. We are all especially interested not only in occurrences in our own community but in occurrences anywhere that particularly involve or concern the people or the welfare of our community.

But happily our interest in the news is not limited to our individual or community associations. While these most intimately and directly concern us, we want to know what is going on elsewhere in the world. And the response to this interest, and its encouragement, constitutes one of the most important tasks of journalism. For the wider the field of our interests the larger the field of knowledge from which we may draw, and the broader our understandings and sympathies. In the selection of such news the principle of relative proximity, or association, is still of importance, interest ordinarily decreasing with the distance, as has been said. There are many and important exceptions to this rule, but none the less it is not to be ignored in the choice of general news. There is, first of all, a regional field about the point of publication to be considered, the territory outside its own particular community in which the newspaper circulates more or less extensively. The news of this region has special claims to consideration, second only to local news, and is judged by much the same principles of relative values. The state as a whole may come within this field, or only a part of it may be included, but in either case the official news of the state, the operations of state government, is of prime importance, having more or less interest to every part of the state and to every individual within it. News of the action or proposals of the federal government is, of course, of particular interest to every section of the country, as a rule, without regard to distance from the seat of government, but there is much news from this source of special local or sectional interest which it is the province of journalism to distinguish. The foreign news that is of most interest, generally speaking, is that which touches or affects our own national relations, whether political, economic or social, but still we may be vastly interested in an event which does not touch us at all, particularly if it has dramatic elements.

But in the selection of all news. whether local, regional, state or national, certain elemental principles apply. The first consideration it should be repeated, is the presumption of public interest and the estimate of the measure of that interest. This is not the only consideration, and it is the duty of journalism to publish much news that is lacking in public interest. But nevertheless public interest is to be desired as to all news, and as to most news it is essential if the newspaper is to have readers. But aside from proximity or personal concern. already discussed, what are the qualities in news that appeal to public interest?

Most active among these is that quality that is termed "human interest," which may be defined as an appeal to the emotional rather than to intellectual appreciation, an appeal to instinct rather than to thought. This embraces the whole drama of life in all its varied and contrasting aspects. Tragedy and comedy, suffering, sorrow and joy, pleasure and pain, virtue and vice, riches and poverty, destruction and construction, are all to be found in the news of the day, appealing to human sympathy, pity, admiration and emulation, to righteous indignation and condemnation, as well as often to baser instincts. At the basis of the sources of human interest, for example, may be placed the universal attraction of a struggle between opposing forces of any character. Life itself being a continuous conflict it follows that conflict not only produces more news but arouses a greater degree of interest, in the generality of mankind, than anything else. Whether the contest is one of skill or of strength, one of principles or of force, whether it is material, intellectual or spiritual, the fight's the thing that appeals most strongly to human interest. The sporting pages and their myriad readers testify to this attraction, and it is this instinctive attraction which draws absorbing attention to the news of a prize fight or a war, of a political campaign, of a conflict between capital and labor, of the trials in court, of moral and religious controversies. Some of these, to be sure. involve intellectual understanding and appreciation, but no contest ever reaches so high an elevation of intellect or spirituality that there is no element of interest in the fight simply as a fight. And that is not an instinct to be disparaged, however low some of its manifestations may be. There can be no progress without struggle, and it is essential to progress that there be a public interest in the struggle from which to draw support for the advancement.

But in the technical sense the term "human interest" is seldom applied to matters of large importance. It pertains more particularly to the sentiments and attractions of social relations, the minor manifestations of humanity or inhumanity, the things that appeal to the heart, to the passions of hatred, avarice, envy or lust, or merely to the curiosity, whether legitimate or illegitimate, as to the condition, movement and conduct of others; things, in short, that may have much of bad or good in them. This class of news is so elemental in its appeal, so attractive to the larger number of people, that the temptation to fill columns with it, to draw special attention to it with big headlines, to seek for it when it does not appear upon the surface of events, to create it by the exaggeration and expansion of trifles, is very great, and in no department of newspaper publication is the privilege and responsibility of journalism so much abused as in this one.

But human interest in the broader sense referred to, and, with limitations, in the more restricted technical sense, is the great reservoir from which journalism legitimately draws extensive support, and thereby contributes to its own influence and value in the public service through the enlargement of the field to which it supplies information and opinion. Moreover, emotional depression rightly directed, has its uses, and is often as important as intellectual impression. At times it is even more important, for many of the greatest advances of civilization have been secured through the sweep of emotions aroused by information. It is no less true that the baser emotions may be aroused in the same way, and it is the task of the conscientious journalist so to discriminate in the selection of news of this character, and so to balance the essential publication of the events of wrongdoing that ever color the news of the day, with the news of the good and with instructive and constructive information, that the total and constant impression of his journal is for the betterment and advancement of society.

And this brings us to the chief function of journalism, the publication of news that has intrinsic value as information, that is essentially instructive through the impartation of knowledge helpful to the individual or the public, that spreads enlightenment as to events of real merit and concern and as to the relations and meanings of such events. Such news may or may not be interesting to the average reader, but the newspaper that fails to supply it in due measure, according to the field it occupies, is neglecting its duty to the public and is evading the obligations laid upon the press generally by the protective laws which give it a peculiar status. Interest, it has been said, is the first requisite of news from the standpoint of journalism. News may have interest without value save as entertainment. Entertainment, however, is an inducement to circulation, and therefore to wider reading of the whole paper, that is not to be entirely neglected. But this class of news is a means to an end, and that end is the larger dissemination of that news of information having intrinsic value which is here under consideration. News of this character may have, and often does have, a public interest as wide and absorbing as the news of mere entertainment. It may, indeed, take first place in the public interest. There is, therefore, news, much news, which has both interest and value, and such news is the best news. But there is also news of importance and value that is lacking in public interest which it is continuously necessary to print if journalism is to fulfill its responsibility to th e public.

"Table-talk", says Herbert Spencer, "proves that nine out of ten people read what amuses them or interests them rather than what instructs them." The truth of this is not to be denied, and the recognition and application of this principle is essential to successful journalism, whatever its purposes. But this does not alter the fact that instruction is as necessary to the nine as to the one;

and for a very great deal of instruction, essential to the maintenance of democracy and to material and spiritual progress along many lines, the newspaper is the only vehicle of knowledge, the only didactic instrument. It is the task of the newspaper to chronicle the events of the day, and it is its duty to give space to news of importance, which the public should know, even though the public lacks interest in it. It is its duty to inform and instruct, to inform and instruct, continuously, as to important matters developing in the news, even in the face of public indifference.

For that is one of the obligations of journalism. And notwithstanding indifference it is never lost motion. For there is always at least the one in ten who seeks instruction, and the aggregate of all of the ones in all of the tens is not only considerable but it generally comprises the most influential elements in any community. In effect, therefore, it is much more than one in ten. But that is not all. The reader who does not seek news of this character and does not want it can rarely escape some impress from it, however slight. To find what he desires he must at least glance at the headlines which call attention to and briefly epitomize the news of the day. Each of these catches his eye for an instant, and from each he has acquired, willy-nilly, a bit of the information it conveys. Moreover, if he recognizes in that fleeting glance that here is something important, something that he ought to know about, regardless of his personal interest, if he is not to appear ignorant before others, he gives more than a cursory reading of headlines to the item, and often finds himself interested where he least expected to be.

But it is frequently the duty, and the pleasure, of the editor to cultivate public interest in news of this nature. Indeed, it is in the stimulation of public interest in matters of public concern that journalism contributes most to public service. Local movements for civic betterment, for example, are largely dependent upon popular support, and such support can seldom be obtained until popular interest has been awakened through continuous newspaper publicity and advocacy. Of still greater importance, though perhaps of less intimate concern to the individual or to the community, is the stimulation of public interest in state, national and international matters, to much of which the public is normally indifferent and requires the urge of persistent information and comment.

In the publication of news, therefore, journalism does not fulfill its obligations, either to itself or to the public, when it makes immediate interest the sole test of judgment in determining what to print. On the other hand, it cannot best serve itself or serve the public unless it makes interest the predominant consideration in such determination. Most news, that is to say, must be selected on the basis of the interest it is likely to awaken at sight in the average reader of the publication, and in that judgment human instincts, human sentiments and human emotions, as well as human intelligence, must be considered and served; but there is much news that it is the duty of journalism to print regardless of public interest.

Chapter V
The Rejection of News

It has been shown that constant and varying limitations of available space compel a constant adjustment of news to meet the varying restrictions of room. Always there is more news than can be printed. Always there must be more or less rejection and condensation. The newspaper does not create events nor do events consider its convenience. It must take events as they come, whether in great volume or less, and adjust accounts of events to the capacity of publication. The item that is rejected to-day might have found a place yesterday. The item that fills a column to-day might have been entirely excluded, or greatly condensed, yesterday. Or an item accepted early in the day may be necessarily rejected before the paper goes to press.

Conditions under which discrimination is exercised are, therefore, different each day and change with the hours. But in reducing the volume of news to fit the capacity of publication that which is of least importance or of least interest is first sacrificed, the effort being to crowd into the paper, not all of the news of the day, for that is rarely, if ever, possible, but the best of the news. In the exercise of this discrimination the editors in direct charge of the news must act upon their judgment of news values, and act instantly as a rule. When doubt arises there may be deliberation and conference, but in the daily publication there is little time or opportunity for this. In nearly all cases immediate decision is essential. In the continuous stream of news that flows through the hands of news editors items are accepted or rejected, given full space or condensed, upon their instantaneous estimate of relative importance or interest, always, however, under the restraints of varying conditions of available space, always subject to sudden and unexpected demands for space for fresh and important news, requiting radical readjustment of all that has been done, and the elimination or reduction of much that has been previously accepted.

In all other productive enterprise the relation between demand and capacity is comparatively uniform, or is at least calculable for a short period of time. The editor is always confronted by unknown quantities. Each day he begins a new creation with no definite knowledge of the volume or the nature of the materials with which he must create. He has, to be sure, the expectation of certain pre-announced events, and he has certain routine sources of daily news, but he does not know what will develop from them nor what they will demand from him. No foreknowledge or prescience can enable him to see through the day, or even through an hour, to make definite calculations in advance. The news, most of it utterly unexpected, may come to him in a steady flow or it may fall upon him as an avalanche. He knows not, nor can he know, what the day may bring forth. All he can be sure of is that he will have more news than he can print, and that he must be prepared for the worst.

And his task differs from other productive enterprise in that he is dealing wholly with ephemeral materials. In the manufacture of a newspaper the principal raw material is news. In all other manufacturing material that which is not used to-day may be used to-morrow or later. It may be perishable, as in the canning industry, for example, but not immediately so. There is no necessity for waste of good stock. But news that cannot be used at once, to-day, is generally worthless to-morrow. Moreover, in all other manufacturing the supply of raw material can be regulated by the capacity of production. The editor cannot regulate supply. He must take each day all the news that comes to him through his established sources, no matter how great-the volume may be. All that he cannot use is waste, unavoidable and irrecoverable waste. And this waste is not limited to the news he rejects upon examination. The uncertainty with which he constantly contends compels the daily sacrifice of much that is accepted and "put in type." Usually every daily newspaper has more news in type each day than it can find room for on its pages and this excess, or "overset," is waste that to some degree is inescapable.

Knowledge of all these conditions is necessary to an understanding of the difficulties under which diurnal journalism labors and must labor. The newspaper must be created within the day. It must be created from materials of varying nature and volume. It must take all the news that comes to it, but it can print no more than its pages will hold. Necessarily, therefore, judgment as to what shall or shall not be printed must be exercised with rapidity upon a flowing current that may be at one moment a gentle stream and at the next a freshet. Necessarily, also, more or less news must be rejected solely because of space limitations, and frequently news that has been accepted and put in type must even then be rejected for the same reason. The fact that an item of news is not published indicates either that the judgment of the editor as to its value, from the standpoint of interest or importance or propriety, warrants its rejection on its merits, or that mechanical limitations compel its rejection as relatively unimportant or uninteresting to the readers of the publication, in comparison with other news of the particular day which is printed.

A veteran newspaperman once said that the judgment of "what not to print" was the supreme test of editorial ability. This may be an exaggeration, but at any rate the negative side of discrimination is as important as the positive. The limitations of space compel a continuous balancing of values for this reason alone—upon a basis of value that may vary with each day or each hour, according to the volume of news. Often the weight of a hair influences the decision for or against publication, but judgment upon each item must be rendered and rendered instantly. To kill an item that ought to be used is as bad judgment as to use an item that ought to be killed. But all this refers to decision in response to the insistent demands of space. Decisions upon the considerations of safety and considerations of propriety are no less essential and no less important.

The newspaper is responsible under the law, and may be held to answer in civil or criminal proceedings, for injury done to persons by untruthful statements affecting their reputation or welfare. The truth is no libel, but the truth is not always clear, nor the means of substantiation certain. Moreover, there is no agreement among legal authorities as to what constitutes a libel. Libel suits are unprofitable even when the newspaper is vindicated, and unless some distinctive public service justifies the risk, no avoidable opportunity for action at libel should be given. Yet it is the business of the newspaper to print the news; that is the primary purpose of its existence; and in doing this it is constantly in danger of unconsciously perpetrating a libel, or of publishing something that prompts an action for libel. No respectable newspaper libels any man with intent. No such newspaper prints a statement reflecting upon the integrity of any man unless it believes it to be true and its publication justified as a matter of news. Both self-interest and right demand that libelous charges, which mean false charges, be avoided. It is, therefore, the task of the editor to scrutinize all news with care and to reject all items containing charges that would be libelous if untrue, if the evidence of truth is not clear, or to eliminate any statements that hold the danger of action at law. There is a general rule of the railway-tram service which applies equally well to this, which is, "in case of doubt always take the safe side," and it was a frequent warning of the veteran editor already quoted that "you never get a libel suit for what you don't print."[①] Considerations of safety require a careful discrimination in the matter of news for the rejection of that which is libelous.

[①]　Joseph B. McCullagh.

But considerations of propriety are also importantly involved in that discrimination. It has been said that there is a difference between giving the people what they want and giving them what they ought not to have. But what is it that the people ought not to have? "There is a great disposition in some quarters," said Chas. A. Dana, once upon a time, "to say that the newspapers ought to limit the amount of news they print; that certain kinds of news ought not to be published. I do not Know how that is. I am not prepared to maintain any abstract position on that line; but I have always felt that whatever the Divine Providence permitted to occur I was not too proud to report." But in practice few editors exercised a finer discrimination than he between news that was "fit to print" and news that was not, recognizing by his own editorial management that there was a distinction, that there were lines beyond which respectable journalism could not go in the publication of news. The printing of news of crime and vice presents a problem about which there has been much controversy, both within and without the field of journalism. This is the class of news to which Mr. Dana referred in the remark quoted, and it was to the contention, from without, that such news should be rejected *in toto* that he applied the view that has become a classical utterance in journalism. And in principle his position is correct.

News of crime and vice should be printed. It is not only proper to print such news but it is a public duty to print it. Crime and vice constitute problems with which society must constantly deal. And if it is to deal with them with any degree of effectiveness it must have knowledge of them, of their nature, extent, and the forces and influences behind them. Public opinion is as important a factor in the prevention, suppression or punishment of crime as in any other field of human activity, but public opinion is never exercised in any field until it is aroused by public events. Crime and vice are menaces to society, and as such must be continuously and actively opposed by the agencies which society creates for its protection. But in the protection of society the law, the courts and the police must have the public support which can only come from a measure of acquaintance with the facts and conditions with which they have to deal. If the news of this character were suppressed the people would be deprived of the only general and constant source of knowledge as to such events.

All social progress is dependent upon information. If we do not know there is wrong, how are we to perceive the need of right? If we do not know what is wrong, how are we to know what to attack? If we do not know the extent of wrong, how are we to arouse and array the forces of good? Right is might only when its eyes are open, only when it sees and appraises the power opposed to it, and only when it is urged to action by the knowledge of the danger that confronts it. To suppress the news of evil would be to blind the eyes of right and to deceive it with a sense of security in the face of peril. Evil always flourishes most in the darkness. It grows upon concealment. It fattens under public indifference resulting from ignorance of its activities. It is essential that the light of publicity be thrown upon it, that its nature, its scope and its habits be revealed. The publication of evil is a public duty and a public service.

But aside from that there is a constant public interest in things evil. Is this interest wrong? It is a universal instinct of humanity. Are we given any instinct that is not designed primarily to promote our welfare? Granting that much evil, possibly all evil, grows out of the abuse or misapplication of instinct, is it not true that our instincts normally operate for our good? "The active part of man," says Newman, "consists of powerful instincts. Some are gentle and continuous, others violent and short; some baser, some nobler, all necessary." The proper use of our instincts never causes evil; it is only their abuse that creates it. And this abuse is a departure from normality. We are interested in crime because it is abnormal, and this interest, in reference to society in general, is self-protective. It makes evil conspicuous, impresses it upon our consciousness and our imagination, compels us to examine it, to realize its wrong and its dangers, and constantly to fortify ourselves against it. Here and there the associated instincts of imitation or acquisition may make interest an influence for evil in certain individuals, but generally speaking its result is an abhorrence of, and an antagonism toward, evil.

If this were not so goodness would long since have perished from the earth. For mankind has ever been attracted by the abnormality of evil, by its departures from the innate standards of right, by its violence, its tragedies, its catastrophes. The literature of all time is permeated with it. It runs like a crimson stream from the beginning to the end of the Bible. It is the theme of poetry, of fiction, of the drama, of opera, and history is crowded with it. "The reign of Antoninus," says Gibbon, "is marked by the rare advantage of furnishing very few materials for history, which indeed is little more than the register of the crimes, follies and misfortunes of mankind." If interest in crime and attention to crime promoted crime, evil would have triumphed over good long ago. But, on the contrary, that interest has always operated to restrain evil by revealing its character, its dangers to the individual and to society as a whole, and its usual results in sorrow or punishment.

But, it is said, the publication of news of crime and vice has a bad influence on the young. For reasons already stated that may be denied, unless in the presentation of the news evil is cloaked in such garments as to make it enticing. That there is wrong in the world every child discovers very early in life. The attempt to conceal from youth the existence of evil has never succeeded. On the contrary, the effort invariably throws a glamour over evil and arouses a curiosity to know more about it. Somehow, sometime, somewhere, youth learns the nature and extent of evil, and this in some measure it must learn before it is fully equipped for the battle of life. The important thing is that it be taught to distinguish right from wrong, and to realize clearly that right is ever good and that evil, however garbed, is always bad, and always destructive, It is true that the publication of crime acts now and then upon the instincts of imitation, but this occurs as a rule only when there is lack of that knowledge, or where there is evil association or inherent disposition in the direction of wrong; and given any one of such conditions criminality is likely to result regardless of publication. As a general proposition neither youth nor maturity would profit by the elimination of legitimate news of crime and vice from the press, while the public would be deprived of information that it needs for self-regulation and self-protection.

But unquestionably there is news of crime and vice that ought not to be printed, news that is of no consequence from the standpoint of public welfare and that appeals only to a prurient curiosity. And there is news of public importance from which salacious details should be stricken in the interests of elementary decency. The newspaper should go into the home, where it should be welcomed and treasured. Much of its value and much of its influence depends upon the domestic confidence it inspires. Therefore it should be clean, in spirit and in speech. It is its duty to present the events of the day, and many of them may be ugly, but ugly news can be reported in clean words. And ugly news when presented should be unmitigated. There should be no gloss upon it to make it attractive. Its importance should not be exaggerated by conspicuous position, by the volume of space given to it, or by its garment of words. It may, indeed, be important enough, however ugly, to justify such position and such space, but the warrant for that should rest upon its news value from the standpoint of respectable public interest and of the public right to know the facts. Valuable public lessons are frequently given by the exposure of whited sepulchers, but service and not response to salacity should be the motive of publication and should govern the manner of its presentation. To devote columns of space to a crime or a scandal solely because of its prurient attractions may be momentarily helpful to circulation but it stains the character of journalism and lowers the newspaper in public esteem, by which it suffers loss in its best asset.

The service of journalism in the publication of news of crime and vice is to reveal them in their ugliness, to show their magnitude and their danger, and this is a real and a necessary service. Upon journalism, however. rests the responsibility of discriminating between what is of service and what is not, between what is of proper public interest and what is not, between what is of value as legitimate news and what is a mere response to lewd curiosity, in short, between what is fit to print and what is not fit to print, judged by its own standards of fitness. It cannot wholly eliminate such news and perform its duty. On the other hand, it cannot let itself become a purveyor of sewage without offense to decency and a lowering of public confidence in its rectitude.

The newspaper is to no little extent a guardian of public morals through its constant revelation of wrong. With most people the fear of publicity is a more potent influence in behalf of uprightness than fear of the law. There are, to be sure, men and women who care little for exposure except for its results in the application of the law. There are some, indeed, who glory in the notoriety that comes from the publication of their offendings. But generally speaking the great majority of men and women fear any publicity that is to their discredit or shame, and to all such it is a wholesome preventive of misdoing. To those who have no such sense of disgrace the fear of the law should be made more potent by the increased certainty of punishment. That, of course, is a problem for the administrations of the law. But journalism might well contribute to the fear of the punishments of the law by giving more attention in the news to the convictions of offenders against the law. A crime is committed of sufficient interest to justify publication but not one that arouses great public interest. The case pursues its slow way through the courts. The evanescent interest in the crime disappears and when conviction results no word of it appears in the press. This is in accord with the rule of interest, but a valuable public service could be rendered if convictions for criminal offense were more generally reported.

It is the business of the newspaper to print the news, as has been repeatedly said, yet "suppression of the news" is one of the most frequent complaints against journalism. It is, however, one of the least justified, if any sinister significance be given to the charge. All the problems of discrimination that have been under discussion involve rejection of news for many proper reasons. And the failure to print news for which there is no room, or which in the judgment of the editor ought not to be printed, whether because it is unimportant, unfit, or relatively uninteresting to his readers, is the only basis for most of the complaints that are made, usually by people who have been disappointed by the absence from the paper of items in which they were personally interested. It is the duty of the newspaper to print the news that is important; it is to its own interest to print the news that is attractive to the public, within the limits of propriety that have been mentioned. But what is important, either actually or relatively, and what is attractive, are questions that must be decided by the individual judgment of the editors of each newspaper, acting always of necessity under the pressure of time and space. There should, however, be no exterior or ulterior influence on that judgment. it should be founded solely upon the conception of news values in general, and, in particular, of its values for the section of the public which the newspaper serves. While a considerable proportion of news is of manifest importance to all newspapers alike, or to all alike in a country, region or community, there is much news whose importance depends upon the nature and purposes of the publication and the character of its readers. That is to say, some news that is of value to one newspaper may be of no value, or relatively little value, to another. The editor must consider not only the comparative importance of news of general interest but the particular interests and tastes of his territory and constituency. Naturally, too, there are differences of judgment among editors, resulting from individual variations of temperament, association and opinion, which cause one editor to reject an item which another would print, or to put in a few lines what another would present with prominence. These, however, are but the differences of personality that give variety to life, as they do to journalism, which is an epitome of life. But whatever these differences, the conscientious editor—most editors are conscientious and all should be-holds the publication of news that is of real importance to his readers to be a paramount duty.

Chapter VI
Truth in The News

The essential element of all news is truth. If news is not substantially true the label is as false as the report. For news is the report of events that have occurred, or of conditions that exist. If the events did not occur, if the conditions do not exist, the report is untrue, and being untrue, is not news. Fiction, fabrication, falsehood, may appear in the guise of news but it is an imposture. The imposture may be deliberate, or it may be the result of deception or misunderstanding, but in either case the product, being wholly false, is something for which language provides many terms but "news" is not among them. The test of the reality of news is truth.

And the measure of truth within the news is the test of its quality. Absolute truth is a difficult attainment in any communications from man to man, whether by word of mouth, by letter, or by publication in book, magazine or newspaper, unless it is limited to a single and bare statement of fact. One man tells another that John Smith is dead. This is absolute truth, incapable of denial or modification. But when he begins to relate the circumstances of death the chances of error increase with the extent of the details. Even if he is a witness of the circumstances leading, to the death, the limitations of observation, of knowledge, and of memory render absolute and complete accuracy in every detail of his narration a difficult accomplishment. And this difficulty is increased when he has his information from others, however careful they may have been, and however truthful he may desire to be.

This difficulty and these human limitations are constantly in evidence in the courts, where numerous witnesses testifying to their knowledge of the same event vary widely in their testimony, though every one may be perfectly honest. Here are men and women under oath to tell the truth, the whole truth and nothing but the truth and conscientiously striving to do so, yet as a rule failing in some degree in the fulfillment of that obligation. Any two, three or four men seeing the same occurrence will tell different stories about it, varying with the points of observation. the nature of the impressions made upon each individual mind, and the personal qualities which make one a better observer or narrator than another. Each one may be entirely trustworthy, and yet no two can tell exactly the same story as to every detail, though all may agree as to the major facts. All of them may be telling the truth notwithstanding the apparent differences, but it is more probable that all of them are wrong in some degree.

Now if these natural limitations and obstacles to the communication of truth are effective to an extent in preventing the ascertainment of the absolute truth, "the whole truth and nothing but the truth," when the will to literal and exact truth is uppermost, they are still more effective where they are influenced by habits, desires or purposes that are against accuracy of statement. The habit of exaggeration is a common failing. The desire to impress the hearer of news with its important or dramatic interest is almost universal in the bearers of news. But not infrequently there are persons who for purposes of their own seek to give false impressions by describing an event, or phases of it, with deliberate untruth. Some or all of these influences are likely to cloud the water in the well of truth.

Upon journalism rests the responsibility for the dissemination of news of public importance and interest. If, then, truth is the test of the reality of news and the measure of truth within the news is the test of its quality, it is by that test that journalism should be judged and must expect to be judged. Absolute truth is an ideal that is often no more attainable than absolute sanctity in human personality, but the nearer the approach to it the nearer will it come to the consummation of perfection. Yet in the collection and publication of the news journalism must work with the human agencies and deal with humanity under the limitations of human qualities that make the ascertainment of truth one of constant difficulty.

News is obtained locally by the reporter and afield by the correspondent and the news agency. The newspaper is, first of all, dependent upon the character and ability of its own news gatherers. A reporter, for example, is directed to "cover" a certain event. It is his duty to obtain the essential facts and embody them in the report he makes to the office or prepares for publication. Upon him rests primarily the responsibility for truth and accuracy. If the editor accepts the report and prints it the responsibility is transferred to, and assumed by, the newspaper. In local news the editor generally has some knowledge of the matter to which the reporter is assigned, and if in doubt may take steps to verify the report. Still it is largely upon the reporter's skill in ascertaining facts and his conscientious care in reporting that the editor must rely.

In news outside the local field he is entirely dependent upon the character of the correspondent. Whatever the correspondent sends him, whether upon direct order or otherwise, he must assume it to be true, and use or not, according to his judgment based upon its face value. Seldom is it practicable within the tune available to verify a "story" that comes over the wires, Yet the newspaper is just as responsible for the news sent by a correspondent as for that which it obtains through the local reporter, and the newspaper's accuracy. and, what is more important, its reputation for accuracy, rests almost entirely upon the quality of its newsgathering representatives. Errors, to be sure may be discovered by the copy reader and corrected, and doubtful statements may be eliminated. But none the less both veracity and accuracy depend upon the character and ability of the men who cover the news.

And these men, or women, are rarely witnesses of the events they report, unless the events are expected. If they are not witnesses, most if not all the information they obtain must be secured from others, in which they must contend with the human limitations in accuracy of observation and of statement. If the event is expected and the reporter is at the scene, he may not see or hear all that occurs and is again dependent upon others to piece out the information he has acquired by personal observation. And even if he sees or hears all that happens he is still a human being with more or less of the human tendency to error. In all consideration of truth in the news these limitations and circumstances should in fairness be taken into account. And there are other elements of error. News when obtained must be transmitted to the newspaper, must be put into writing, and the writing put into type. All these processes involve the possibility, or probability, of mistakes, that may be of no consequence or that may be serious; mistakes that may or may not be discoverable before publication.

But none the less it is the task and the duty of journalism to obtain and to publish the news. and it is not performing this task efficiently, nor doing its duty to the public it serves. unless its reports are substantially true. The measure of service which a newspaper renders to its readers, whether that service be collective or individual, depends absolutely upon the accuracy of the information it supplies. And the measure of public confidence in the integrity of the newspaper must depend upon the constant evidence of the essential truth of the news it presents. There are, therefore, two compelling reasons for making the standards of accuracy as high as possible. It is true that a publication can attract readers by pandering to the sensational at the expense of truth, by expanding a little fact into impressive fiction, by appealing to the sense of the monstrous by exaggeration or by utter falsehood, but such a publication is not a newspaper, in the proper sense, and the process of its creation is not journalism, in the proper sense. For falsehood is not news, fiction is not news, and the publication that deliberately and habitually presents untruth in the garment of news is not only an imposition upon the public but an offense to journalism. The measure of truth within the news is the test of journalism, and upon this test alone can it justify its existence or merit public respect and confidence.

Truth, however, in relation to news. needs definition. News primarily is a report of an occurrence or a condition. If the report presents the salient facts accurately, the concrete facts, it is presenting the truth. For news deals fundamentally with events, with things that have happened or are happening, that are susceptible to observation, and that may be verified, as any other concrete facts, by the evidence of the senses. The truth it presents is the truth of narration. It is not concerned, in the first instance, with the interpretation of events, although, as a secondary function, it may delve into causes and purposes and report opinions of others bearing upon them. The newspapers own interpretation of events belongs in the companion field of journalism wherein truth may take on other definitions and incur obligations of a larger scope, The specific province of the news is to present the account of an event with substantial accuracy. When it has done that it has told the truth and fulfilled its purpose to the best of its ability. Nor can it properly be charged with untruth if it fails to narrate every phase or every detail of the event. How much or how little it tells, may depend upon the extent of the facts obtainable, upon the judgment of the editor as to the relative importance or interest to his readers of the event, or upon the space he has available. If the essential facts are accurately given, however concisely, the truth is presented.

But the claim of truth can hardly be justified if the news is not reported impartially. It is as important to the standing of journalism, and to its effectiveness, that news be unbiased, as it is that news be true, If journalism is to provide the people with information upon which public opinion is to be based it is essential that its news of events be uncolored by prejudice, that facts be presented fairly as well as accurately. This does not mean, where issues of any sort are creating news, that each of two sides should be given the same space, or that where an event concerning one side is reported search should be made for counterbalancing material affecting the other. News being a report of events is subject to events, not superior to them. Somebody must do something, or something must occur, of public interest or importance, before there is any news to report, and the space given to this news depends upon its intrinsic value, whatever may be its bearings upon the controversy. It may be that one side is creating news day after day while the other side is creating none, and the one side is in consequence being given continuous publicity, whether to its advantage or disadvantage, while the other side is given little. In a great strike, for example, the unions initiate the event which brings the controversy into public notice, and they, being on the offensive, as a rule, create more news than the employers, who are on the defensive. It is the strike and the events growing out of the strike whatever they may be, rather than the internal merits of the controversy, that constitute the news. It is not the function of the news to try causes, but to present the facts that are revealed in occurrences touching the public interest. Statements of leaders on both sides convey information, helpful or otherwise, to public understanding, and are classed as news because of their relation to events and the light they may cast upon them. How far a newspaper may permit its columns to be used as a forum for public discussion, however, depends upon the circumstances of the event, the degree of public interest aroused, and its actual public importance. It may invite and warrant particular investigation by the newspaper to bring hidden facts to light, or to make clear those already revealed. But all this is but incidental to the publication of the news of the overt acts of the occasion, a subsidiary or auxiliary service that may or may not be undertaken, inasmuch as no obligation rests upon the newspaper to go beyond the salient facts of occurrences. It is not the task of journalism, in its news department, to interpret or to justify events, but to present the events themselves, as fairly, impartially and accurately as possible, leaving the expression of opinions to its editorial department, or to statements from persons or groups of persons whose views may have news value in connection with a specific event. Opinions may also find a proper place m the reports of special correspondents whose names are signed to their correspondence. Their task is often not only to report events but to endeavor to interpret them. Their views, however, are individual, and should be so understood.

The degree of accuracy with which an occurrence can be reported depends upon the completeness of the event, the accessibility of the facts and the dependableness of the sources of information. A completed event may be observed as a whole. The facts in relation to it are within definite boundaries. Certain information is to be obtained, and if obtainable from personal observation or reliable authority, the report, like the event, may be complete, and with a near approach to absolute truth. In the case of a fire, to take a simple example, the event is complete when the fire engines withdraw from the scene, if there are no criminal complications. The identity of the owner of the property, the estimate of the loss, the extent of the insurance, are details easily obtainable as a rule. The item is finished, the important facts are presented, and there is nothing more to be said. But suppose there are evidences of arson. Then the fire is not a completed event. It is a continuing event which may develop aspects of much larger importance and interest in what follows the fire than in the fire itself. The bare fact of the fire may be reported with as much accuracy as if the event were completed, but the criminal circumstances bring in elements of uncertainty. The evidences of crime may be direct or circumstantial, or both direct and circumstantial, and the less accessible and verifiable the facts the greater must be the liability to error in the news, just as the trial court finds greater difficulty in ascertaining the truth where the truth is obscured. The news-gatherer is not trying a case, but he is seeking the facts that are necessary to the presentation of the news, and he is confronted with the same obstacles with which the court must deal, without the powers of the court to extract evidence, and with a responsibility for libelous error that does not rest upon the court.

All this is stated, not to excuse untruth, which when deliberate is inexcusable, nor to excuse error, which is excusable only when unavoidable. Its purpose is to show that facts are not always simple and to be acquired merely by going and getting them; that they are, on the contrary, often complex, often obscure, often difficult of access and identification; that often they have different aspects when seen from different viewpoints by different observers, and are therefore conflicting; it is to show that the newspaper has no magic wand to reveal the truth, but when it is veiled or concealed must make the best of the information obtainable and seek laboriously for more facts where the importance of the event warrants, even as the courts and other fact-finding agencies of government must do; it is to show that truth in the news, even as in these authoritative agencies of law, is a relative quality, sometimes reaching the absolute, but more often merely an approximation Rarely, in law or in news, is there such a thing as "the whole truth and nothing but the truth." Approximate truth is, because in the nature of things it must be, sufficient for the purposes of everyday life. No one claims that even history, wherein facts have been weighed and scrutinized and analyzed through years of inquiry and deliberate study, is more than an approximation to truth. How then can it be expected that the news of the day can be perfect in its accuracy and completeness, can be always, if ever, "the whole truth and nothing but the truth"!

Yet the newspaper that understands its mission and realizes its responsibility as a purveyor of news, places accuracy at the head of professional virtues and seeks constantly to attain it. To what extent does it succeed? To what extent can it succeed. It has been said that the degree of accuracy depends upon "the completeness of the event, the accessibility of the facts and the dependableness of the sources of information." The factor of completeness has been briefly discussed. Where facts are readily accessible and the sources of information reliable, newspaper reports are, as a rule, substantially accurate. "Wherever there is good machinery of record the modern news service works with great precision. There is one on the stock exchange, and the news of price movements is flashed over tickers with dependable accuracy. There is a machinery for election returns and when the counting and tabulating are well done, the result of a national election is usually known on the night of the election. In civilized communities, deaths, births, marriages and divorces are recorded, and are known accurately, except where there is concealment or neglect. The machinery exists for some, and only some, aspects of industry and government, in varying degrees of precision for securities, money and staples, bank clearances, realty transactions, wage scales. It exists for imports and exports because they pass through a customhouse and can be directly recorded."① Formal acts of public officials, decisions of the courts, passage or rejection of measures by legislative bodies, movements of shipping, military and naval orders, results of sporting contests-all such matters are, generally speaking, correctly reported. All that is accessible, that is definite, that is authoritative, that is complete in itself, may be, and usually is, recorded in the news with precision. There is, to be sure, the chance of error in transmission, in editing and in typographical composition. but relatively such errors in such material are infrequent. And news of such character constitutes the staples of journalism. They include in very large measure the information of utility and of value that the public requires.

But if newspapers printed nothing else they would be dry reading. It is written that man cannot live by bread alone. Bread and water, in sooth, are fundamentals of diet, but limitation to them is considered one of the severest punishments in penal institutions. Human welfare as well as human taste requires a variety of condiments, some of which contribute only to pleasure. And the same variety of desires and of needs controls the operation of

---

① Walter Lippman, *Public Opinion*.

journalism. The newspaper, therefore, cannot confine itself to recorded facts, but must spread upon its table reports of an infinite variety of events for the accuracy of which it must assume entire responsibility, though the facts may be difficult of access, though they may be only partially obtainable, though the event itself may be incomplete. And within this vast field of news where there is usually more or less uncertainty and indefiniteness, where ascertainable facts are clouded by the presumption of other facts at the moment inaccessible, the newspaper is expected to present the news as precisely as possible, to present the truth as completely as the truth may be obtainable at the time the report is made. It is in this field that journalism finds its hardest tasks, and in this it wins its greatest victories. It is in this field particularly that it needs to strive constantly for accuracy and greater accuracy to the full extent that truth is attainable in each instance.

And this brings us again to the means of attainment, the quality and character of the reporter, and his training for the work, the quality, character and training of the copy reader, who handles the reports. "How few there be," said Sir Philip Sidney long ago, "that can discern between truth and truth-likeness, between sham and substance!" Yet such discernment is as essential to the good reporter or the good copy reader as that necessary, fundamental instinct of journalism which we term the "nose for news." It is only by stressing accuracy, fidelity to truth above all things, and the necessity of discernment between truth and truth-likeness, upon the foundations of news-gathering and newspreparation that journalism can approach the ideal of truth to which it must never cease to aspire.

Chapter VII
Getting and Handling The News

Getting the news is, of course, the fundamental task of journalism. Events do not consider the convenience of the press, nor do they report themselves. News, it is true, travels by its own momentum, and the more important the event the swifter the flight. But in its spread it inevitably accumulates error and exaggeration. The newspaper cannot accept the news that comes to it on the winds of rumor save as a call for investigation. Getting the news, in the journalistic sense, is getting the facts, going direct to the seat of the event and by observation and inquiry ascertaining the salient truths of the occurrence as accurately as may be possible in the particular circumstances. Whether the event is at home or abroad, whether the instrument is the reporter or correspondent under the direct control of the newspaper, or the news agency which gathers its own reports for distribution to many newspapers, the principle of action is the same. The newsgatherer must go to the scene and get first hand information of the event.

The newspaper reporter is, first of all, a fact-finder. When he is assigned to cover an event, or some phase of an event, his task and his duty are to get the facts. But that usually involves much more than going after a bundle and bringing it home. It calls for the exercise of qualities of the intelligence, the intuitive discrimination between what is important and what is not, between the essentials and the nonessentials; and the reasoning which deduces presumption from indication and thereby brings out vital facts that are obscured by circumstances or design. The smallest routine assignment may contain possibilities of great news, if the discernment to distinguish news is present. What is termed the "nose for news" is more than instinct, although it may seem to be instinctive. It is a quality of the intelligence, of the mind, which, though a gift of nature, needs to be associated with reason and developed through experience, as any other natural talent, The faculty of the artist, who sees beauty where others see nothing attractive; of, the musician, who discerns harmonies not distinguished by the duller senses; of the poet, who finds in the primrose by the river's brim divine secrets not revealed to those to whom it is but a flower—all are endowed with that superior quality of discernment and distinction which in the reporter is the news sense, and which is essential to the highest success m any department of the profession of journalism. For journalism is fundamentally an art, an art of expression, and even as the colors of the painter must be mixed with brains, so the ascertainment and the presentation of the truths of daily events must be directed by both the intuitive and reasoning qualities of an intelligence adapted to this art if it is to depict life truly upon its ephemeral canvas.

A painter cannot be made of one who has no sense of color; a musician cannot be made of one who has no sense of harmony; nor can a journalist be made of one who has no sense of news. But having the intuitive sense, or talent, one is not, because of it, a painter, a musician or a journalist. Poets, it is said, are born, not made, but like many sayings this is not true. Poets are born *and* made. There is no such thing as a born poet. The quality is born, but the poet is made by life, by experience, by training, by study, by education, all combining in the exercise of the quality It is only through experience and application, indeed, that the quality is disclosed and developed. This is no less true of the journalist. There is no such thing as a born reporter, or a born editor. The news sense is essential, but that faculty must be cultivated by training and experience, must be developed by study, education and observation, which alone can make the journalist, "Journalism demands of its practitioners the widest range of intelligence, of knowledge and of experience, as well as natural and trained powers of observation and reasoning." [1] To the natural powers must be added the acquired powers in some degree, even at the beginning of journalistic practice, if the news is to be intelligently and accurately reported. Nor can the element of character be ignored. For if the measure of truth within the news is the test of journalism then it is obvious that the practice of the profession

---

① From preamble to *Canons of Journalism*, adopted by the American Society of Newspaper Editors, April, 1923.

must be founded upon character.

All this is said to emphasize the importance of the qualities, natural and acquired, that are essential to news-gathering and publication upon the high plane of truth to which all reputable journalism aspires. The progress of journalism toward and upon that elevation depends very largely upon the character and capacity of the news-gatherers and news-handlers, to whom is intrusted the primary and fundamental tasks of getting the facts and preparing the reports for publication. It is useless for editors or publishers to entertain ideals of perfection if the quality of the sources of production is unconsidered. No degree of care, of energy or of intelligence at the editorial desk, or in the managerial office, can make a dependable newspaper unless the reportorial and copy-reading staffs are dependable. That they are largely so is one of the distinctions of journalism, and one of the chief causes for its great advancement. The annals of journalism are filled with deeds of heroism and devotion by news-gatherers in search of truth, not to be excelled in the ranks of any other profession, and the loyalty, intelligence and activity of unrecorded thousands of such workers, in the field and at the desk, have constantly promoted and ennobled the Fourth Estate. It is, however, no disparagement of these to say that there is not enough of them, not enough of the right kind. Journalism is an institutional profession, and as the institution grows the demand for competent workers increases, while the supply, from the casual sources so long depended upon, decreases. But the demand is insistent and it calls more and more, not only for men and women in greater number who have the gift of nature that adapts them to the profession, but who have a foundation of education, general and specific, and some measure of preliminary training. It demands, that is to say, not only more workers but workers who are better equipped *at the beginning* of professional practice. Granting the advantage of training through practical experience in actual newspaper work, the fact remains that opportunities for experience in all the elementals decrease with the increasing complexity and specialization of that work, particularly in the metropolitan field. General and technical education as a preparation for professional practice is demanded as much by circumstances as by the growing necessity for a sound and dependable foundation for professional dignity, standing and progress.

The schools of journalism, in short, must be increasingly relied upon as the sources of supply from which the ranks of journalism are to be recruited Following the same road over which other and older professions have traveled it must eventually reach the point where for its own protection it will set up definite standards of qualification for admission to practice. But in the meantime it cannot, without loss, fail to demand the best obtainable material for its service, in the quantity needed. To accomplish this it is essential to encourage the aspiration to journalistic service in the youth of the land, and to impress the conviction that it is an honorable and desirable calling, whose direct awards are attractive and one which offers exceptional opportunities for individual usefulness and achievement. The best agency for such impression is the school. Educational preparation is as requisite to success in journalism as in other professions. Newspapermen are not to be made in schools, nor are lawyers or doctors, but properly conducted schools may lay a foundation of useful knowledge, impart the elements of professional practice and inculcate professional ideals, all of which are requisite to the best results in journalism, and must be acquired in actual practice if not obtained beforehand. Moreover. the school may be helpful in establishing a professional spirit, in laying the groundwork of professional ethics, in fixing fundamental principles within the callow mind. Only by practical experience, hard work and continuous study, added to natural fitness, can a proficient journalist be produced, and these are essential to proficiency, and success, in any profession; but preparatory education is not less useful in this than in other callings, and journalism as a profession is as fully worthy of the respect which the demand for such a preparation implies as is any other.

Getting the news, getting it with substantial accuracy, depends then upon the quality and character of the news-gatherer. It is his task, first of all, to get the facts, the salient facts, of the event to be reported. It can never be too strongly impressed, not only here but in every newspaper office, that fact is the fundamental element of journalism. But fact alone is but the bare bones of the news. It is the essential material of production, and the highest skill, the most intelligent observation, discernment and discrimination, the most ardent and arduous labor, may be necessary to its acquirement. It is in the attainment of fact that one finds the romance of journalism, the contacts with events and with people that give it its most fascinating experiences, the spice of adventure that appeals to some of the finest of human qualities, the elation of achievement over dangers and difficulties, though much of it, it is true, is but the drudgery of routine labor. But the fine art of journalism lies in the presentation of the facts, in the preparation of the news for the eye and the interest of the reader.

Two men reporting the same event may so differ in their qualities that the report of one will be dull and unattractive, the report of the other be bright and interesting. The difference may lie in the superior news sense of the latter, the greater ability to recognize and grasp the phases of the event that appeal to human interest in the larger degree, or that merely serve to adorn the salient facts and thereby make them more attractive. But it may lie wholly in the superior power of narration. in the gift of clear, coherent and connected statement, in the better selection and arrangement of words, in the more effective emphasis of the details that impart interest. For, although getting the facts is the primary essential, and often calls for the exercise of intellectual and instinctive qualities of a high order, it is still but the collection of the materials of production, and the value of the materials, in the news sense, depends very largely upon the character of the narrative that is produced from them. And it follows that the value of the newspaper depends no less upon the manner in which it presents the news, upon the degree of the art of expression exercised in the narration of events, upon the interest which that art gives to the news; provided, however, that neither truth nor proportion is sacrificed in the expression.

It is the task of the newspaper to get the news. It is fundamental, first of all, that it get the facts of the news. It is fundamental, second, that it tell the news as interestingly as the circumstances of each event warrant or permit, consistent with the truth. But there is a third fundamental, and that is the judicious selection of the reported news in relation to the available space, the careful discrimination between events, and the adjustment of reports in relation to their importance, the construction of suitable headlines, and the proper arrangement of the news in the printed page, which constitute the final editorial processes in the making of a newspaper. The matters of selection and adjustment have been discussed in previous pages, but these processes are grouped here to bring into view one of the most important fields of journalistic activity, the preparation of the news for the press.

The news may be thoroughly gathered, the facts ascertained and the reports excellently written, but unless copy readers and news editors are competent much of the value of that labor may be lost. To know where, to what extent, and how, to use the blue pencil, to catch inaccuracies of statement, to discover assertions likely to be libelous, to recognize in an obscure item the possibilities of important news. to discern the relation of a report in hand to events occurring at another place than its source, to grasp at once the import of an item and write a headline that will correctly express that import—all these are tasks that call for the exercise of broad knowledge, intelligence and judgment. To the copy desk comes the news of the world in all its, variety of character and meaning, to be judged upon its merits in relation to the needs and capacity of the particular newspaper. The reports come from hundreds or thousands of sources, the work of many men of many minds and diverse abilities, some of it poorly done and requiring rewriting, some of it profuse and redundant, requiring condensation, some of it of little importance to one section. While possibly of great importance to another, some of it calling for expansion with other related facts in the possession of, or obtainable by, the editors. Whatever it is, or wherever it is from, the copy desk is the point where the chaff is winnowed from the wheat and the grain made ready for the readers' daily bread. If there is inadequacy, inefficiency, incompetency at this point the product is defective. No degree of excellence in the reportorial staff, or of editorial direction of that staff, can overcome the handicap of an inefficient or insufficient copy desk.

Nor can accuracy be maintained if accuracy is not demanded at the copy desk with the same degree of insistence as in the reportorial and correspondence departments Accurate reports may be made inaccurate by incompetent or careless handling in the office. The same sort of workmanship may take the point or interest or vitality out of a good report, or give to a rewritten report aspects quite different from the original. A conservative statement of facts may be made grossly exaggerated, or a well-constructed story robbed of continuity or coherency by injudicious editing. But, on the other hand, a competent copy-handling force promotes accuracy, gives coherency where it is lacking, strengthens the weak points, corrects errors of diction, often by a deft reconstruction gives life to a dull narrative without sacrifice of truth.

The copy desk is the finishing board, the polishing block, in the process of newspaper making, and the responsibility that rests upon it is very great, for its proper conduct is essential to the making of a good newspaper. And its competent workers fill a high place in the profession of journalism, though they are ever anonymous. They do not have that direct contact with life that gives attraction and often thrill to the task of the news gatherers, but there are compensations in the kaleidoscopic view of varied events that unrolls before them as a continuous moving picture; in the news that passes through their hands, and in the excitement of the sudden break of big news of which they are among the first to hear. Nor is there anywhere in journalism more loyalty, more devotion, more intelligence or more knowledge shown than at the copy desk that is properly manned. The desk has its heroes, its geniuses and its artists no less than the field.

In the duties of the copy desk no task is more important than the "building" of headlines, It is an art in itself, one that demands peculiar qualities for its best expression. The headline, in American journalism, has two functions : first, to indicate the nature of the news; second, to draw attention to the news. In the exercise of these functions it serves another purpose, that of denoting to the readers the relative importance or interest, in the judgment of the editor, of the various items presented. Up to the second half of the last century the headline in America was nothing more than an indicator, a reticent indicator, of the purport of the matter. A single line was generally considered sufficient for even the most important news European journalism still holds, as a rule, to this view and practice, though less conservative in its announcements than formerly. The American practice grows out of the urge to awaken interest in the news presented. rt aims not only to tell the reader the general subject of the item but to present and to emphasize its leading features. It frequently gives him in effect a concise synopsis of the event with its maim details accentuated.

But whatever the merits of the system it creates two serious difficulties. First, the more extensive the headline the greater the possibility of error. No amplification can alter the fundamental fact that the essential purpose of a headline is to tell the reader what the item is about, and it fulfills its purpose only when it indicates to him, clearly and correctly, the nature of the news it heralds. If it does not do this it is not a good headline But obviously the more a headline is expanded the greater the chance of misstatement and misrepresentation. A four-line head, each line presenting a distinct phase of the item, offers twice as many opportunities for error as a two-line head. The second difficulty is that the desire to attract attention to the item is a constant temptation to an exaggeration of its merits, to make it seem more important than it really is. The headline that does not thunder in the index is an evidence of commendable restraint upon the part of copy reader or editor.

The system has also an unforeseen effect which is not desirable, and which presents a problem of a somewhat serious nature to journalism. The purpose of the headline, as has been said, is to indicate the nature of the item and to arouse interest in it. But the headline too often appears to tell the story, and in itself conveys sufficient information to satisfy the hurried reader. The result is that a great many people get the news from the headline, or think they do, and are content. One of the purposes of the headline is thus defeated. It does not tempt to a perusal of the item, and it makes perusal of any part of it except the head unnecessary for the superficial reader. The effect of this casual skimming of the headlines, so common a practice in America, is not good for journalism, nor is it good for the public. It is not good for journalism because it makes so much of its labor go for naught. The reports of events are written to be read. The time and the labor, the intelligence and skill, applied to the collection of news are expressed in the finished articles that are laid before the reader. In each of them the writer has endeavored to present the collated facts in such detail as to give the reader a clear understanding of what has occurred, or at least of what is known as to the occurrence. But the care for accuracy, for clarity in construction and for effective diction is wasted effort for the reader who finds enough information to satisfy him in the headline.

It is not good for the public because the public value of a newspaper lies in the information it supplies as a foundation for public opinion. If public opinion is to be intelligent it must be founded upon information to the fullest degree obtainable. The meager knowledge to be drawn from headlines cannot create intelligent opinion. It is not the aim of the headline to supply knowledge but to direct attention to the report which contains the collected information. The headline, however amplified, can but point to the salient facts, and only a few of these. No one can get a clear understanding of an event from a headline, however accurately it may indicate its character. No man can acquire a knowledge of the contents of a book by reading the index. The title and the index can but tell him the nature of the book. The newspaper headlines are but the titles and indexes of the news it contains, and knowledge of public events and movements is not to be acquired from them. But if in the effort to attract attention and arouse interest they tell so much that the reader thinks he has sufficient knowledge of the event without perusal of the matter to which they point, they have failed in their purpose, from the standpoint of journalism, and have deluded him into the belief that he has obtained the news when he has only read an index to the news.

The primary function of the headline, as has been stated, is to indicate the nature of the news. That is a convenience for the reader to which he is entitled. There are few who care to read all that a newspaper contains and such thoroughness of perusal is expected of no one. But by glancing over the headlines one may discover the news that naturally appeals to one's interest and taste, and, if one pleases, ignore all the rest. But if a headline is so constructed as to arouse a justifiable interest in an item among those readers to whom the subject itself would but slightly appeal, if at all, it has fulfilled its secondary function. It has to that extent enlarged its field of interest; to that extent it has added value to its service. For interest being the essential source of circulation, it is quite important that the interest it arouses be wide as well as deep. The more thoroughly a newspaper is read by the mass of its readers the better it is for the newspaper and the better it is for them—if the news is worth while. Therefore the awakening of a legitimate interest in an item by means of the headline is a proper function. That it is an essential duty of journalism to stimulate public interest in public questions is not to be denied. Indeed much of the public value of journalism is created by the exercise of that duty. And in arousing that public interest the headline may be helpful in no small degree. But the effort to awaken interest in any news by means of the headline must in every case be justified by the nature of the item. To arouse an interest by a headline that is not warranted by the item is to betray the confidence of the reader, to lower his opinion of the editorial judgment and to weaken his respect for the value of all headlines in the paper. There is never any excuse for overstatement or overemphasis in a headline. It gives the reader a false idea of the news if he reads only the headline, and he immediately realizes its exaggerations if he reads the item. In the one case the reader is injured, in the other the newspaper.

For the same reason it is particularly important that the headline be accurate. It is one thing to misrepresent the news by overemphasis in the headlines, it is another to misrepresent the news by inaccuracies of statement which the most conservative of headlines may contain. Exaggeration is usually, though not always, deliberate. Inaccuracies of statement that are not exaggerations are usually unconscious mistakes, resulting from haste, from lack of understanding of the real import of the item on the part of the copy reader, from lack of care in making the facts in the headline accord with those in the item, or from misuse of words in the headline. It is often the case that a single word wrongly used will give the reader an entirely false conception of the nature of the news. It is not infrequently the case that a headline makes a statement that is absolutely contradicted in the item. Not a few headlines betray the complete ignorance of their writers as to the matter they caption. These are as a rule errors of incompetent, careless or hasty workmanship, committed unconsciously. There is none at the copy desk, or anywhere else, so competent and careful as to be without error, but none the less there is nothing that so reveals the efficiency of a copy staff as the general accuracy of the headlines and their harmony with the news they introduce. The reader is entitled to assume that any headline correctly indicates the nature of the news it heralds, and it is essential to the establishment and maintenance of his respect for the character of the newspaper as a whole that this assumption be constantly justified, as completely as it is humanly possible to justify it. Truth in the headlines is just as important as truth in the news.

The editorial process in the newspaper publication leads from the headline to the "make-up" the arrangement of news and other reading matter in the pages. This is something more. indeed much more than a mechanical task. It is in no small degree the work of an artist, one who has the sense of balance, of proportion and relation that is essential to the architect. It is an editorial task because a knowledge of the nature of the materials and of their comparative importance and value is necessary. It is in this operation that the varied products of journalistic enterprise and labor in numerous fields are assembled and visible form given to that personality which daily meets and greets the reader. To the director of the make-up is intrusted not only the face and dress of the newspaper but its heart and soul wherewith to present to the public a living body whose readers will recognize its identity at a glance and welcome it as a friend. The character of a newspaper, as of a man, is, or should be, deeper than surface appearances, but it is none the less much to be desired that it have a clean and pleasing face and a dress that, like the garb of a gentleman, proclaims his quality without attracting undue attention to itself. All personality is more or less influenced, both subjectively and objectively, by looks. An attractive countenance not only invites acquaintance but may be, without vanity, a source of satisfaction to its possessor. It is, at any rate, an indication of character, and not less so in a newspaper than in a man. And equally is dress an influence in the impression made by personality, and upon the personality itself. "Dress," says an old writer, "has a moral effect upon the conduct of mankind. Let any gentleman find himself with dirty boots, old surtout, soiled neckcloth, and a general negligence of dress, and he will in all probability find a corresponding disposition to negligence of address." The truth of this is apparent to all, and so too is the contrary fact that clean raiment is a mighty help toward clean conduct. A well-dressed newspaper, one, that is to say, whose appearance is clean and attractive to the eye, is not only a constant pleasure to those who read it but a constant inspiration to those who serve, however humbly, in its creation.

But the make-up involves not only the general appearance of the paper, but the arrangement of the news to suit the convenience of the reader and the display of news for the promotion of sales. One of the values of newspaper acquaintance is the familiarity of the reader with its customary arrangement of the news. He knows where to find what he particularly wants and the knowledge is one of the influences that hold his allegiance to the paper which he favors. The selling function of the make-up is limited almost wholly to street sales, and, in its application, to the first page. This page may, indeed, be termed the show window of the newspaper. Here it exposes to view its most attractive goods, its most important, or most interesting, news. To choose from the events of the day those which should merit the greatest attention or arouse the greatest interest, is the task of the director of the make-up, and this involves a quick and accurate judgment of news values and of the tastes of the readers. The first page, therefore, is at once a test of editorial judgment and a test of the editorial artist, in the quality of the news selected and in the arrangement of the news to please the eye of the regular reader, as well as to attract the attention and immediate interest of all who are possible buyers. This last is of more importance to the afternoon paper than to the morning paper, as the former ordinarily derives more of its circulation from street sales because the time of its publication is more favorable for such sales. The afternoon paper, therefore, places more emphasis upon its first-page features, cries its wares somewhat louder, as a rule, than the morning paper, but in both the aspect of the first page has an influence upon sales.

There are thus several considerations involved in the make-up of the first page and not infrequently they conflict. If that page is regarded as the face of the paper it is highly important that its appearance be respectable if the paper as a whole is to inspire respect, Its countenance should express character, and there is, indeed, no better selling quality for a newspaper or a man than character revealed in the face. It is an influence that establishes permanent relations, if the body and soul prove that the countenance has not lied. This view of the function of the first page makes the impress of its general appearance the first consideration. It aims to attract constantly, by a well-balanced arrangement of news that gives a pleasing effect to the whole page regardless of the quality of the news it contains. It is essential, of course, that the quality justifies the appearance, but there is no little value in the impression made by the mere looks of the first page of a newspaper made up on that principle. One likes to read a newspaper whose face looks intelligent, friendly and clean, and one is likely to stand by such a newspaper when it is found that its looks are not deceiving.

If, however, the first page is regarded primarily as a show window; if, that is to say, the commercial influence predominates in the make-up, then the arrangement of the first page for sales purposes is the first consideration. This theory of the function of the first page is incompatible with the other. It is not mainly concerned with impressing its character upon the reader but with extracting pennies from his pocket. Character it may have, but the make-up is at no pains to reveal it. The make-up, on the contrary, labors to assemble the most startling items under the most startling heads, and character, if it exists, is concealed or misrepresented by the countenance. In the effort to increase street sales by striking the eye with sensational appeal, good appearance is sacrificed to immediate effect upon the beholder. That sales are made by this is not to be doubted, but the standpoint is not an elevated one. and the practice tends to promote exaggerations in headlines and in the news that in turn tend to lower the public confidence in the reliability of journalism generally.

If, however, selling appeal is a secondary rather than a primary consideration in the make-up, the show-window idea need not be inconsistent with the idea of character expression. For a show window may be in itself both an affirmative expression of character and an inspiration to confidence as well as to sales. To realize the truth of this it is only necessary to consider the development of the mercantile show window. It was at first, and for a long period, merely a place to display the nature and variety of goods for sale within. The custom was to crowd as much into the window as it would hold. Little attention was given to arrangement and so much was placed within the space that the mass impression was a collection of junk whose details were virtually lost unless time was given to inspection. There was little to attract or to please the eye in such a show window and nothing to create respect for the institution responsible for it. It has largely disappeared with a better understanding of the psychology of salesmanship, and is to be found only in back streets or in backward communities where merchandising methods are primitive. But this type of show window is presented in the first pages of many newspapers, whose practice it is to pack as many items as possible into that page, each with a bold heading designed to convey the idea that it is important. The mass effect is confusion rather than attention. The selling influence is thereby diminished, if not lost, because no particular detail in such an assemblage can be impressed upon the eye with the force that is possible when a fact that is really impressive is presented in a way to make it stand out, separate and distinct, even as a great tree challenges attention when standing alone but is unobserved in a forest.

So, with a clear understanding of this, the modern mercantile show window displays a few things so attractively that detail is emphasized to the eye, and the selling appeal thereby materially strengthened, while the composition as a whole is pleasing to the taste and inspires respect for the institution responsible for it. The character of the institution, in short, is indicated to a degree by the character of the display, which at the same time promotes sales. It has been said frequently in this discussion of journalistic principles that the first essential of a newspaper is that it be salable. Therefore, any honest device that tends to increase sales without lowering the newspaper in public esteem and confidence is to be considered as a legitimate contributor to that essential. From this viewpoint the show-window theory of the function of the first page is not to be condemned if it is made subordinate to the impress of character on the eye of the observer, the impress which alone can create and maintain continuous favor and faith in the mind of the reader. Any fine window display of a mercantile establishment is a lesson in the fundamental principles of first-page arrangement. Therein is shown the same judicious selection of items most likely to appeal to public interest, the same balance and artistic grouping, and the same avoidance of crowding, that are the primary qualities of a first page that combines good taste, dignity and character with a strong and continuous selling appeal.

Chapter VIII
Personality in the Newspaper

It was said at the beginning of this discussion that news and views constituted journalism. News alone is but one of the two functions of journalism. Views alone lack the primary element on which journalism is founded. A newspaper without opinions or a periodical without news may be accepted as within the field of journalism but neither can be said to cover that field. Opinion, as has been shown, is a constant associate of news Whenever and wherever news of interest is imparted it stimulates thought, if the mind is capable of thought, and the resulting expression of opinion, if the time and opportunity for expression are present. Give out a bit of news to any group of men, or women, and if it interests them a discussion will follow, and varied views of its nature or import will be voiced. Moreover, if the news is important and the one who bears it commands respect, his opinion of its meaning will be desired. He will not only be questioned for details but will be asked what he thinks about it. In the communication of events between men news and views are inseparable and they have always been so.

Journalism, being a product of the interest in events which is characteristic of all humanity, is incomplete unless it combines both information and opinion in the service it renders in response to that interest, for both are essential to its satisfaction. This has been recognized almost from the beginning of journalism, though for a long time the dissemination of opinion in connection with the news was repressed by authority, and it was not until the battle of the press for the freedom of expression was won that public opinion began to develop the power which has since made it the controlling influence in the progress of mankind.

A newspaper without opinion is at the best but a purveyor of current information. It creates a merchandise of events which it presents for sale in the public market. Great as is the importance of the public service thereby rendered, and fundamental as it is as a function of journalism, it is none the less true that it is essentially commercial in its nature. The newspaper so limited is simply a commodity, an insensate product of a manufacturing process the raw materials for which are drawn from the ends of the earth. It may, like the phonograph or the radio, collect and disseminate thought as well as information, but having no thought of its own it is without inherent vitality. It is thought and the expression of thought that breathes the spirit of life into a newspaper, that makes of it a living, moving, speaking entity, with a mind and a will and a purpose, a personality in every sense of the word.

Personality is as essential to the newspaper as it is to a man. Man cannot escape it. No man, however colorless, is without it.

It is, indeed, himself, the identity of which he is conscious and which distinguishes him from others. It is not a superficial quality resting in face or form though face and form contribute to its revealment. It is something within, which thinks and wills and prompts to action, and though we may identify a man to the eye by his physical appearance, we do not and cannot know him save as he gives expression to that which is within him by speech or conduct, save as he somehow reveals his thought. The countenance, the manner, the dress, do not constitute personality. They are but outward indications of the inner self, which alone is personality.

So it is with the newspaper. It is not possible to create a personality out of merchandise. The newspaper, like any other product, may be identified by its appearance. Its face and dress, the character and arrangement of its news, may, it is true, indicate personality, but they cannot constitute personality. It is only thought and the expression of thought in the editorial columns of the paper that reveal the existence of a mind and a soul within it, without which there is no such thing as personality anywhere. The news may be said to compose the body of the newspaper, that part of it which shows to the eye lineaments, form and garments, but the editorial page is its soul. If the soul is not there the body is but a lay figure.

And this personality, this mind-encompassing soul, inevitably reveals its quality to the eye. the ear and the understanding by its constant self-expression In revealing its thought the newspaper reveals its character and its intellectual capacity. Whatever may be the surface indications of its countenance it is the editorial page that shows what it really is. Many a man has a weak and cowardly soul beneath an imposing exterior, and a powerful mind often exists within a fragile body. Surface appearances may or may not be misleading. But whatever the exterior the personality within discloses itself through its own expression It is the same with the newspaper. It presents itself for public inspection daily Its face and dress may indicate character or the lack of it, but the real test of its character, the actual revelation of its personality, is to be found only in the expression of its own thought.

Superficially the newspapers have perhaps lost something in the way of individual distinctiveness. To a large extent they present much the same news in virtually the same form. Typographical differences, though always existing, are somewhat less marked than in the past. The great development of general news-collecting agencies supplying identical matter to numerous papers contributes to uniformity of content. The growth of syndicate service is an important influence to the same effect. This, however, is the usual and almost inevitable result of large production in any field of manufacture. Both the process and the product of the process tend to certain uniformity, to become more or less standardized along particular lines This is due to improvement of methods or design whereby a better product may be obtained, whereby the cost of production may be lessened, or whereby volume of production may be largely increased. The first automobiles for example, varied greatly in appearance and in mechanical device. Gradually, however, as experience established definite principles of construction they began to assume a relative uniformity of mechanism and design until distinction became rather a matter of quality than appearance, though enough differences of appearance have been maintained to permit ready identification, But this approach to uniformity increased the value of the product as an instrument of service and facilitated its larger distribution.

The influences that have contributed to a similar trend in newspaper production have enlarged its sphere of usefulness, have increased the facilities of manufacture and the field of circulation, and have given to the newspapers and therefore to their readers a larger news service than any individual newspaper, with perhaps a few exceptions, could otherwise obtain. That they have tended to establish some uniformity of appearance is not to be unduly deplored in the face of these facts. Distinctiveness or individuality in a newspaper is not a matter of aspect. Personality alone gives distinction to a newspaper, and although personality may be indicated by appearance it is not in the appearance that it exists. All men are much alike. They have the same form. All, with some unfortunate exceptions, have the same number of arms and legs, attached to the body in the same thoroughly standardized way. The features of all are "made up," to use the newspaper term, according to a fixed and virtually invariable rule of place and balance. Even in dress, a matter that is subject to his will, there is comparative uniformity. Yet who will undertake to say that individual distinctiveness is any the less apparent? There are enough differences of form and aspect among men for the purpose of identification, and that is all that is externally necessary. It is the soul and mind within, the personality revealed in thought and word and conduct, that in reality distinguishes one man from another. And so it is with the newspaper Influences that tend to uniformity can never go so far as to make all newspapers exactly alike. There are and will always be differences in appearance sufficient for the purpose of identification, differences in quality, manner and conduct that reflect in some degree the personality, differences in the form and direction of individual initiative which no trend toward superficial similarity can entirely remove.

But while these influences have been at work in the progressive development of the newspaper in its physical aspect, these and others have effected a change in its inner self. It has become more and more of an entity, more and more of a living being; having its own rather than a borrowed vitality. We often speak of the passing of personal journalism, sometimes with an air of regret. That personal Journalism had its values and attractions is not to be questioned. But the newspapers in that day were not, and could not be, personalities in themselves. Each was but a medium of expression for the human personality directing it. It registered what Greeley said, or what Dana said. It was the man who spoke, not the newspaper, and the man rather than the paper impressed the public mind. Personality was no more embodied in a newspaper than in a book or a pamphlet.

But as newspapers have developed in size and circulation, as their fields and activities have increased, they have of necessity become institutional, and individual human personality has given place to a composite personality which rests within the newspaper itself. People no longer speak of what Greeley or Dana or Raymond said, but of what the *Tribune*, the *Sun* or the *Times* says. For it is no longer a man who speaks. It is the voice of the paper that is impressed upon the public mind, revealing its own thought, its own character, its own personality. It is no longer a mere insensate instrument of expression, it has in effect become a self-conscious, self-expressive ego, a living being that is respected and loved, hated and feared, regarded with contempt or with admiration, according to the nature of the personality it discloses

Chapter VIII   Personality in the Newspaper **225**

and its impress upon the individual mind.

And this personality, resting within the newspaper itself, rather than within any individual man, acquires, or may acquire, a larger, deeper and more pervasive influence upon public opinion than it could ordinarily obtain as the mere medium of individual expression. There is something about this institutional personality that gives its thought and its utterance a weight and impressiveness that no person who contributes to that utterance can give to his own words as an individual opinion. John Jones, the editor of the *Eagle*, is no oracle among his acquaintances. His views, personally imparted to them, are received with no more attention than is paid to those of others among them. His intelligence, his knowledge, may be respected, but he is John Jones, one of themselves. But when the *Eagle* speaks the effect is different. It may be that it expresses the same opinion that Jones has given to them personally, and they may know that it is in reality the voice of Jones, but they are seldom, if ever. conscious of Jones when they read. It is the *Eagle*, the newspaper, that now speaks to them, expressing a personality of its own, making an impress of its own, exercising an influence of its own. as a distinct entity; and that personality, if worthy of respect, is respected as Jones could never be, and its opinions. accepted as conclusive when those of Jones personally would not be. Jones, indeed, may pass, giving way to Smith, and Smith in turn to Brown, without affecting the personality of the *Eagle* which seems undisturbed by human mutations, unmoved oy the incidents of death. Constantly renewing its vitality with fresh blood it holds the possibilities of immortality within itself and need succumb to nothing so long as that blood is untainted and kept red with corpuscles of abounding life.

Chapter IX
The Editorial Page

There is, then, such a thing as personality in the newspaper. a living entity that exists quite apart from the human personalities that sustain it. It cannot, of course. be independent of them. It draws its life from them, even as every man draws the means of subsistence from others, but it is none the less a living being, with a body, mind and soul of its own. And the editorial page is the tongue which expresses the thought of this personality and thereby reveals its character, its conscience and the measure of its intelligence.

With this conception of the newspaper the editorial page cannot be regarded as a mere feature, an incident of journalism, whose value or importance is open to question, something which may be neglected or even dispensed with. It is, on the contrary, essential to the functioning of journalism, in the complete sense, essential to the expression of that personality which, without expression can hardly be said to exist, and which alone, by its expression, can give distinctiveness and vital individuality to a newspaper. It is here that it discloses its personality. It is here that it reveals what it thinks about things, and in the revelation exposes its intellectual capacity, its standards of right and wrong, the quality of its judgment, its likes and dislikes, its prejudices and passions, its sentiments and its aspirations, its sincerity or hypocrisy, reveals, in short, its own character. It is here that it speaks to the public in its own voice. preaching, propounding, interpreting, advocating, condemning, utilizing that audience which it acquires primarily by the dissemination of news to spread knowledge of the meaning of public events, to arouse and maintain interest in public affairs, to promote activities for the public welfare and to defend principles of public and private righteousness It is here that it makes its personality felt in its impress upon public opinion, and renders that service to the people, to liberty, democracy and civilization which is the primary reason for its constitutional protection.

This being true the character and quality of the editorial page is a matter of the first importance in journalism. The personality it reveals must be one that justifies a measure of public respect and public confidence if the newspaper as a whole is to be fixed firmly in public esteem and public support. It would be far from the truth, however, to assert that the value of the newspaper is measured by its editorial page. People as a rule do not buy a newspaper for its editorials, however high their quality There are exceptional newspapers whose editorials form the chief attraction to the larger number of their readers, but such cases are rare and when they exist there is something lacking in the balance between news and editorials. There are people, many of them, to whom the editorial page of any paper, if it is a good one, has first place in their interest, but they are in the minority. Generally speaking people buy a newspaper for the news, interest in opinion being secondary. And this is the natural and fundamental order of precedence. Events necessarily precede the study of events. There must, that is to say, be an occurrence before there can be any opinion about the occurrence. There must be a condition to arouse thought before there can be any occasion for the expression of thought. Our first concern as human beings is in events, in what is going on-in the news. The primary function of a newspaper is to present the news, and primarily it is to obtain the news that people buy it. In a very large degree, therefore, they measure the value of the paper by the extent and quality of its news service.

But interest in the news stimulates thought about the news and the reader who seeks an understanding of the meaning and import of events turns to the editorial page for such enlightenment as he may find there. And in so doing he turns from consideration of a product to a direct communion with a personality that is the spirit within the product. He realizes that the news he has been reading, whatever its value as information, is but a statement of facts, a record of current events. But that which he reads, when he refers to the editorial page, is an expression of thought from a living personality, one that talks to him daily from this page, one that he feels he knows though he may never attempt to visualize it, and for which he may acquire, through that continuous communion, a respect and attachment that are the foundations of loyal support. Such feelings are not, and cannot be, created by news, by records of events. There is nothing in a page of current chronicles to inspire affection for the paper on which it is printed or for the publication of which it is a part. The manner of its presentation may be pleasing to the eye, the customary truthfulness of the record may develop a confidence in its accuracy and it may be highly valued for its general trustworthiness. But these are the impressions of the inanimate, such as may be made by any worthy product. From the editorial page, on the other hand, a personality speaks, and the sentiments it arouses are personal in their nature, the sentiments of the heart and mind that are created and actuated by personal relations. Happy and fortunate is the newspaper with a personality that inspires and justifies the esteem, the trust and the affection of its readers. It is to them more than a sheet of paper; it is an intimate friend, a trusted counselor.

But how is that confidence and attachment to be Won? Manifestly by the revelation of the same qualities that inspire confidence and attachment in all personal relations—integrity, sincerity, intelligence, humanity. There is no essential difference between character in a newspaper and character in a man. Newspaper personality is, indeed, but an embodiment of human qualities within paper instead of flesh. It is of necessity created out of human personality, composite though it be, and inevitably takes the form and character of the human attributes, good or bad, or good and bad, which enter into it. It is, moreover, subject to the ordinary human limitations. However it tries it cannot be inerrant or infallible, nor can it maintain itself in the rarefied atmosphere above the human level. It is of mankind and inevitably presents the variations of weakness and of strength to which mankind, even at its best, is subject.

We do not ask nor expect perfection in our friends or in those to whom we look for counsel, and we have no right to ask it or expect it in the newspaper to which we give our friendship and support But we do ask and expect of friend or counselor that he be true, that he be faithful, that he be dependable, that he be honest; and we have a right to ask and expect of the newspaper personality with which we daily commune that it have, within its human limitations, the same qualities of heart and mind. It is but necessary to think of the newspaper as in effect a human being in order to understand the qualities it must have if it is to obtain and maintain public appreciation and confidence. And the vocal organ of this being, the instrument with which it makes these qualities known, is the editorial page. Therefore, the newspaper, in its editorial columns, is not merely presenting something to read, not merely furnishing comment on events, not merely interpreting the news, not merely expressing or guiding public opinion; it is revealing its own mind and soul, its own intelligence, its own conscience, its own standards of right and wrong.

All of this argument leads to the assertion that the primary and fundamental function of the editorial page is self-expression; not, let it be understood, the self-expression of any individual contributing to the page, but the self-expression of the living entity that is embodied within the newspaper. The editorials may be the product of one person or of a number of persons; they may present the opinions of one man or the conclusions of a conference of editors; but it remains true none the less that whatever is said, or by whomsoever written, becomes the thought of the newspaper when it is printed. The reader as a rule does not know from what individual pen an editorial comes. or by what joint and concurrent cerebration its conclusions may have been reached. If he does happen to know he rarely thinks of the connection. It is to him not the voice of any man or any group of men. but the voice of the newspaper, and that, indeed, is what it is in reality. It is no illusion And this voice, if it has merited his respect and confidence, impresses him, as the spoken voice of no individual contributing to its editorial columns in his own personality can ever do. It is not that it is anonymous. Anonymity in fact lowers the weight of any utterance. In reality it is not anonymous. It is the *Sun* that speaks and as the voice of the *Sun* it is recognized by the reader.

In the production of the editorial page, therefore, there is involved, as the primary task, the creation and maintenance of a personality that will speak with the voice of the newspaper, that will express the consciousness and the conscience of the newspaper, and that will reveal a character worthy of the respect and the confidence of the readers. The breath of life must be breathed into it that it become a living soul. How is it to be accomplished? By no tricks of artifice or of legerdemain; only by putting into it the best that is in its creators. And if the character of the newspaper personality is to be made one that is worthy of public respect it is essential that there be the qualities of such personality in those to whom the task of creation is intrusted. No man can put into an editorial page what he himself does not possess. He may, to be sure, often preach what he fails to practice. In that more or less frequent failing all humanity is akin. But unless the editor has a mind and a conscience. unless he himself has intelligence, judgment, truth and sincerity, which are the fundamental requisites of character, he cannot put these qualities into the newspaper; and only to the extent of his possession of them can he impart them to that other personality for which he is responsible. Whatever he lacks in these qualities is bound to be revealed more or less clearly in the page he directs He can through this channel make the paper greater than himself, because of the larger sweep of its personality, but it cannot escape from the limitations of its maker.

It follows, therefore, that the higher the character of the editor and the editorial staff in charge of the editorial page the higher will be the character of the newspaper personality which they create and sustain, and the greater will be the respect which it commands, provided, of course, that they are so earnestly devoted to the task that they put the best of themselves, the best of which they are capable, into the creation. It follows also that the editorial page is no place for the novice in journalism, nor for the superficial application of talents however experienced. Its direction is not to be safely entrusted to one lacking maturity of mind or of judgment, which, however, by no means implies gray hairs, nor to one lacking in broad knowledge of public affairs or a comprehension of the obligations of journalism in its relation to public affairs. The direction of the editorial page of a newspaper is a serious task, an office of the highest responsibility, not only to the newspaper service but to the public, and the character and qualities applied to it should be the highest obtainable.

Chapter X
Editorial Responsibility

It is essential to the development of the individual newspaper, and the profession of journalism generally, that editorial responsibility to the public be recognized and realized by editors, particularly those in charge of or contributing to editorial pages This assertion does not mean that the sense of responsibility should be a heavy burden on the mind or the conscience. The man upon whose shoulders it weighs painfully is out of place in the editorial chair. Rather should it be accepted as a privilege and a joy, an opportunity for service and for accomplishment. But whatever the feeling as to the responsibility, it must be realized if the newspaper is to serve worthily, if it is to fulfill its function either in the guidance or reflection of public opinion. and if the newspaper man himself is to give to the paper and to the people the best that is in him.

For the editorial office is essentially a public office, though the public may never see or know the editor. Daily he speaks to the public in regard to matters that are of public concern. And he speaks not to a few hundred and but now and then, as does the preacher, the lecturer or the politician, but to thousands and even to hundreds of thousands every day throughout the year. His hearers are not limited, as theirs are, to those who can get within the sound of his voice, There are no limitations upon the reach and pervasiveness of his speech save the extent and the spread of the circulation of his newspaper, and even that is not a boundary, for every newspaper has many readers that are not numbered among its subscribers, and in particular instances what it says is often reprinted by other newspapers thereby reaching other and more distant circles. The editor, therefore, addresses a greater audience than is possible for any other public speaker and he speaks to his audience daily. Moreover, he speaks far more directly and intimately, for he enters the homes, sits by the fireside, as it were, and talks perhaps to the whole family. He goes into the offices and the places of business and addresses the merchant, the manufacturer, the banker, the salesman, the clerks and the industrial workers. He goes into the country and talks to the farmer. Every street car and every passenger coach feels his presence. Wherever there is a man or a woman, no matter how far retreated, there he may find a hearer. The ubiquity, the pervasiveness, the continuity and the persistency of the newspaper voice give it the means of an influence attainable by no other agency in the creation, guidance or expression of public opinion or public sentiment.

"In this and like communities," said Abraham Lincoln,

"public sentiment is everything. With public sentiment nothing can fail, without it nothing can succeed. Consequently he who molds public sentiment goes deeper than he who enacts statutes or pronounces decisions. " Lincoln was careful in his choice of words, and it is to be presumed that he used the term "public sentiment" deliberately as a broader or more comprehensive term than "public opinion. " Opinion, as Webster defines it, is an intellectual judgment. Sentiment includes opinion and feeling or emotion, whether the one or the other preponderates. "The word sentiment, agreeably to the use made of it by our best English writers," says Dugald Stewart, as quoted by Webster, "expresses in my own opinion very happily, those complex determinations of the mind which result from the cooperation of our rational powers and of our moral feelings. " Sentiment, that is to say, is, in this sense, a combined product of the mind and the heart, and it is probably true that what is ordinarily, almost universally, called public opinion is in reality public sentiment, something that partakes of feeling as well as thought.

But however that may be, whether we term it opinion or sentiment, it is undeniable that in the modern world it is the most potent of influences, and he who molds it, in whatever degree, is invested with a privilege and a responsibility. That the press has a large influence in molding public opinion is not to be questioned. That it has a larger influence than any other agency may ba asserted without much fear of successful contradiction, And this not because it is endowed with superior intelligence or prescience-often, indeed, it is unhappily inferior in these qualities—but because it gives continuous and persistent publicity to events and to thought-about events. The news itself is an important, a fundamental, factor in the creation of public opinion. It is upon this that virtually all opinion as to current affairs is founded. But people as a rule have little time or inclination to analyze or to study events, to seek for themselves an understanding of their import or relation. Each man and each woman, speaking generally, is too deeply absorbed in his or her occupation or individual interests, to devote much thought or attention to the personal interpretation of public events. The opinions of those who have taken time to study them, to think about them and to express their thoughts, are likely to be accepted, if they do no violence to individual prejudices or to one's inherent sense of rationality. And this is particularly hue if the source of the opinions has become a customary source of reliance, whether through mere habit or through a developed respect for its judgment.

So it is that the newspaper, expressing its thought daily through its editorial page, exercises a constant influence upon the opinion of its readers, whether they are conscious of it or not. The press, says Charles A. Dana, is a powerful agent. It takes men when their information is not complete, when their reasoning has not yet been worked out, when their opinions are not yet fixed, and it suggests and intimates and insinuates an opinion and a judgment which oftentimes the man, unless he is a man of great intelligence and force of character, adopts as something established and concluded. It is a power and influence which is exercised over the minds of the people, often without any knowledge or any criticism on the part of the person who is subject to it. In that way there is a real and remarkable power of the press, and it is a power that inspires me always with a very solemn sense of responsibility. Here you take the mind of a man, and, without his knowing it, you shape it, you direct it, you send him along a road which he does not know, and, very often, which you do not know."

Such a power as this is not one to be used carelessly. The possession of it lays upon the press a very great obligation that cannot be fulfilled unless the responsibility is realized and earnest effort made to exercise it for the public good. It is an obligation that rests upon all newspaper ownership and direction, but particularly upon the editor or editors who are entrusted with the task of expressing the thought of the newspaper The fact that the editor never sees, and rarely hears directly from, his audience, prevents him often from realizing that he is actually addressing an audience, perhaps a vast one He is then apt to regard his task merely as one requiring the preparation of a certain amount of copy to fill a certain amount of space; so many words and the day is done, also his duty. That attitude is not incompatible with a sense of obligation to his newspaper to fill his allotted space with something worth reading, but it is incompatible with a sense of responsibility to the unseen audience which he is in fact addressing, and unless that responsibility is realized he cannot do his duty to the public which his newspaper serves, nor, for that very reason, can he do his full duty to the newspaper itself. For it is only as the newspaper serves the public that it can serve itself, and it cannot render the best service either to the public or to itself unless it recognizes this fact and keeps it in mind.

Every editorial is an address or a statement to the public. Any man who makes a speech understands that his audience measures his intelligence, and perhaps his character, by what he says. Certainly if he speaks with some frequency both character and intelligence will be estimated from his utterances. Knowing this he will, if he has the opportunity, prepare himself with some care, study his subject and arrange his thoughts, so as to make the best impression he can upon his hearers. He will have his audience before him, and usually he may discern some indications of the effect upon it of his words and his personality. The editor cannot see his audience and rarely has he any sign of the immediate effect of his words. But none the less he is a speaker addressing an audience, a much larger one than any man can reach with vocal speech, and the intelligence, the character, the general personality of the newspaper will be measured in the main by what he says from day to day. It is important, therefore, that he likewise consider his subject, in each instance, with as much care as the circumstances of time permit, if he is to create, maintain or enhance for his newspaper a reputation to justify public confidence and respect.

This is his duty to the paper, for the interests of the paper, but he cannot perform that duty, as has been said, unless he realizes that he is not talking to himself, not merely filling a certain space with words, but is speaking to a public, to which he and his paper owe a real and definite responsibility for the character, purport and import of his words. That responsibility is all the greater because it involves a power and influence over the minds of the people which is often exercised, as Dana says, "without any knowledge or any criticism on the part of the person subject to it." Few readers are conscious of the extent to which the newspaper molds their sentiments. Day after day they read what their paper has to say on public questions, if what it says is worth reading, and unless its opinions on a given question arouse antagonism because it conflicts with their prejudices, traditions or judgment, they accept them as their own. Many, of course, those who give real thought to the meaning of events and are accustomed to forming their own conclusions, weigh the newspaper expression as they would any other, and accept or reject its opinions upon their own judgment of their merits, but these are in the minority. They constitute, however, the element of the population having the largest influence upon public opinion, and the highest test of the intelligence, accuracy and soundness of newspaper thought is the approval and support of this element. But they, being able and disposed to judge for themselves, are not such a charge upon newspaper responsibility as that great majority which is too deeply absorbed in individual vocation and interest, or is too indifferent, to give much thought to the import of events or to the personal development of opinion through its own intellectual processes. That does not mean that this majority lacks in intelligence. Much of it does, to be sure, but it includes a great many of a high order of intelligence who limit their thinking to matters of direct personal concern, and customarily, though perhaps unconsciously, take their opinions ready made from external sources of thought, particularly and mainly the daily newspaper.

This being true the newspaper cannot afford, either from the material or the moral standpoint, to trifle with the power that lies in its hands in the expression of its thoughts. To be content with superficial comment, with unconsidered opinions, with poorly digested facts, is a dereliction of duty and a betrayal of trust. Every reader of a newspaper should be justified in feeling that the views presented to him in its editorial columns are founded upon the best information accessible at the moment, and are the sincere product of the best thought of which the editor or the editorial staff is capable. This refers particularly, of course, to the discussion of the things that matter, the things that affect or may affect the public attitude toward public questions, whether local or general There is much editorial that has no such bearing, that is not likely to influence public opinion one way or another, that treats subjects of more or less interest but which are of no, or of relatively little, importance in the molding of public sentiment. It is the small talk so to speak, of editorial expression, and it is valuable in itself not only in adding attractiveness to the editorial page, but in revealing qualities of the newspaper personality that make it more humanly companionable. The editorial page is defective without it, and the better it is done the better for the paper.

But this is not the character of editorial expression in which the public responsibility lies that is here under discussion It is in the treatment of matters of public concern. the questions of the day that affect or may affect the public interest, the current events that have a bearing upon public welfare, that the newspaper exercises the trust imposed upon it, and in the manner of its exercise reveals its sense of that responsibility, and no less its capacity to fulfill its obligation to the public. The highest and greatest test of the newspaper is in the extent and character of the influence it brings to bear upon society, and that test applies collectively to the whole profession of journalism.

Chapter XI
The Freedom of The Press

But there is another phase of editorial responsibility that involves obligations to the public no less serious, and it lies in what is termed the freedom of the press. That freedom is one of the inherent rights of civil liberty and its maintenance is vital to hunan welfare. To maintain it to the highest degree compatible with the safety of society is a solemn duty of journalism, not only for itself but for the people; less, indeed, for itself than for the people. For its exercise is essential to the public interest, essential to the security and progress of democratic institutions, essential to the preservation of all the other liberties that constitute the most prized possessions of humanity. These liberties, where they exist, have been acquired only after ages of struggle, and such are the destructive forces of human propensities that they can be kept only by maintaining a firm hold upon them. In retaining liberty once acquired, as in securing it in the first instance, no influence is so powerful as that of a free press.

This is universally admitted, and in America it has been so fully recognized from the beginning that the freedom of the press is given the sanction and protection of the Constitution, which declares that it cannot be abridged. The press is the only private institution that is so shielded by the mandate of that fundamental law, and this was due not to any desire to confer a special privilege upon the press for its own benefit, but for the sole purpose of protecting the rights and liberties of the people. "During the revolutionary epoch," says Cooley,[1] "the press had been the chief means of disseminating free principles among the people and in preparing the country to resist oppression, and its powers for good in this direction had appeared so great as to cast its other benefits into the shade. It is a just conclusion, therefore, that this freedom of public discussion was meant to be fully preserved; and that the prohibition of laws impairing it was aimed, not merely at a censorship of the press, but more particularly at any restrictive laws or administration of law whereby such free and general discussion of public interests and affairs as had become customary in America should be so abridged as to deprive it of its advantages as an aid to the people in exercising intelligently their privileges as citizens, and in protecting their liberties."

The freedom of the press, let it be repeated, is commanded and guaranteed by the American Constitution, not as a measure for the protection of a private interest but as a measure for the

---

[1] *Constitutional Law.*

protection of the people in the preservation of their liberties. It is a right, that is to say, which is recognized, authorized and guarded by the fundamental law, not for the emolument or aggrandizement of the press, but to be exercised by it for the benefit of the people. The very nature of this right makes any limitation of its exercise a paradox unless the limitation is in itself essential to the protection of society. There are some, indeed, who hold that any limitation whatsoever is a violation of the right. But if that were true of this form of civil liberty it would be true of all forms, and it is the conunon experience of mankind that civil liberty of any sort can be maintained only in the degree in which its exercise is for the general good. Liberty unless united with law inevitably destroys itself. "To imagine liberty without a law," as Clarendon says, "is to imagine every man with his sword in his hand to destroy him who is weaker than himself." That does not mean the law of statutory enactment simply, but the law of custom, of reason and conscience, that society has in all times enacted for self-protection from liberty unrestrained. "I should wish to act, no doubt, in every instance as I pleased," says Paley, "but I reflect that the rest of mankind also would then do the same; to which state of universal independence and self-direction I should meet with so many checks and obstacles to my own will, from the opposition and interference of other men's, that not only my happiness but my liberty would be less than whilst the whole community were subject to the domination of equal laws."

The freedom of the press, as any other form of liberty, is subject to such restraints as are necessary for the preservation of other rights, subject to restraints upon the abuse of liberty. The press must recognize the fact that there are other rights than this and that these other rights must be respected if its own right is to preserve that public sanction which placed the protection of the Constitution around it. "The freedom of the press, says Cooley again, may be defined to be the liberty to utter and publish whatever the citizen may choose, and to be protected against legal censure and punishment in so doing, provided the publication is not so far injurious to public morals or to private reputation as to be condemned by the common law standards by which defamatory publications were judged when this freedom was thus made a constitutional right." The right goes farther than that, for the principle that the truth is no libel was not then established. But none the less the limitation on the exercise of the right as to defamatory publication obtains in principle and in law, and there are other restrictions of a similar nature that are accepted as compatible with the public interest without improper restraint of this freedom.

Statutory law, however, does not cover all the restraints that are laid upon journalism by a sense of decency, fairness and right. The very fact that the freedom of the press is so guarded by the Constitution and so little restrained by law throws upon the press as an agency of public welfare an obligation to exercise that liberty, wisely, fairly, righteously and for the public good. "The liberty of the press," said Alexander Hamilton, "consists, in my idea, in publishing the truth, from good motives and for justifiable ends, though it reflects upon the government, on magistrates, on individuals. If it be not allowed it excludes the privilege of canvassing men. and our rulers." Therein is stated the principle, and the proper rule of practice, in the exercise of the freedom of the press. To justify that freedom it is essential to publish the truth, or what one sincerely believes to be the truth.

The difficulties that surround the ascertainment of truth in the news have been fully discussed in this volume, and inasmuch as editorial opinions are founded largely upon the news the same difficulties are encountered in editorial expression. But in such expression truth can be and should be sought with more care than is practicable in the publication of news, for the editorial writer has usually more time to sift the evidence, and because he is expressing the thought and the personality of the newspaper itself, by which its character is to be estimated, he has a larger responsibility for the discernment and publication of truth, both for the welfare of his journal and the we are of the public.

But in the exercise of that freedom in the expression of opinion it is not sufficient that the truth be stated. It should be "from good motives and for justifiable ends." These motives and ends are implied and assumed in all discussion of the acts of public men or the acts of any men m relation to public affairs. But it is important to the standing of each individual newspaper and to the standing of journalism generally that these assumptions be justified by the sincerity of the discussion. Within the truth there can be no proper limitations by law of the right of such discussion other th an the restraints already mentioned and a possible reservation for acute emergencies presently to be stated. To put any other limit upon the expression of opinion is to endanger not only that liberty but all liberty. "No one," says Justice Story, "can doubt the importance, in a free government, of the rights to canvass the acts of public men and the tendency of public measures, to censure boldly the conduct of rulers and to scrutinize closely the policy and plans of the government. This is the great security of a free government. If we would preserve it public opinion must be enlightened, political vigilance must be inculcated, free, but not licentious discussion, must be encouraged." Free discussion is essential to a free government, but licentious discussion is an abuse of the privilege which lowers its standards, weakens its influence and imperils its security. It can never be warranted by "good motives" and "justifiable ends," and it is to the honor of journalism that it has recognized this and has gradually and voluntarily abandoned in a large degree the scurrility which so often characterized its discussions in past days. Yet it should never be forgotten that the right of free speech, however unlimited, is a sacred privilege that in itself confers an obligation to use it with decent moderation for the public purposes which alone can justify its maintenance. It can exist only so long as it contributes to the permanence and security of free government, only so long as it is an instrument for the support of all civil liberty. And the responsibility for maintaining it in usefulness and purity, in beneficence and in power, rests upon journalism, which is at once its expression and its guardian.

In the preceding paragraph reference was made to "a possible reservation for acute emergencies." There are conceivable circumstances in which a temporary restraint upon the gross abuse of the freedom of the press may be necessary for the security of society. This freedom, it has been stated, "is commanded and guaranteed by the American Constitution not as a measure for the protection of a private interest but as a measure for the protection of the people in the preservation of their liberties." This being the case if the abuse of this freedom seriously and imminently imperils the constitutional liberties of the people and the existence of a free government its restriction might be imperative. "The safeguarding and fructification of free and constitutional institutions," said Chief Justice Waite in a notable decision, "is the very basis and mainstay upon which the freedom of the press rests, and that freedom, therefore, does not and cannot be held to include the right virtually to destroy such institutions." We do not need to endorse the specific application of this assertion in approving it as fundamentally sound in itself. But it does not warrant a restraint upon free speech unless free and constitutional institutions are actually and immediately imperiled. It is of the essence of these institutions that they are subject to change in accord with the popular mandate and it is essential to such evolution that the constitution itself, as well as all government under it, be open to the fullest discussion and criticism, for it is only by such processes that political progress can be made and political rights maintained. And if change is to be permitted through condemnation of what is believed to be wrong, as a result of altering conditions or altering convictions, then it is necessary that the right of condemnation, to whatever extreme it may go in utterance, should be preserved. "No errors of opinions can possibly be dangerous in a country where opinion is left free to grapple with them," says Simms, and this is true where time can be given for the operation of the processes by which error of opinion may be corrected. It is only when, in a time of national crisis, that these processes of correction can not be effectively exercised, and when dangerous opinions *are being translated into dangerous action*, subversive of free government and popular rights, that a limitation of this freedom may be conceivably justifiable. "We should be eternally vigilant against attempts to check the expression of opinion that we loathe and believe to be fraught with death," says Justice

Holmes, "unless they so imminently threaten immediate interference with the lawful and pressing purposes of the law that an immediate check is required to save the country." That is the sole condition under which a limitation upon the right of the press to express opinion may be warranted, and that only to the extent necessary for the immediate purpose and no longer than to serve that purpose.

In relation to the freedom of the press journalism has two responsibilities laid upon it: First, to guard that right from any encroachment upon it that is not justified by an immediate, urgent and obvious peril to the free government and the civil liberties that it is its province to proteet; and, second, to exercise that right wisely and sincerely for the public welfare.

Chapter XII
Editorial Policy

There rests, then, upon the editor or editorial directors the task of creating and sustaining a newspaper personality whose intellectual and ethical qualities command respect, and of fulfilling the obligation that rests upon the paper to serve the public interest to the best of its ability. He, or they, have, that is to say, two interests to serve, that of the paper and that of the public. There is no necessary conflict in this, for as a rule the best service to the paper is that which gives the best service to the public. The interest of the paper, however, comes first, inasmuch as material subsistence is the primary essential of all service. With every man, whatever his aspirations, whatever his ideals, bread must be provided for if he is to make any progress toward their attainment The means of existence are necessary to the purposes of existence, and must be established both as a preliminary and a constant accompaniment to their accomplishment. Therefore it is essential that the editor labor to sustain and promote the material welfare of his paper, not only because his own material welfare is involved, but because it can contribute to the public service only upon the material foundations laid for itself. The building up of a great newspaper, the building up of any newspaper, that exercises the proper and legitimate functions of journalism is in itself a public service, and the newspaper is entitled to all the honest rewards that may come from the exercise, and in the assertion that it must first consider its own interest there is no implication that it should in any measure sacrifice, or go contrary to, the public interest, for in all the rightful serving of the one there is necessarily the serving of the other.

In this construction it is essential that the newspaper have an editorial policy. It is not essential that it be expressed in definite terms, even to itself, but it is necessary that there be a consciousness of aims and ideals. It may be that the creator of a newspaper has no other purpose in view than the publication of a newspaper to supply the news to a certain field. He may, that is to say. have no specific object to be accomplished through and beyond the publication. He may have no thought of using it to advance the interests of any party, class or condition, or to promote any definite plans or principles of public conduct and action. None the less a conscious policy is necessary. For the mere publication of a newspaper, however limited its purposes and aspirations, involves public information, public observation, public criticism and public judgment that must result in a measure of public approval if it is to attain success, simply as a newspaper. And if that approval is to be obtained and maintained there must be in the product itself evidences of studied concern for its own character and efficiency. Unless thought has been given to these qualities the product will be worthless, and unless that thought is founded upon some understood and accepted principles it is without guidance or aim, and therefore ineffective. One moved by the urge of journalistic creation decides that he is going to publish a newspaper. But coincident with that decision, if they have not preceded it, as usually they have, are the questions, what kind of a newspaper and what for? And whatever may be the answers to these questions they compel a conception of policies, of purposes and the means to their attainment. If the answer to the first is merely "a good newspaper," and to the second, "to publish the news," he is at once confronted with the problem of what constitutes a good newspaper and how it is to be made good, leading his consideration inevitably to the adoption of standards of some sort.

And once in operation the daily contacts of the newspaper with life and events, the response that it must make to the kaleidoscopic aspects of the news. the obligations that it necessarily assumes as a disseminator of current information and as an exponent of public opinion, demands not only a continuous application of these elemental standards but a continuous adjustment of policy in consonance with them to the varing events, conditions and issues of the procession of days. A newspaper policy can be fixed only as to fundamental principles. These determine its character, reveal its qualities, both as a purveyor of news and as an interpreter of events, and indicate in a general way its aims and ideals. Nor are these necessarily immovable. They may develop through growth and experience, or through a change in the spirit behind them, into something vastly finer and greater than the original conceptions, or they may be allowed to deteriorate both in quality and activity, bringing in the latter case deterioration to the newspaper, unless they were originally too visionary for practical application. But aside from these principles that are the permanent guides of policy, the events of each day constantly raise up new questions requiring expression of editorial opinion by which its policy as to these questions is indicated.

Editorial policy, therefore, is a constant adjustment of opinion and the expression of opinion to more or less fixed principles of conduct and action, and to varying events and issues. Or, to put it another way, it is the application of relatively fixed principles of opinion to the protean aspects of life in its public manifestations. Its direction is not unlike the piloting of a boat upon a stream, where the landscape is constantly changing, and where there are shifting currents, stretches of comparatively still water, rapids at times, with sandbars, rocks and snags to be seen and evaded; but if the boat is staunch and the pilot alert the voyage is safe and continuously diverting. The pilot, however, has a double responsibility to make the voyage worth while for the owners of the vessel, and to guard the lives and the goods intrusted to him, that the journey be made secure and beneficial for all. He cannot follow his own whims; he cannot take unnecessary risks; he cannot play fast and loose with his employer's interests, or with his own interests if he is perchance the proprietor; he cannot ignore the rights nor imperil the security of his precious freight. His task and his duty are to steer the boat and carry the freight to port. It is a task that involves constant watchfulness, a steady hand upon the wheel, with such a sense of obligation and responsibility that no self-interest opposed to its performance can divert him from the course.

So it is with newspaper policy. Given staunch principles of integrity and purpose, its direction is but a matter of steering with a steady hand and a watchful eye through the varying conditions and issues which the events of the day develop. But the dual responsibility of the helmsman cannot be forgotten. The material interests of the newspaper must be served if it is to carry on, while at the same time the interests of the people, material and spiritual, which are its precious freight, must be guarded and safely guided. He cannot imperil or sacrifice either, nor can he advance one at the loss of the other. Their interests are inseparable. To betray the public is to betray the newspaper. Loyalty both to press and people is essential to editorial guidance.

But, abandoning nautical symbolism and coming ashore, it is necessary that newspaper policy be, as Lincoln said of his legs, long enough to reach the ground. An editor cannot profitably or successfully soar above the heads of his readers. He may be in advance of them, but never out of touch with them. If he is to lead it must be along a road which they can follow, and leadership must be expressed in terms which they can understand. Moreover, the fiduciary relation which he bears to them must be exercised with a decent respect for their opinions, their emotions, their prejudices and passions, if he is to carry them with him. Journalism should be independent, but it cannot carry the independence so far as to separate itself from the public it serves without loss of public support and consequent loss of opportunity to service. A fiduciary office, that is to say, cannot be exercised save in association with the objects of the trust it involves.

"This fiduciary relation," Dr. Talcott Williams[①] well says, "carries with it the obligation of service and the consciousness of a great public duty on the part of the journalist. It is never true of him, as is sometimes unkindly said, that, like the drum-major, he leads the procession along a predetermined route, from which he cannot vary, and that the apparently spontaneous twirl of his baton and surprising gyrations of his wand of office really follow a prescribed tune which is already written, as he walks before those who pipe and drum it, from the thundering bass of the great newspaper to the flageolet of the country weekly piping on its rural reed. But it is true that the instant the journalist turns into a side street and the procession leaves him and goes its own way, as has happened to many an independent journalist, he ceases to be a journalist and becomes that admirable but costly person, to himself and to his publisher, the pamphleteer, who pays the price of printing, careless whether men take it or leave it. A journalist cannot be careless at this point. If men leave his newspaper he may be publishing a most admirable history of the world for a day, freighted with the wisest opinion ever uttered, but the publication is not a newspaper. It is, instead, a book published daily by its author and creator at an extravagant cost, in a form which renders its preservation impossible, its present penally costly, and its future a safe oblivion."

The truth of that is not to be questioned. But, on the other hand, neither can the journalist sit with his ears open waiting for the *vox populi* before he dares to speak. It is one thing to be in

---

[①] *The Newspaper Man.*

general accord with the tendencies of opinion in that part of the public which a newspaper serves; it is quite another to be a mere echo of that opinion. The newspaper cannot be too far ahead of or oblivious to its public, nor can it sink to the level of a camp follower. In the nature of things, newspaper opinion must be formed and expressed in relation to questions as they arise, and the newspaper must constantly declare opinions, whether tentative or positive, before the public in general has time or opportunity to form opinions for itself. It may, it is true, comment without hazarding a direct expression of view until some signs of the trend of public reaction appear, but this is to withhold from the public the suggestions and guidance for which it so largely depends upon the press, and which it is the function of the press to supply. It is a cautiousness, not to say timidity, that is not compatible with the fundamentals of journalism. There are occasions. however, when information is too incomplete or too conflicting to permit an intelligent opinion to be formed, and its definite formation should wait upon better knowledge and clearer light. There are circumstances also when the scales of judgment are so nearly evenly balanced that it is difficult to decide upon what is right or what is best. Under such circumstances it is wisdom and not timidity that cautions careful deliberation. The public has a right to the best judgment and the clearest definition of which the editor is capable, and, moreover it is upon the character and quality of that judgment that public respect for a newspaper's opinion, and the consequent influence of its opinion, must be founded. "Hair-trigger" opinion or "half-baked" opinion is not good journalism under any circumstances.

But these exceptions to the utterance of opinion in advance of public expression are relatively of unusual occurrence, and they operate only to defer initial and independent judgment where such judgment is not at once practicable or proper. Ordinarily the editor must form his own opinions upon the events and questions coming before him for comment, without any other knowledge of the public attitude toward them, present or prospective, than that derived from his experience with the expression of public sentiment, and the acquaintance with its trends that constant association and study gives to him He is, therefore, always, and must always be, a little in advance of public opinion if he is to fulfill this important function of journalism properly and influence the direction of public opinion. In this, of necessity, he constantly risks the possibility that the public will refuse to follow him, but this risk is not great if he has learned through experience, and the intuition growing out of experience, to estimate the public feeling and will in relation to any given question. However, there are often times when he must express opinions that he knows to be in opposition to public sentiment, and be prepared to battle for his convictions of right against popular prejudice, passion or error until he has won or lost, if he is to justify his independence, his sincerity, if he is to fulfill his duty as a guide and protector of the public welfare. For the public is not infrequently misled by its own emotions and its own lack of knowledge, or misguided by influences that are consciously or unconsciously antagonistic to its real welfare, and must be urged into the right against its own convictions.

Therefore, while it is important that an editor should consider his readers—their intelligence, disposition and tastes and the nature of their customary attitude toward public questions; that he should endeavor generally to be in accord with them if he is to expect them to be in accord with him and to march with him along the road he follows—the fundamental conditions of his calling and his service demand that he precede them on the way; and he must trust to his knowledge of them, of their interests, their needs and their feelings to keep himself and his paper in touch with them and in sympathy with them, thereby maintaining their approval and support in his general policy even though he may often find it necessary to go contrary to their wishes and feelings in some details of it.

Indeed, if it were attempted it is not possible for the opinions of a newspaper to please all of the readers all of the time, or, for that matter, to please all of them any of the time, if its opinions have any force of character, and therefore any value, whatsoever. No expression of opinion that is definite and positive enough to have any weight can fail to be more or less distasteful to some, however homogeneous and accordant the body of readers may be in general. It is as certain a rule in journalism as it is in individual life that to attempt to please everybody is to please nobody. On the other hand, the newspaper that tries to please nobody is usually successful in doing so. The safer course is to please oneself, within the limitations created by the necessity of public support and the obligations of public service. A newspaper's opinions, that is to say, should be of its own creation or acceptance, founded upon its own knowledge and study of facts, and agreeable with its own conceptions of right, if it is to respect itself and acquire the respect of the public. But in arriving at its judgment of right it has to remember that it is a newspaper, not a pamphlet, that in the expression of its views it occupies a fiduciary relation to its public, that the purpose of the expression is not to air one's opinions for the mere pleasure of the airing but to interest, inform and guide its readers in the right way.

That involves an essential independence of thought that is limited as to its expression by considerations of public feeling, public interests and public needs. Independence in the forming and expression of opinion is a fundamental quality of journalism. This has no reference to what is termed an independent newspaper in the political sense, for independence is not incompatible with the most intense partisanship. What is meant by it, in this connection, is the inalienable right to form and publish one s opinions in accordance with one's conception of right, whether that conception is right or wrong, whether it is partisan or unpartisan. There are honest men who are so imbued with party spirit that they are unable to conceive of anything being right politically that does not bear the stamp of their party, and if that is their voluntary conviction they are not lacking in individual independence in its expression. But that type of journalism is passing with the passing of that type of men. There will always be partisans as long as there are parties, as long indeed as there are issues which cause sharp differences of opinion. for one may be intensely partisan in other fields than politics. But journalism, even that which is frankly partisan in the political sense, has become more or less discriminating in its judgment, more or less disposed to weigh men and measures on their individual merits. This tendency of journalism in general has caused the virtual disappearance of the all-inclusive and all-indorsing partisanship of the past, and the growth of a journalism that is expressed in "independent" newspapers, by which is meant, not neutrality, as some imagine, nor general opposition to parties and party purposes, but such a detachment from party allegiance as will permit the expression of independent views on all questions arising without regard to party interests. It does not inhibit the strongest kind of support to party aims or action if in the circumstances of a particular moment that support is believed to be justified, but judgment is based, in theory at least, upon the conception of the merits of the specific situation and not upon attachment to the party. In short, independent journalism in this restricted sense, claims the right and the duty to support what it believes to be right and to oppose what it believes to be wrong, in relation to every question or condition that arises affecting the public interest, untrammeled by party connection.

Naturally this trend is not favorable to party solidarity or unity, and parties being apparently necessary in a democratic government it raises the question of the responsibility of journalism in relation to parties and to public officials. Is independent journalism a better promotive of the public welfare than partisan journalism? The trend is itself an answer in the affirmative. For it is a development that is a result of a growing professional consciousness that the interests and rights of the people are its paramount concern, that party existence and power are justified only by its contribution to public welfare, an that parties, however meritorious, are but means to ends which they can accomplish only so long as they are in fact the agencies of the people, responsive to their will, and conducting the affairs of government honestly and efficiently in the interest of the people. This consciousness, therefore, while it may or may not lessen individual attachment to the party, demands a discriminating consideration of party positions and of party conduct as it is expressed through its representatives in office. The tendency of this development, that is to say, is to impel the examination of public questions and of public acts more and more upon their individual merits in relation to the public interest rather than exclusively in relation to party interest. Its influence, of course, is felt and manifested in varying degree but it has made even the most partisan papers less blindly partisan, so that the party organ, the mere mouthpiece of party, has virtually vanished, while its call for independence of thought and expression has created innumerable newspapers that declare their entire independence of party control or party obligation.

This consciousness is a natural and inevitable accompaniment of the developing realization that journalism is a profession of public service, that if it is to serve effectively it must be founded upon truth, in its opinion as well as in its news, and that it is a betrayal of trust to deceive the people even for partisan ends. It is, therefore, an ethical and a political as well as a professional advance. And like all such advances it has had its prophets and its leaders, men who recognized the reasons, and the public necessity, for independence in journalism, long before the realization affected the mass of the profession. John Thaddeus Delane, of the London *Times*, was one of these. In 1852 Lord Derby and Lord Grey, incensed by Delane's criticisms of British governmental policy in its relation with Louis Napoleon both hotly denounced him, though they were of different parties. "If in these days," said Lord Derby, "the Press aspires to exercise the influence of statesmen, the Press should remember they are not free from the corresponding responsibilities of statesmen." To this Delane replied in an editorial in the *Times*, recognizing the responsibility of journalism but denying that it is "bound by the same limitations, the same duties, the same liabilities, as those of the Ministers of the Crown."

"The purposes and duties of the two Powers," he said, "are constantly separate, generally independent, sometimes diametrically opposite. The dignity and freedom of the Press are trammeled from the moment it accepts an ancillary position. To perform its duties with entire independence, and consequently with the utmost public advantage, the Press can enter into no close or binding alliance with the statesmen of the day, nor can it surrender its permanent interests to the convenience of the ephemeral power of any Government. The first duty of the press is to obtain the earliest and most correct intelligence of the events of the time, and instantly by disclosing them to make them the common property of the nation. The Press lives by disclosures. Whatever passes into its keeping becomes a part of the knowledge and history of our times. It is daily and forever appealing to the enlightened force of public opinion—anticipating if possible the march of events—standing upon the breach between the present and the future, and extending its survey to the horizon of the world. The duty of the Press is to speak, of the statesman to be silent. We are bound to tell the truth as we find it, without fear of consequences-to lend no convenient shelter to acts of injustice and oppression, but to consign them at once to the judgment of the world.... It may suit the purposes of the statesman, purpose of the statesman to veil the Statue of Liberty.... Governments must treat other Governments with external respect, however black their origin or foul their deeds; but happily the Press is under no such trammels, and, while diplomatists are exchanging courtesies, can unmask the mean heart that beats beneath a star, or point out the bloodstains on the hand which grasps a scepter. The duty of the journalist is the same as that of the historian to seek out the truth, above all things, and to present to his readers, not such things as statecraft would wish them to know, but the truth as near as he can obtain it.... Let those who will preach silence on crimes which they cannot deny and dare not even palliate; we have been trained in another school, and will not shirk from boldly declaring what we freely think, though it should be our disagreeable duty to tell Lord Derby that he condescends to be the tool of the party which he pretends to lead, and Lord Grey that he is the scourge of the party which he is permitted to govern." ①

That is the spirit and these are the principles that in general should govern independent journalism, as much so now as they governed Delane so long ago. But in their exercise it should never be forgotten that the newspaper bears a responsibility of its own as great as that which rests upon the statesman. The public welfare is as much in the keeping of one estate as of the other, and though journalism is subject to no law that restrains its speech and is bound to its duty by no oath of office it is none the less under an obligation equally solemn to protect, conserve and promote the public welfare within the field of its influence to the best of its ability. Its declaration of independence and its constitutional right of free speech constitute no license to run amuck amid the public interests. It is its constant duty to watch the course of e-

---

① Cook, *Delane of the Times*.

vents in their relation to the welfare of the people, to consider and discuss the questions that concern or affect the interests of the people, to point out error, to criticize vigorously unfaithful or incompetent public service, to expose violations of the public trust in any office however exalted, to condemn the wrong and support the right, and all of this upon the individual opinion as to what is wrong and what is right. It is not infallible, and can lay no claim to inerrancy. On the contrary, it is subject to the variations and the weaknesses of judgment that affect all of humanity. But it is nevertheless the source of the information on which virtually all public opinion is founded, to a very large degree it is the voice of public opinion, however varied that opinion may be, and the development and guidance of public opinion is its particular and recognized function.

It follows, therefore, that it is its duty to consider the effect upon public opinion, and therefore upon public welfare, of all that it says in its own person. It cannot, consistent with the performance of that duty, permit personal prejudices or antipathies to govern the expression of its opinions if they blind it to truth, to justice, or to fair and intelligent judgment. Law and order and the conduct of government being essential to the public welfare, adverse criticism of the agencies of government should be based upon fact, and on honest convictions of error or of wrong. The agencies of the law are entitled to the respect of journalism as of the people so long as they justify that respect, for it is only in the degree of the respect in which they are held that they can be effective in the public service, Indiscriminate and unjust attacks upon them tend to lower them in the public estimation and therefore to lower the quality of the public service. It is of the utmost importance in the conduct of government that it have the support of public opinion in the largest degree possible, and that opinion should be founded upon the merits of governmental conduct, general and specific. Public opinion, in fact governs the character of government in a democracy, and that opinion promotes good government in the degree in which it is truly and correctly informed and its impressions fairly influenced for good. False and misleading information in regard to the persons or acts of government, and opinions which unjustly impugn motives or integrity, are, for that reason, to be deprecated, not only as influences inimical to the public welfare, but as unworthy of journalism when it is deliberate The difficulty of ascertaining and identifying the truth under all circumstances has been fully discussed in this volume, and what is fair or unfair in the discussion of public men or measures depends so largely upon view and feeling that no comprehensive rule can be laid down by which either can be always distinguished. But one may venture to assert that the test of proper journalistic conduct in this relation—indeed, in all relations involving the expression of opinion—is sincere conviction based upon knowledge. The evidences of that sincerity and that knowledge are the evidences of character which justify and secure the respect and confidence of the public in the measure of their constant impress upon the public mind.

Chapter XIII
Editorial Construction

And now let us turn from editorial policy in general to the editorial in particular, the instrument by which editorial policy is expressed. There is, to be sure, or ought to be, an editorial policy relating to the news, which involves the manner of collection, preparation and publication of the news, but the principles applying to this division of editorial policy have been discussed in the chapters devoted to that department. We are here considering editorial policy as it is revealed in the expression of opinion on the editorial page.

The editorial page. it has been said, is the seat of the mind and soul of the newspaper personality, and the editorial is the tongue which "expresses the thought of this personality and thereby reveals its character, its conscience and the measure of its intelligence." This conception of the place and function of the editorial gives to it a dignity and importance that must be regarded if the personality to be created and sustained is to merit and receive the respect for its qualities of mind and heart that must be the foundation of public support and the foundation of its influence upon public opinion and action. The thought of the living personality of an institution is to be expressed, and this thought is not necessarily in exact accord with the thought of the individual within the institution that is formulating the expression, though undoubtedly the thought is much better expressed and more impressive in its sincerity if that accord exists. Indeed, it must exist to a large degree if the strongest impression of a sincere and vital personality within the newspaper is to be made. But none the less there is a difference between the relation of the newspaper to the public and the personal relation of the editor to the public. The editor as an individual is not different from other individuals, his public responsibilities as a man. separated from the exercise of his office, being no greater than the public responsibilities of other men. What he says or does in his personal relations are not usually matters of public concern. He may express his views among his acquaintances as freely, and perhaps with as little effect, as any other. But when he undertakes to express the thought of the newspaper personality he is giving voice to something larger than himself, something with great, conspicuous and definite responsibilities, which it is incumbent upon him to recognize and respect; and in the exercise of his office in relation to that personality it is often necessary to restrain, to modify or to expand what may be his individual views, or even, particularly if he is one of a group responsible for editorial direction, to express views with which he does not wholly agree as an individual.

For because of its public relation and responsibility a newspaper may not always properly say what an individual may say with impunity; it may be expedient, purely as a matter of conserving the public welfare, to say only in guarded terms what the individual could express freely, or it may be its duty to declare with vigor what the individual would be reluctant to say at all. The point that it is desired to express here is that the newspaper personality must be regarded objectively as something that has distinct interests, duties, obligations, responsibilities, rights and privileges separate from, and generally superior to, those of the individual personalities which create and sustain it. Moreover, it has, or may have, a permanency that does not pertain to any individual within it at any time, it has perhaps an established reputation for distinguishing qualities of character that it is necessary or desirable to protect and maintain, however changing the individual forces behind it. All of which comes to this, that in editorial direction and guidance and in editorial writing, one has more to consider than one's individual opinions, and there is an obligation not merely to do the best work one can, but to respect the rights and perform the duty of the institution that one serves, and so to express thought for public consideration that an institutional personality may be maintained that is distinctive. consistent, and worthy of public regard and confidence.

The past of the newspaper is therefore to be regarded. For whatever position it may have in the mind and feeling of its readers is due to its past conduct. There may be at times sound reasons for a decided change of principles, policy and course, because it has failed to keep abreast of the day, because it is necessary to reverse a downward tendency, or because it is desirable by such a change, it being considered consistent with right, to expand its field of usefulness. These, however, are matters of deliberate adjustment with a full consideration and understanding of the obligations and risks involved. They refer to possible crises in a newspaper's career that do not often confront it, if ever. Lacking the need for such changes it is to be assumed that its past is worthy of respect and its continuity something to be maintained, in so far as the personality it embodies is concerned. That is no impediment to its growth, expansion and progress. For it is true of newspapers as it is of men that they "may rise on stepping stones of their dead selves to better things," and the past of a good newspaper is an accumulation of assets upon which the present and the future should profit.

That being conceded, what are the essential principles of editorial construction for the maintenance and growth of such a newspaper personality, or the creation of such a personality if it is still in the stages of conception? First and foremost, the editorial being the expression of the thought of the newspaper it is necessary that it be a product of thought. It is an easy matter for a practiced editorial writer to fill an allotted space with words that look well and read well but which having little or no thought behind them convey little or no thought to the reader. If an editorial page has no readers to speak of, it is because its editorials little meaning, little relevancy, bear; because they fail to interest, to inform and to guide; because being written without thought they have no thought within them to impart. If an editorial page is not read it is the fault of the editor, not of the readers. An editorial page is always read if it is worth reading. Not by everybody, to be sure. Nothing in a newspaper is ever read by everybody. But editorials worth reading will be read by many if exceptionally worth while, by the great majority, and always such editorial readers constitute the most intelligent and therefore the most influential element of any community. In proportion to the number of such readers, the newspaper is able to impress its thought, its character, its personality, and therefore its direct influence, upon the field of its circulation. There is no privilege in journalism so great as the development of a constituency that gives attention to its words because it knows them true, because it knows them intelligent, because it knows them sincere, and therefore trusts them; and there is no asset so valuable as this. But such a constituency cannot be developed unless earnest, sincere and intelligent thought is given daily to editorial utterance.

And obviously such thought must be founded upon knowledge. Not the learning of the schools or the lore of the past, though much of that is foundationally necessary; but particularly knowledge of the day, of circumstances and conditions, of persons and peoples, of questions and needs, of the immediate present. Such knowledge can be acquired only by constant study and observation of events, of their causes and nature, their import and trend. The conscientious editor is of necessity an industrious reader. He draws his stock of information from many sources, and is not content with that which coincides with his own point of view or predilection. He wants to get at the truth and he weighs and analyzes facts to that end. Nor can he be satisfied with the knowledge that pertains to affairs which are at the moment of pressing public interest or importance. Events or conditions that seem unworthy of notice to-day may develop great issues to-morrow. Whatever is going on in the world, and particularly in his field of activity, that affects or is likely to affect the public interest or welfare, is worthy of his attention though it may never justify his comment.

That is not to say that an editor should cram his head full of details. It is easily possible to store so much lumber in the mind that there is no room left for construction. The "walking encyclopedia" is often useful as a piece of office equipment but usually it is only valuable for reference purposes. All the editor needs to retain is the salient points of a subject, the impressions that enable him to recall the outlines of information. Details are generally accessible when the needs of discussion require them. Even then it is seldom desirable to load the mind with the minutiae of information. When one is unable "to see the town for the houses," the objective view of the whole question, which is so essential to editorial judgment, is difficult to obtain. The great value of editorial opinion, judicially formed and expressed, lies in the fact that it is objective, that it is the result of observation of a thing from the outside, viewing it in more or less clear perspective, with all its visible parts revealing their relation to the whole, much as a passenger in an aeroplane looks down upon a city and sees it as a unit while at the same time his eye picks out its topographical distinctions. An opinion based upon a single aspect of an event or a question, seen so closely as to prevent a view of the other aspects, of all sides of it, is bound to be biased by the narrowness of the perspective, and therefore misleading. It is not always possible to view a question in the objective clearly, because of defects of vision or because all the facts essential to such a view are not at hand, but none the less it is necessary to the best and soundest judgment, and the editor is, or should be, in a better position to obtain such a view than any other observer. Even though his purpose be partisan, in any sense, he cannot do his best unless he knows what he opposes as well as what he supports.

But the value of thought and knowledge is dependent very largely upon the form and manner of their expression. An editor can never afford to forget that he is talking not only to a great audience but to all sorts and conditions of people, men and women—and, it is to be hoped, youths—of varying degrees of culture and education. If the editorial page is read to the extent that is always to be desired, if it is to have the weight in its field that only wide reading can command, it is essential that the thought of the newspaper be expressed, so far as possible, in terms of commion understanding within the limitations of good English that comprehends the vocabulary of the day. At the same time if the thought, and the personality behind the thought, are to be respected it is necessary that the thought be clothed in language that justifies respect for its own qualities of diction. That does not imply fine writing but good writing, by which is meant writing that expresses thought clearly in words that ordinarily require no reference to the dictionary by the average reader. Writing that is over the heads of the common people may win the applause of the few and elevate the writer in his own esteem, but it does not promote that large interest in, and attachment to, the page that is the foundation of its influence.

It is always to be assumed that the reader has sufficient intelligence to understand clear statements in plain English. The editorial page cannot be adjusted to the intelligence of the moron or to the ignorance of the illiterate. But it is not always to be assumed that the reader, however intelligent, is fully informed as to any subject of editorial discussion unless it is one so fully covered in the news, or one that is in general so well known that there is no excuse for lack of information. If the possession of that knowledge or information is doubtful the subject of the editorial should be made as clear as the thought about it, if the reader is to understand the opinion. The editorial, that is to say, should under such circumstances convey sufficient information in itself to enlighten the reader as to the theme of discussion. Moreover, the statement of opinion without the reasons for the opinion is not desirable unless it can be presumed that the reasons are already well known. With the growth of education, and of interest in public affairs, both of which it is the task of journalism to promote, the people become less and less disposed to accept opinions ready made, and more and more inclined to resent dogmatic assertions that do not justify themselves by logic. They want, or many of them do, the reasons for editorial opinion, and they are entitled to them. Editorial discussion that discloses the processes of reasoning by which conclusions are reached, as well as the conclusions themselves, is the most convincing form of expression, if the reasoning is good. And such discussion is not only a tribute to the intelligence of the reader but it is a proof of the intelligence of the newspaper and *prima facie* evidence that it does its own thinking, a reputation for which is much to be desired.

And that brings us to another essential of editorial expression, that it be honest. Honest opinion can only b e founded upon truth, or at least upon a belief in the truth of its premises, Exact truth, of course. is always more or less difficult to determine, particularly so in relation to current events, and the estimate of what is true is often as much a matter of individual judgment as is the opinion regarding its meaning and import. It is, however, upon the editorial judgment of the truth, as well as upon its judgment in opinion, that the public largely depends for its conceptions of right. Honest editorial expression, therefore involves honest statement of fact, as it appears to the editor, as well as sincerity of the views based upon it. It may be wrong as to both, it can never be always right as to either, it can only hope to be right, and to convince its readers that it is right, most of the time. But honesty and sincerity, which in this connection are synonymous, are essential to that conviction, essential to the establishment and maintenance of the public confidence, and, it follows, essential to the material as well as the spiritual welfare of the newspaper.

But still more is needed for that impression. It is just as desirable to win the heart of the reader as his mind. Intellectual respect is necessary to the highest regard, but that respect is not likely to be active nor dependably loyal, unless there is developed with it a degree of attachment that approaches, or reaches, a sentiment of affection. To that end newspaper editorials should be imbued with human feeling. That is not to say that the newspaper should ever be temperamentally emotional, but that it should always realize that the qualities of humanity are necessary to personality, and that these qualities are not to be fully expressed unless feeling as well as thought actuate them. The newspaper, in other words, must feel as well as think, must put feeling into its thought as well as reason, if it is 'to be regarded as a friend as well as a counselor. Feeling, to be sure. must be restrained by reason. It is always easier to feel than it is to think and there is nothing more dangerous to the public interest, or to the real interest of the newspaper, than feeling that is uncontrolled by thought. There is, indeed, much editorial, that is more the expression of emotion than of sense, and it would be unnecessary to speak of feeling, save to condemn its excesses, were it not that it is indispensable, when under control, to the earnest and vigorous utterance of deep conviction, and indispensable to the strongest impress upon the public mind and conscience. Opinion, under circumstances that arouse and justify feeling, may array argument with skill, but if it rigidly suppresses feeling it lacks the vitality that strikes the answering spark in the reader. Being "icily regular" it is likely to be "splendidly null." Moreover, it is through feeling that the highest sentiments of humanity, in its ethical and altruistic relations, and its highest spiritual aspirations and ideals, are expressed, subject to the direction and guardianship of the mind. Newspaper personality, in short, must have a heart as well as an intellect, and be as unafraid to reveal the one as the other, if it is to be in accord with the humanity it represents and presents, if it is to be a fit and influential companion and mentor for mankind. There is no greater field of usefulness and of public service for journalism than the exercise of its power, when occasion warrants, to awaken the sentiments of the heart within the breast of the people and make them active for good works, and it cannot exercise that power effectively unless it has a heart of its own, a heart that ever responds to human suffering, human needs, and human aspirations toward the good—unless, in short, it has a soul, that encompasses and controls both heart and mind.

Chapter XIV
Ethics of Journalism

The newspaper of each day is more or less a record of events that involve ethics in one way or another. They present violations more often than observances of ethical rules and principles, because such violations are departures from the normal which arrest, and require, public attention. It is the abnormal, the unusual, that rouses interest and curiosity and that creates much of what is termed news; and, misanthropes to the contrary notwithstanding, violations of moral law and duty of sufficient magnitude to get into the newspapers are still, as they have always been since civilization came into existence, manifestations of the abnormal in human conduct. The great mass of the people rarely depart, in any degree sufficiently marked to attract public notice, from the standards of conduct laid down ages ago as the essentials of human relations in a civilized society. But the newspaper of each day may also contain observances of ethical principles so conspicuous or unusual as to constitute news. and record movements for the promotion of such principles that make themselves worthy of a place in the public news by their public acts.

The newspaper, that is to say, deals to a considerable extent with the phenomena of ethical violations, whether negative or affirmative, and it is in itself, or should be, and usually is, a great influence for the advancement of ethical principles and conduct. Being in that degree an exponent of such principles it is peculiarly subject to them. It lives, and must live, in the open, Whatever it does, good or bad, is necessarily exposed to public view and criticism, for it is by public exposure of itself that it exists, The newspaper can have no private life. Living by disclosures it cannot conceal itself. Its motives, to be sure. may be construed one way or another, but its acts are each day in evidence before the bar of public opinion. Therefore its own ethical conduct is constantly involved by the diurnal creation of itself, and ethics becomes a matter of special importance to the practice of the profession, and no less to the business, of journalism.

Journalism, dealing as it does almost wholly with human relations and having constant and insistent obligations in connection with the exercise of its public office, its essential principles are largely, and necessarily, of an ethical nature. Throughout this entire volume ethical considerations predominate because they are inescapable, but it would seem to be desirable in bringing this discussion of journalistic principles to an end, to consider specific standards of ethics in the conduct of journalism.

It is quite probable that many a journalist having the direction of a newspaper in his hands and being responsible for its conduct, has gone to his grave after a successful and honorable career without ever a thought of ethics as such, or without ever formulating in his own mind a single definite rule of ethics in relation to his work. Nevertheless it is just as probable that he conducted his newspaper with a due observance of ethical principles. Doubtless there have been millions of men who never heard of the Ten Commandments but who observed their rules as fully as those to whom they were well-known and divine commands. Every man. whether he is conscious of it or not, is influenced by some sort of moral standards. They may be high, they may be low, they may be broad or extremely restricted, they may dominate his acts at all times or only now and then, but in some way and to some extent their influence is expressed in conduct, even though he may not be aware of the existence of such standards as something definitely formulated. The influence of a moral standard, that is to say, once accepted as such and put into practice, is much broader and more pervasive than the knowledge of it. Ethical principles were in operation ages before ethics, or any similar definitive term was applied to them, and also before any moral standards were formed or adopted. But none the less it was necessary to establish such standards in order to have recognized measures of right by which men might be guided in their conduct to the observance of the right, or condemned either by law or by society for their failure to do so. And by their adoption and application among those who realized not only their essential rightness but their need as regulating agencies. of human conduct, their influence was spread to those who realized none of this but who found it necessary to conform in some degree to their principles in order to maintain a standing in the society controlled by them. No people have ever progressed morally who did not have conceptions of right impressed upon them by moral leadership, and these conceptions embodied in more or less definite rules for human guidance; and material progress, it is worth while to say, has never been long maintained that was not accompanied by moral progress. For the higher the state of material development the more complicated the state and the relations of society, and the greater the need for moral standards by which society may be guided in these relations.

As it is with people in general so it is with groups of people having a common interest. Each individual of such a group may have a conception of right which he puts into practice in his own way, or he may have no conception of right and conduct himself without regard to considerations of right. Having no recognized standards of right for the whole interest each is guided by the nature of his own personality. If his personal standards are high his conduct in relation to the common interest will be high. If his personal standards are low his conduct in that relation will be of the same order. There is nothing but the individual conception of right by which one may be guided, and there is no means of impressing the one having low ideas of right with the desirability or necessity of higher ones. But it is in accord with the customary manifestations of human nature that the application of low standards within a group has a more far-reaching effect upon its reputation than the application of the higher ones. The conduct of the majority of the members may be irreproachable but the group as a whole must suffer from the reproach that the conduct of the minority brings upon it. Much of that conduct of the minority, however, is due not to deliberate preference, but to a lack of knowledge of better principles of action, or a lack of thought about principles. In the absence of any recognized standards of conduct one is apt to be governed by one's individual conceptions of right, or, having no such conceptions, or giving no thought to ethical distinctions, by one's desires propelled upon the level of one's personality. Not until the group establishes standards of conduct for the individual guidance of all of its members is there any definite measure by which the conduct of the individual may be judged in its relation to the whole, or whereby the thoughtless or the ignorant, as to such principles, may discover wherein he is lacking, and by the revelation of the sentiment of the majority of his fellows be supplied with an inducement to raise his own standards to conform with theirs. It is upon some such considerations as these that professional and other groups have found it necessary to establish codes of ethics, for the protection, the elevation and advancement of group interests, and no less the interest of each individual member of the group.

But in no instance has this ever been done until individuals had commenced to give thought to ethical principles, to formulate standards for their own guidance, and thereby to develop something concrete to attract the attention and thinking of others in the same field, Usually it is a slow development, and not until it is realized that there is a group interest that is distinct from and yet essential to the individual interest; that the group interest must be sustained and promoted as a means to the general and individual progress, does the question of moral standards become acute and impelling. In other words, it is first necessary to realize that all are members of one body, and upon that to establish a collective interest and purpose. If the common interest is to be advanced, common standards, as well as common aims, are essential means to advancement. If a group is to progress as a whole, morally or materially, it must first regard itself as a unit, and then move forward as such upon a definite course of progress.

Perhaps journalism has never been without representatives who gave serious thought to the ethical responsibilities of the press. and many an editor has given form and action to his thoughts in this direction by the creation of something in the nature of a code for the guidance of his individual newspaper. Long ago, for example, when George W. Childs published the Philadelphia *Public Ledger*. William V. McKean, its managing editor, adopted a system of editorial ethics for that paper which comprehended almost all the requirements of ethical conduct in journalism. It follows:

Always deal fairly and frankly with the public.

A newspaper to be trusted and respected must give trustworthy information and counsel. It is a serious thing to mislead the people.

Understate your case rather than overstate it.

Have a sure voucher for every statement, especially for censure.

There is a wide gap between accusation of crime and actual guilt.

Deal gently with weak and helpless offenders.

Before making up judgment take care to understand both sides, and remember there are at least two sides. If you attempt to decide you are bound to know both.

Do not say you know when you have only heard.

Never proceed on mere hearsay. Rumor is only an index to be followed by inquiry.

Take care to be right. Better be right than quickest with the news, which is often false. It is bad to be late, but worse to be wrong.

Go to first hands and original sources for information; if you cannot, then get as near as you can.

It is the reporter's office to chronicle events, to collect facts; comments on the facts are reserved for the editor.

Let the facts and reasoning tell the story rather than rhetorical flourish.

Don't be too positive. Remember always it is possible that you may err.

All persons have equal rights in the court of conscience, as well as in courts of law.

Never add fuel to the fire of popular excitement.

There is nothing more demoralizing in public affairs than habitual disregard of the law.

Uphold the authorities in maintaining public order, rectify wrongs through the law. If the law is defective, better mend it than break it.

Nearly always there is law enough. It is the failure to enforce it that makes most mischief.

There is no need, and therefore no excuse, for mob law in American communities.

Numerous as bad men may be, remember they are but few compared with the millions of people.

The public welfare has higher claims than any party, cry.

Grace and purity of style are always desirable, but never al-low rhetoric to displace clear, direct, forcible expression.

Plain words are essential for unlearned people, and these are just as plain to the most accomplished. ①

This contains no little sound common sense and no little admirable philosophy, as well as ethical principles that reveal a keen conception of right and justice in the mind of the creator of this private code. Similar in character and purpose. though it has more of the heart and less of the head in it than the foregoing, are the rules adopted by Warren G. Harding for the conduct of his newspaper :

Remember there are two sides to every question. Get them both.

Be truthful; get the facts.

Mistakes are inevitable, but strive for accuracy I would rather have one story exactly right than a hundred half wrong.

Be decent, be fair, be generous.

Boost; don't knock.

There's good in everybody. Bring out the good in everybody, and never needlessly hurt the feelings of anybody.

In reporting a political gathering give the facts, tell the story as it is, not as you would like to have it. Treat all parties alike.

If there's any politics to be played, we will play it in our Editorial Columns.

Treat all religious matters reverently.

---

① Payne's History of Journalism in the United States.

If it can possibly be avoided never bring ignominy to an innocent man or child in telling of the misdeeds of a relative.

Don't wait to be asked, but do it without the asking, and, above all, be clean and never let a dirty word or suggestive story get into type.

I want this paper to be conducted so that it can go into any home without destroying the innocence of any child.

Another, and a very fine, personal expression of the ethical principles of journalism is found in The Journalist's Creed, the creation of Walter Williams:

I believe in the profession of journalism.

I believe that the public journal is a public trust, that all connected with it are, to the full measure of their responsibility, trustees for the public; that acceptance of a lesser service than the public service is a betrayal of this trust.

I believe that clear thinking and clear statement, accuracy and fairness, are fundamental to good journalism.

I believe that a journalist should write only what he holds in his heart to be true.

I believe that suppression of the news, for any con-sideration other than the welfare of society, is indefensible.

I believe that no one should write as a journalist what he would not say as a gentleman; that bribery by one's own pocketbook is as much to be avoided as bribery by the pocketbook of another; that individual responsibility may not be escaped by pleading another's instructions or another's dividends.

I believe that advertising, news and editorial columns should alike serve the best interests of the readers; that a single standard of helpful truth and cleanness should prevail for all; that the supreme test of good journalism is the measure of its public service.

I believe that the journalism which succeeds best-and best deserves success—fears God and honors man, is stoutly independent, unmoved by pride of opinion or greed of power, constructive, tolerant but never careless, self-controlled, patient, always respectful of its readers but always unafraid; is quickly indignant at injustice; is unswayed by the appeal of privilege or clamor of the mob; seeks to give every rnan a chance, and, as far as law and honest wage and recognition of human brotherhood can make it so, an equal chance; is profoundly patriotic while sincerely promoting international good will and cementing world-comradeship; is a journalism of humanity of and for to-day's world.

These examples are sufficient to show the ethical ideas and ideals of individual journalists. No one can say how many similar codes have been created for the private guidance of particular newspapers, but it is safe to assert that the majority of journalists who are responsible for newspaper direction and have given thought to the matter of ethical conduct in the practice of journalism consciously recognize some such principles as these and endeavor to apply them, And many, as has been said, apply them unconsciously because they are that sort of men and could not do otherwise.

But such statements of principles, being individual, and applied to the conduct of individual enterprise, have no influence upon the profession as a whole save as the effects of their application impress others. It is, that is to say, the influence of example, which is limited in its impress to its contacts, and, moreover, it seldom reveals the specific principles which actuate it, Individual standards ever remain individual, and are always as varied as individual nature. Common standards recognized by all can only be established by collective consideration and action, resulting in a definite declaration of ethical principles for common observance, serving both as a guide to right and as a measure of right. Such a code, applying to the profession of journalism generally, is that adopted by the American Society of Newspaper Editors in 1923. It is entitled *Canons of Journalism* [①] and it reads as follows:

> The primary function of newspapers is to communicate to the human race what its members do, feel, and think. Journalism, therefore, demands of its practitioners the widest range of intelligence, of knowledge, and of experience, as well as natural and trained powers of observation and reasoning. To its opportunities as a chronicle are indissolubly linked its obligations as a teacher and interpreter.

To the end of finding some means of codifying sound practice and just aspirations of American journalism these canons are set forth:

---

① These canons were formulated by H J. Wright, editor of the New York *Globe* and Chairman of the Committee on Ethical Standards of the American Society of Newspaper Editors.

I

Responsibility. —The right of a newspaper to attract and hold readers is restricted by nothing but considerations of public welfare. The use a newspaper makes of the share of public attention it gains serves to determine its sense of responsibility, which it shares with every member of its staff. A journalist who uses his power for any selfish or otherwise unworthy purpose is faithless to a high trust.

II

Freedom, of the Press. —Freedom of the press is to be guarded as a vital right of mankind. It is the unquestionable right to discuss whatever is not explicitly forbidden by law, including the wisdom of any restrictive statute.

III

Independence. —Freedom from all obligations except that of fidelity to the public interest is vital.

1. Promotion of any private interest contrary to the general welfare, for whatever reason, is not compatible with honest journalism. So-called news communications from private sources should not be published without public notice of their source or else substantiation of their claims to value as news, both in form and substance.

2. Partisanship in editorial comment which knowingly departs from the truth does violence to the best spirit of American journalism; in the news columns it is subversive of a fundamental principle of the profession.

IV

Sincerity, Truthfulness, Accuracy. —Good faith with the reader is the foundation of all journalism worthy of the name.

1. By every consideration of good faith a newspaper is constrained to be truthful. It is not to be excused for lack of thoroughness or accuracy within its control or failure to obtain command of these essential qualities.

2. Headlines should be fully warranted by the contents of the articles which they surmount.

V

Impartiality. —Sound practice makes clear distinction between news reports and expressions of opinion. News reports should be free from opinion or bias of any kind.

This rule does not apply to so-called special articles unmistakably devoted to advocacy or characterized by a signature authorizing the writer's own conclusions and interpretations.

VI

Fair Play. —A newspaper should not publish unofficial charges affecting reputation or moral character without opportunity given to the accused to be heard; right practice demands the giving of such opportunity in all cases of serious accusation outside judicial proceedings.

1. A newspaper should not invade private rights or feelings without sure warrant of public right as distinguished from public curiosity.

2. It is the privilege, as it is the duty, of a newspaper to

make prompt and complete correction of its own serious mistakes of fact or opinion, whatever their origin.

VII

Decency. —A newspaper cannot escape conviction of insincerity if while professing high moral purpose it supplies incentives to base conduct, such as are to be found in details of crime and vice, publication of which is not demonstrably for the general good. Lacking authority to enforce its canons, the journalism here represented can but express the hope that deliberate pandering to vicious instincts will encounter effective public disapproval or yield to the influence of a preponderant professional condemnation.

Here is epitomized most of the fundamental principles of journalism that have been discussed in the preceding pages of this volume and specific application is given to such of those principles as pertain directly to ethical conduct in the broadest sense. These canons constitute a standard of right for the practice of journalism generally, and they were given collective approval by a body of directing editors of newspapers of the largest circulation and influence. Therefore they may be assumed to express a consensus of professional opinion as to the nature of ethical principles applicable to journalism everywhere.

But in journalism as in all professions, as, indeed, in all life, it is one thing to declare principles and another thing to apply them; it is one thing to believe in principles and another to put belief into action. Formulas of right, save where they may be enforcible by penalties, can do no more than point to the right, can do no more than present standards for the guidance of all who are disposed to recognize them and who will endeavor to conform to them; and serve as a measure of the delinquencies of those who are not disposed to observe them. And every man must apply such standards according to his own interpretations of them and according to the urge of his own consciousness in relation to them. Therefore, even among those who wish to do right, there are ever differences in the degree or character of observance. The minds and consciences of men cannot be standardized by any rules or laws.

None the less the development and definite statement of moral standards is essential to moral progress beyond the stage of individual effort in every field of hunan endeavor, for until principles of right are conceived and given form there can be no general understanding of what is right. But once formed, and once accepted as a general measure of right, they become by common consent an ever widening and growing influence in shaping and directing the trend of the mass.

The physical progress of journalism is one of the wonders of the modern world. That progress is something to be proud of. And it has not been accomplished without a degree of moral progress that is gratifying to the journalist who loves his profession. It is not difficult to find exceptions in this, as in all vocations, but generally speaking journalism has advanced, and is continually advancing, in its conceptions of right, in the character of its service, in the realization of its responsibilities and obligations, in the increasing emphasis it gives to truth, in the greater fairness of its discussion, and in its larger and profounder devotion to the public interest. And with this has been developing a professional consciousness that permits and promotes a broader outlook upon the field and sphere of journalism, with a desire to advance the standing and the welfare of the profession as a whole, with an impulse to collective study of common problems and to common action for the general good. The *Canons of Journalism* is one of the fruits of this development, itself an impressive indication of the moral progress of journalism as a profession worthy to rank with the highest, and as a great and powerful agency for both the moral and material advancement of mankind, and an assurance of greater progress in the future.

Index

Accuracy, in the news, 60—66; depends upon accessible facts, 66; Walter Lippman on, 66; necessity of in headlines, 82.

American Society of Newspaper Editors, code of ethics, called "Canons of Journalism," 161—164.

Canons of Journalism, 161—164.

Constitution, guarantee of freedom of the press, 115.

Copy desk, responsibility for accuracy, 77; general importance of, 78; building headlines, 78.

Copy readers, must be dependable, 72; requisites of, 76; high places: in journalism, 78.

Crime, in the news, 48—53.

Dana, Chas. A. , definition of news, 22; on printing the news, 47; on power of the press, 109

Delane of the Times, on independence in journalism, 135—137.

Distinctiveness in the newspaper, 94—95.

Editor, responsibility of, 106—114; holds a public office, 106; his audience, 107; power of, 104—110; duty to paper; 111—126; duty to public, 111—114.

Editorial, construction of the, 140 — 150; principles of, 143; form of, 146; information in, 147; necessity of honesty in. 148.

Editorial page, 98—105; soul of the newspaper, 92; essential to journalism, 98; selfexpression fundamental function of, 102; creation of personality in, 103.

Editorial policy, 123 — 139; essential to newspaper, 124; defined, 126; fiduciary relation to public, 128; formation of, 129.

Ethics, of journalism, 151 — 166; regard for essential, 152; nature of, 153; code of William V. McKeon, 156—157; code of Warren G. Harding, 158; code of Walter Williams, 159; code of American Society of Newspaper Editors, 161—164.

Facts, fundamental element of journalism, 74.
Flour, compared with newspaper, 12.
Features, value of, 12.
Freedom of the press, 115 — 122; subject to restraints, 117; essential to free government, 120; in acute emergencies, 120—122.

Harding, Warren G. , code of newspaper ethics, 158.
Headlines, importance of, 78; functions of, 78 — 83; essential purpose of, 79; dangers of exaggeration in, 79; overstatement in, 80; necessity of accuracy, 82.

Honesty, in editorial policy, 148.

Information, value of in news, 38—39—40; in editorial, 147.

Interest, essential quality in news, 31; measure of in news, 31; degrees of in news, 31—32; "human" importance of, 36; "human," nature of, 36—37—38.

Journalism, beginnings of, 6; primary duty of, 28; chief function of, 38; responsibility for truth, 58; educational foundation, 72; schools of, 73; incomplete without opmion, 90; development of institutional, 94; independent, 132—135; ethics of, 151—166.

Journalist's creed, 159.

Libel, avoiding, 46; limitation on freedom of the press, 118.

Lippman, Walter, on accuracy in news, 66.

Make-up, importance of, 84; art in, 84; value of in news arrangement, 85; first page a show window, 87—89; selling appeal, 87.

McKeon, William V., code of ethics of, 156—157.

Moral standards, 153—155.

"News," origin of word, 3.

News, passion for, 2; and views associated, 5; early methods of dissemination, 6; primacy of, 20; definition of, 21; complete and incomplete distinguished, 24; serial, 24; processional, 25; entertainment in,

27—29; selection of, 29—41; space limitations, 30—45; truth in, 30, 55—68; interest essential quality, 31; measures of interest in, 32—33; local, superior interest of; information in, 38, 39, 40; rejection of, 42—55; supply and demand, 43; judgment in rejection, 45; of crime anc vice, 48—53; suppression of, 53—55; getting and handling the, 69—89; relation to space, 76; at the copy desk, 78; headline to indicate nature of, 81; arrangement of, 85.

Newspaper, beginnings of the, 7; influence of, 7—13; principles of production of, 9—19; a manufacturing enterprise, 9; must be salable, io; circulation, necessity of, 10; circulation, basis of influence of, 11; necessary agency of public welfare, 13; business management, 13; lives by scrutiny, 14; profit secondary, 14; character of ownership, 15; must be sold daily, 17; raw materials of 44; character indicated in make-up, 84; clean countenance important, 84; a well—dressed, 85; personality m, 90—97; soul of, 92; causes of uniformity, 93; function of editorial page in, 98—105; responsibility of, 106—114; editorial policy of, 123—139; independence of, 132; partisanship in, 133; selfrespect, 142; honesty in editorials, 148; must have a heart, 149—150; ethicsin, 151—166.

Obligations, of journalism, 40.

Opinion, associated with news, 5, 90; influence of public, 107—109; expression of, 129—133; must be honest, 148.

Ownership, newspaper, Melville E. Stone on character of,

15; must be primarily concerned in publication, 16.

Personal journalism, passing of, 95.
Personahty, in newspaper, 90 — 97; expressed in editorial page, 92; importance of, 96; qualities of, 101.
Policy, editorial, 123—139. Press, freedom of, 115—122; subject to restraints, 117.
Production, newspaper, principles of, 9.
Pubhc opinion, influence of, 107 — 109; consideration of, 138—139.

Reporter, responsibility of, 58; character of, 68; a fact-finder, 69; qualities of, 69—71.

Space, limitations of, 30.
Stone, Melville E. , on newspaper ownership, 15.
Truth, in the news, 30, 55 — 68; difficulties of ascertaining, 57; test of quality of journalism, 58; definition of, 61; impartiality essential to, 62.

Vice, news of, 48—53.

Williams, Talcott, on fiduciary office of newspaper, 128.
Williams, Walter, journalist's creed, 159.
Wright, H. J. , formulated ethical code American Society of Newspaper Editors, note, 161.

索 引

（所注页码均为原书页码，即本书边页码。）

Accuracy, in the news　新闻准确性　60—66
depends upon accessible facts　取决于所接近的事实　66
Walter Lippman on　李普曼　66
necessity of in headlines　标题的要素　82
American Society of Newspaper Editors, code of ethics, called "Canons of Journalism"　美国报纸编辑协会；伦理准则；所谓"新闻记者规约"　161—164
Canons of Journalism　《新闻记者规约》　161—164
Constitution, guarantee of freedom of the press　宪法，新闻自由的保证　115
Copy desk, responsibility for accuracy　编辑室，准确性的责任　77
general importance of　普遍的重要性　78
building headlines　制作标题　78
Copy readers, must be dependable　文字编辑，必须是可靠的　72
requisites of　要求　76
high places in journalism　处在新闻业的很高地位　78
Crime, in the news　犯罪，新闻　48—53

Dana, Chas. A., definition of news　查理斯·A·达纳，新闻界定　22

on printing the news　关于刊载的新闻　47

on power of the press　关于报刊的力量　109

Delane of the Times, on independence in journalism　德莱恩在《泰晤士报》发表关于新闻独立的评论　135—137

Distinctiveness in the newspaper　报纸的区分　94—95

Editor, responsibility of　编辑，职责　106—114

 holds a public office　担任公职　106

 his audience　他的受众　107

 power of　力量　104—110

 duty to paper　报纸的职责　111—126

 duty to public　公众的职责　111—114

Editorial, construction of the　编辑结构　140—150

 principles of　原理　143

 form of　（表达的）形式　146

 information in　（评论中）的信息　147

 necessity of honesty in　（评论）真诚的必要条件　148

Editorial page　评论版　98—105

 soul of the newspaper　报纸灵魂　92

 essential to journalism　对新闻业的必要性　98

 self-expression fundamental function of　自我表达的基本功能　102

 creation of personality in　（报纸）个性特征的创新　103

Editorial policy　评论政策　123—139

 essential to newspaper　对报纸的必要性　124

 defined　被界定　126

 fiduciary relation to public　与公众的信用关系　128

 formation of　形成　129

Ethics, of journalism　新闻伦理　151—166

 regard for essential　注视（新闻伦理的）必要性　152

 nature of　（伦理）本质　153

 code of William V. McKeon　威廉·V·麦基恩的准则　156—157

code of Warren G. Harding 沃伦·哈丁的准则 158

code of （新闻伦理）准则 167－168 Walter Williams, 沃尔特·威廉姆斯 159

code of American Society of Newspaper Editors 美国报纸编辑协会准则 161－164

Facts, fundamental element of journalism 事实，新闻业基本要素 74

Flour, compared with newspaper 面粉，与报纸比较 12

Features, value of 特稿，价值 12

Freedom of the press 新闻自由 115－122

   subject to restraints 服从于限制（约束） 117

   essential to free government 对自由政府的必要性 120

   in acute emergencies 在紧急情况下 120－122

Harding, Warren G., code of newspaper ethics 沃伦·哈丁的新闻伦理准则 158

Headlines, importance of 标题，重要性 78

   functions of 功能 78－83

   essential purpose of 首要目标 79

   dangers of exaggeration in 夸张的危险 79

   overstatement in 夸大事实的陈述 80

   necessity of accuracy 准确的必要性 82

Honesty, in editorial policy 真诚，评论政策 148

Information, value of in news 信息，在新闻中的价值 38－40

   in editorial 在评论中 147

Interest, essential quality in news 31

   measure of in news 新闻价值的评估 31

   degrees of in news 新闻价值的重要程度 31－32

   "human" importance of "人情味"的重要性 36

   "human," nature of "人情味"的本质 36－38

Journalism, beginnings of 新闻业，开端 6

   primary duty of 基本职责 28

   chief function of 主要功能 38

responsibility for truth　为真相所承担的责任　58

educational foundation　教育基础　72

schools of　新闻学院　73

incomplete without opinion　缺失评论的报纸是不完整的　90

development of institutional　机构的发展　94

independent　独立　132—135

ethics of　伦理　151—166

Journalist's creed　记者准则　159

Libel, avoiding　诽谤，避免　46

limitation on freedom of the press　新闻自由的局限性　118

Lippman, Walter, on accuracy in news　李普曼，关于新闻的准确性　66

Make-up, importance of　（报纸）外观，重要性　84

art in　艺术　84

value of in news arrangement　新闻编排的价值　85

first page, a show window　头版，一个展示橱窗　87—89

selling appeal　（报纸）售卖诉求　87

McKeon, William V., code of ethics of　威廉·V·麦基恩　伦理准则　156—157

Moral standards　道德标准　153—155

"News", origin of word　"新闻"的来源　3

News, passion for　新闻，热情　2

and views associated　相关的观点　5

early methods of dissemination　早期的传播方法　6

primacy of　首要　20

definition of　界定　21

complete and incomplete distinguished　完整报道和不完整报道的区别　24

serial　系列报道　24

processional　并列的　25

entertainment in　娱乐　27—29

selection of　选择　29—41

space limitations　版面的局限性　30—45

truth in 真相 30，55—68
interest essential quality 首要的趣味性品质 31
measures of interest in 兴趣性的评估 32—33
local，superior interest of，information in 地方，最大兴趣，信息 38，39，40
rejection of 新闻取舍 42—55
supply and demand 供给与需求 43
judgment in rejection 新闻取舍的判断 45
of crime and vice 关于犯罪和罪恶 48—53
suppression of 压制（新闻自由） 53—55
getting and handling the 新闻的获取和编辑 69—89
relation to space 与版面相关 76
at the copy desk 在编辑室 78
headline to indicate nature of 标题提示性的本质功能 81
arrangement of 编排 85
Newspaper，beginnings of the 报纸，开端 7
influence of 影响 7—13
principles of production of 生产原则 9—19
a manufacturing enterprise 制造厂商（企业） 9
must be salable 必须是可以售卖的 10
circulation，necessity of 发行量，必要性 10
circulation，basis of influence of 发行量，影响力的基础 11
necessary agency of public welfare 必要的公共福利代理 13
business management 业务管理 13
lives by scrutiny 依靠审视而生存 14
profit secondary 利润第二 14
character of ownership 所有权特征 15
must be sold daily 必须每日售出 17
raw materials of 素材 44
character indicated in make-up 报纸外观表明的特征 84
clean countenance important 保持报纸版面整洁的重要性 84

a well－dressed　外观精美的报纸　85

personality in　个性特征　90－97

soul of　（报纸的）灵魂　92

causes of uniformity　统一外观的起因　93

function of editorial page in　评论版的功能　98－105

responsibility of　责任　106－114

editorial policy of　评论政策　123－139

independence of　独立性　132

partisanship in　党派性　133

self－respect　自尊　142

honesty in editorials　评论的真诚　148

must have a heart　（报纸）必须具备灵魂　149－150

ethics in　伦理　151－166

Obligations, of journalism　新闻的义务　40

Opinion, associated with news　观点，与新闻相关　5，90

influence of public　公众的影响力　107－109

expression of　表达　129－133

must be honest　必须真诚　148

Ownership, newspaper, Melville E. Stone on character of　梅尔维尔·斯通关于报纸所有权特征的论述　15；

must be primarily concerned in publication　必须首先关注发行　16

Personal journalism, passing of　个人新闻生涯　95

Personality, in newspaper　个性特征，报纸　90－97

expressed in editorial page　在评论版的表达　92

importance of　重要性　96

qualities of　质量　101

Policy, editorial　政策，评论　123－139

Press, freedom of　新闻自由　115－122

subject to restraints　服从于限制（约束）　117

Production, newspaper, principles of　报纸制作原则　9

Public opinion, influence of　舆论，影响力　107－109

consideration of 考虑 138—139
Reporter, responsibility of 记者的责任 58
character of 特征 68
a fact-finder 事实发掘者 69
qualities of 质量 69—71
Space, limitations of 版面，局限性 30
Stone, Melville E., on newspaper ownership 梅尔维尔·斯通关于报纸所有权 15
Truth, in the news 新闻中的真相 30, 55—68
difficulties of ascertaining 确信（肯定）的困难 57
test of quality of journalism 新闻质量的测验 58
definition of 界定 61
impartiality essential to 公正的重要性 62
Vice, news of 罪恶类新闻 48—53
Williams, Talcott, on fiduciary-office of newspaper 威廉姆斯关于报纸公信力的论述 128
Williams, Walter, journalist's creed 沃特·威廉姆斯，记者守则 159
Wright, H. J., formulated ethical code American Society of Newspaper Editors, note 赖特，美国报纸编辑协会颁布的伦理准则，注释 161

有关新闻学书目

The Principles of Journalism (《新闻学原理》) Casper S. Yost

The Editorial (《编辑学》) Leon N. Flint

Distinctive characteristics of the editorial and how they can be made to function most effectively under modern conditions

The Country Weekly (《乡村周刊》) Phil C. Bing

The methods which successful country editors have found most profitable and effective in their interesting and important field

Practical Journalism (《实用新闻学》) E. L. Shuman

Detailed practical analysis of all the writing departments of a progressive city daily. Inclusive and en-lightening

The Community Newspaper (《社区报纸》) Emerson R. Harris and Florence Harris

What the newspaper can be and do in the community. A new view of journalism in the modern large town and small city

History of Journalism in the United States (《美国新闻史》) George Henry Payne

Entertaining and compact account of the Press from its first appearance in the United States up to the very present

Handbook for Newspaper Workers (《新闻工作者手册》) D. Appleton and Company, New York London, Grant Milnor Hyde's Books on Journalism

The information the newspaper man wants, presented so he can get at it. No factor of effective writing and good newspaper practice is omitted

Newspaper Reporting and Correspondence (《新闻采写原理》)

Practical suggestion on the fundamentals of news-paper writing which the reporter must master in his first few weeks

Newspaper Editing (《报纸编辑》)

The tools and methods of the copy editor, his opportunities, and how the results of his work count in the paper

Course in Journalistic Writing (《新闻采写教程》) D. Appleton and Company New York London

Interesting instruction and thorough drill in the clear, effective English composition which is the basis of good newspaper style

附录一:《圣路易斯邮报》准则(约瑟夫·普利策,1907 年 4 月 10 日)

我相信我的退休对于本报的基本准则不会带来影响,本报仍将永远为发展和改革而奋斗。

从不利税于任何党派,永远反对特权阶级和公共利益的窃取者;

从不对穷苦人缺乏同情心,永远忠实于公众利益;

从不满足于已经发表的新闻,永远最大程度独立;

从不畏惧攻击错误言行,不管这些错误言行是来自劫掠性的财阀们还是来自于劫掠性的贫穷者。

附录二:美国新闻记者协会(SPJ)职业伦理规范(1996 年 9 月)

绪言

职业新闻记者协会成员相信,公众的启蒙是正义的先驱,民主的基石。新闻记者的职责就是通过追求真实,提供关于事件和问题的全面、公平的叙述,达到启蒙公众的目的。来自所有专门领域和媒体的有责任感的记者,都努力彻底和忠实地为公众服务。职业正直感是记者信誉的基础,协会成员因此对于职业道德行为产生共同认识,并采用本规范作为协会实践原则和标准的声明。

追求真实并加以报道

新闻记者应该忠实、公正和勇敢地搜集报道和转述信息。

新闻记者应该:

检验来自所有来源的信息的准确性,小心避免无意的错误。绝不允许故意扭曲。

努力找到报道的主体,给他们对于声称的错误行为做出反应的机会。

任何可能的时候,都要指明消息来源。公众应该有尽可能多的信息来判断消息来源的可靠性。

在承诺保证信息来源匿名之前,永远要质问一下信息来源的动机。要对为换取信息而作出的承诺中各种可能的情况都做出清楚的说明,一旦承诺,则保守诺言。

确保标题、导读和其他突出处理的材料、照片、音像、图表、声音和用语都没有错误表达。

避免在转述和连续性的报道中误导。如果有必要转述别的媒体一条新闻,可以这样做,但要标识清楚。

除非传统的公开的方法不能得到对公众至关重要的信息,不要采用秘密的或窃听的方法获取信息。如果使用了这样的方法,在报道中应该加以说明。

永远不要剽窃。

勇敢地讲述关于人类经验多样性和广泛性的报道,尽管这些经验可能是不经常有的。

检查自己的文化价值观念,并避免将这些价值观念强加给别人。

观察人时不要被民族、性别、年龄、宗教、种族、地理、性取向、是否残障、外貌或社会地位这些因素框住。

支持公开的意见交流,即使这些意见自己很反感。

让无声的人们发出声音,官方信息和非官方的信息被以同样价值对待。

在鼓吹文章和新闻报道之间做出明确区分。分析性文章和评论应被明确标出,以免与事实和报道文本相混。

对广告和新闻做区分,避免出现模糊二者界限的杂交式文章。

认识到自己的特殊使命,要确保公众事务是公开处理的,而且政府记录可以公开查阅。

减小伤害

有职业操守的记者把新闻来源、采访对象和同事都看作值得尊敬的人。

新闻记者应该:

对那些可能因为新闻报道而受到负面影响的人们表示同情。当面对孩子和没有经验的新闻来源或新闻主体时,要特别小心。

当采访和使用受到正在悲伤中的人们的照片时,要特别小心。

要认识到采集和报道信息会引起伤害和不适,报道新闻并不意味着你就可以傲慢自大。

要认识到，一般人比公共官员和追求权力、影响和希望引起人们注意的其他人有更多的权利保有关于自己的信息。只有当有十分迫切的公共需要时，侵入任何人的私人领域获取信息才是正当的。

品位要高。避免迎合任何低级趣味。

在指出青少年犯罪嫌疑人或性犯罪受害人时，要非常谨慎。

在正式控诉文件出来之前指明犯罪嫌疑人时，要非常审慎。

在公众被告知的权利和犯罪嫌疑人被公正审判的权利之间寻求平衡。

独立行动

除了公众的知情权之外，新闻记者不应该对任何其他利益负有责任。

新闻记者应该：

避免自己的利益与采访发生冲突，不管是现实的利益还是可能的利益。

不参加任何可能伤害自己公正和信誉的组织和活动。

如果将伤害记者的正直感，就拒绝一切礼物、好处、费用、免费旅游和特殊对待，并避免第二职业、政治涉入、在公共办公机构或社区机构工作。

如果这些冲突必不可免，那么将它们暴露出来。

勇敢地要求那些拥有权力的人负起责任。

拒绝广告商的优厚待遇和特殊利益，抵制他们企图影响新闻报道的压力。

警惕新闻来源为了好处或金钱而提供信息，避免力求新闻出现的心理。

可信

新闻记者在他们读者、听众、观众的眼中是可信的。

新闻记者应该：

澄清和解释新闻报道，就新闻界的行为邀请公众对话。

鼓励公众说出他们对新闻媒体的不满。

承认错误，并迅速纠正。

揭露新闻记者和新闻媒体的不道德行为。

遵守他们对于别人提出的高要求。

The Principles of Journalism by Casper Yost
Copyright © 1924 by D. Appleton and Company

图书在版编目(CIP)数据

新闻学原理:双语版:汉、英/(美)卡斯珀·约斯特著;王海译.—北京:中国传媒大学出版社,2017.9
(新闻学与传播学经典丛书·大师系列)
书名原文:The principles of journalism
ISBN 978-7-5657-2109-0

Ⅰ.①新… Ⅱ.①卡…②王… Ⅲ.①新闻学 Ⅳ.①G210

中国版本图书馆 CIP 数据核字(2017)第 199076 号

新闻学与传播学经典丛书·大师系列

新闻学原理
XINWENXUE YUANLI

著　　者	[美]卡斯珀·约斯特
译　　者	王　海
策划编辑	司马兰　姜颖昳
责任编辑	姜颖昳
特约编辑	魏　征
封面设计	运平设计
责任印制	阳金洲
出版发行	中国传媒大学出版社
社　　址	北京市朝阳区定福庄东街1号　　邮编:100024
电　　话	010-65450532 或 65450528　　传真:010-65779405
网　　址	http://www.cucp.com.cn
经　　销	全国新华书店
印　　刷	三河市东方印刷有限公司
开　　本	880mm×1230mm　　1/32
印　　张	10
字　　数	259 千字
版　　次	2017 年 9 月第 1 版　2017 年 9 月第 1 次印刷
书　　号	ISBN 978-7-5657-2109-0/G·2109　　定价 42.00元

版权所有　　翻印必究　　印装错误　　负责调换